100 THINGS
RANGERS FANS
SHOULD KNOW & DO
BEFORE THEY DIE

100 THINGS RANGERS FANS SHOULD KNOW & DO BEFORE THEY DIE

Adam Raider and Russ Cohen

TRIUMPH
BOOKS

Copyright © 2014 by Adam Raider and Russ Cohen

No part of this publication may be reproduced, stored in a retrieval system, or transmitted in any form by any means, electronic, mechanical, photocopying, or otherwise, without the prior written permission of the publisher, Triumph Books LLC, 814 North Franklin Street, Chicago, Illinois 60610.

Library of Congress Cataloging-in-Publication Data has been applied for.

This book is available in quantity at special discounts for your group or organization. For further information, contact:

Triumph Books LLC
814 North Franklin Street
Chicago, Illinois 60610
(312) 337-0747
www.triumphbooks.com

Printed in U.S.A.
ISBN: 978-1-60078-917-5
Design by Patricia Frey
Photos courtesy of AP Images unless otherwise indicated

For John

Contents

Introduction

Like the title says, *100 Things Rangers Fans Should Know & Do Before They Die* is a list of the facts you must know and tasks you must undertake to prove your worth as a Rangers fan. Great care was taken to compile a list that was entertaining, informative, likely to spark debate, and certain to ruin what little chance I had of ever being invited to Glen Sather's cabin in Banff.

Here are the greatest players, biggest games, smartest and dumbest trades, best and worst draft picks, most heated rivalries, and club records least likely to be broken. You'll also find my picks for the best places to watch a game when the Rangers are out of town, tips on how to build a proper Rangers fan cave without having to deplete your 401(k), and trivia spanning the entire eight-decade history of the team. Entries are ranked 1 to 100 in order of general importance.

I would have preferred to skip the rankings altogether, but Triumph insisted, threatening to go public with the shameful truth that I once interviewed for a media relations job with the Islanders. For what it's worth, the hiring manager asked me what team I rooted for. I told him the Rangers. There was no second interview.

I wasn't thrilled with the publisher's choice of title, either, since I abhor all reminders of mortality (a Rangers victory in sudden-death overtime being an exception). I can tell you what's at the top of *this* Ranger fan's list of things to do before he dies: to not die. I've found that being dead severely limits one's enjoyment of Rangers hockey.

This book is as much a celebration of playing for the Rangers as it is cheering for the Rangers, which is to say that the fans, with their unique culture and traditions, are as much a part of the story as Mark Messier, Henrik Lundqvist, or Ed Giacomin. Their experiences—some funny, some poignant, some downright disturbing—are sprinkled throughout. What I hope comes through clearly is the passion they have for this hockey team, the unconditional love. Sometimes it's a tough love, but it's a love that lasts a lifetime.

—Adam Raider

1 Now You Can Die in Peace

It was a season that began and ended with a championship.

Training camp for the Rangers' 1993–94 campaign opened early so the team could play a two-game exhibition series against the Toronto Maple Leafs in London, England. New York swept the mini-tournament, which had been sponsored by French's Mustard, and even won a trophy: the French's Mustard Cup.

Players had a good chuckle over that, but it was an important bonding experience for a team coming off a nightmarish 1992–93 season in which virtually everything that could go wrong did go wrong.

Mike Keenan, the Rangers' new coach, went to Madison Square Garden Network producer Joe Whelan and asked him to edit together a video of past ticker-tape parades along the Canyon of Heroes, that stretch of Broadway running from Battery Park at the southern tip of Manhattan up to City Hall. It featured footage from the championship parades of the 1969 Mets and the 1978 Yankees as well as astronauts back from missions in space. Keenan gathered the Rangers together and showed them the video because he wanted them to see what winning a Stanley Cup in New York would be like. If they couldn't visualize it, he reasoned, they would never win it.

Keenan wasn't alone in setting lofty goals for the Rangers. *The Hockey News* went out on a pretty big limb by predicting that New York City would host a Stanley Cup parade the following June.

"RANGERS WILL GO FROM CHUMPS TO CHAMPS IN '94," the magazine declared.

A parade was the last thing on anyone's mind after the Rangers lost five of their first nine games. A humiliating 4–1 loss to the

1

lowly Tampa Bay Lightning on October 22 was their third in a row, but it would turn out to be a turning point in the Rangers' season. A 3–2 win over the Los Angeles Kings two days later kicked off an 18–1–3 run that catapulted the Rangers to the top of the NHL standings. There they would stay.

Winning bred optimism and optimism is contagious. Captain Mark Messier and his lieutenants, Adam Graves and Kevin Lowe, went out of their way to make sure that everyone felt like they were

Captain Mark Messier holds the Stanley Cup during the team's victory parade in New York City on June 17, 1994. (AP Photo/Marty Lederhandler)

part of the team and had played a role in its success. Ed Olczyk was a perfect example. The former 40-goal scorer was good enough to be a regular on most other teams but rarely cracked the top six in New York. Relentlessly upbeat, Eddie O emerged as the leader of the Black Aces, a group of players who didn't get into the lineup very often. He started a ritual of leading the team in a group stretch at center ice after practices, shouting "Heave ho, heave ho, heave ho" as teammates joined in.

That all-for-one, one-for-all attitude carried the Rangers through a 52-win regular season; playoff series victories over the New York Islanders, Washington Capitals, and New Jersey Devils; and the first six games of the Stanley Cup Finals against the Vancouver Canucks.

Just hours before Game 7, on June 14, 1994, Keenan showed his players the same parade compilation video they had watched during training camp, as well as a collection of the season's highlights, set to music. Inspirational stuff.

And there was The Speech, the one Messier called the best he had ever heard. Keenan, channeling Henry V before the Battle of Agincourt (and a little Freddie Shero), told his players that if they won that night, they would walk together forever.

Meanwhile, instead of being thrilled that their team was one win away from the Stanley Cup, fans were beside themselves with worry. To them, history dictated that the curse would rear its ugly head sooner or later in the form of a broken ankle to Brian Leetch, a fluke goal through Mike Richter's legs from 50' out, Martians crashing through the roof to kidnap Messier, or some other unforeseeable calamity.

Backup goalie Glenn Healy cracked, "There are 23 million people in New York today who have already dialed the 9 and the 1 and they're waiting to see if they have to dial the last 1."

The Rangers went on the attack from the opening faceoff and took a 1–0 lead when Leetch, all alone on the left side of Kirk

McLean's net, converted a pass from Sergei Zubov at 11:02 of the first period.

Three minutes later, with the Rangers on a power play, Zubov carried the puck into the Vancouver zone and dished it to Alexei Kovalev, who was skating down the left wing. Kovalev found Graves open in the slot, and Graves ripped a shot past McLean for his first goal in 11 games.

Canucks captain Trevor Linden cut New York's lead to one when he scored a shorthanded goal at 5:21 of the second period. The Rangers answered eight minutes later when Messier, Graves, and Brian Noonan all took swipes at a loose puck in front of the Vancouver net that bounced in off McLean's right pad. Messier got credit for the goal.

The Rangers carried a 3–1 lead into the third period, but when Linden scored a power play goal at 4:50 to make it 3–2, fans started getting anxious. With about five minutes left in the game, the Canucks' Nathan LaFayette beat Mike Richter with a shot that clanged off the goal post. In any other year, that puck goes in and the Rangers lose the game and the series. But this wasn't any other year.

With time winding down, the building was ready to erupt into a celebration unlike anything that anyone on the ice or in the stands had ever experienced. Then Steve Larmer was called for icing with just 1.1 seconds remaining. Officials tacked on five tenths of a

Coolest Job on Earth?

Prior to 1994, the Stanley Cup didn't have its own personal escort. But the Rangers and their fans partied so hard with the trophy that it was damaged and had to be taken back to the Hockey Hall of Fame in Toronto for repairs. The following season, the Hall created a new position, the Keeper of the Cup, whose duty is to maintain a watchful eye on the Cup at photo-ops, pub crawls, and other events where Lord Stanley's chalice might get dinged up.

Priorities

"I was in the Persian Gulf on a carrier when the Rangers won the Cup in 1994. I snuck down off the flight deck in between bomb loads to call and wake up my wife back in Virginia to turn on the TV and let me know who won the game."

Fred Parker, Leonardtown, Maryland
Rangers fan since 1975

second to the clock—enough time for one more faceoff deep in the Rangers' zone. One more chance for the curse to strike.

Craig MacTavish won the draw, the final buzzer sounded, and Messier jumped for joy. It's amazing how high a 205-lb. player in full gear can leap when the weight of 54 seasons of futility is removed from his shoulders.

"The waiting is over!" play-by-play man Sam Rosen screamed. "The New York Rangers are Stanley Cup champions! And this one will last a lifetime."

Fireworks exploded overhead. The curse was broken. The dragon was slain. Delirious Rangers fans mockingly chanted "1940!" one last time to celebrate the end of a half-century of disappointment, torment, and frustration. People hugged. People cried. There was ecstasy and elation, yes, but also a magical feeling that *anything* was possible. And relief. So much relief. Someone held up a banner that read, "NOW I CAN DIE IN PEACE."

NHL commissioner Gary Bettman, in one of his last public appearances when he wasn't met with a chorus of boos, came onto the ice and congratulated both teams for a hard-fought final before announcing Leetch as the winner of the Conn Smythe Trophy as the playoffs' Most Valuable Player.

Then two men wearing white gloves carried the most beautiful object on earth to center ice. "New York," Bettman told the crowd, "your long wait is over. Captain Mark Messier, come get the Stanley Cup."

Mess had won the trophy five times before as an Edmonton Oiler, but this time was extra special. You could see it in his face. He wanted this badly. This was the reason Messier came to New York.

The Cup was passed to Lowe and Larmer, Leetch and Graves, Richter and Zubov. Every player got to hold it, even the ones who didn't dress for the game. Keenan and Smith got their turns, too.

Leetch's postgame press conference was interrupted by a congratulatory call from President Bill Clinton. "Congratulations, man," the President said. "I've been sitting here alone in the White House watching this, cheering for you, biting my fingernails, screaming and yelling."

They chatted for a minute before Clinton hung up. "Was that Dana Carvey?" Leetch asked, wondering if he'd just been pranked by the former *Saturday Night Live* star.

Much champagne (and beer) was guzzled from the Cup that night and for many nights to follow.

Three days later, an estimated 1.5 million people turned out for a victory parade up the Canyon of Heroes that looked and sounded bigger than anything players would have seen in Keenan's motivational video. It concluded with a ceremony at City Hall, where Mayor Rudy Giuliani gave every player a key to the city.

When Olczyk, everyone's favorite cheerleader, grabbed the microphone to lead the crowd in an impromptu chant of "Heave ho, two in a row!" it wasn't hard to envision the Rangers returning to this place in one year's time. We still believed anything was possible.

2 The Curse

There is a pivotal scene in *The Matrix* in which the evil Agent Smith expounds his belief that human beings define their reality through misery and suffering.

For decades, Rangers fans existed in much the same way (in fact, a few still do). For many, it was never a question of, "Will this be the year they finally win the Stanley Cup?" but rather "How deep will they plunge the knife into my heart this time?"

From 1926 to 1940, the Rangers were the class of the NHL, appearing in six Stanley Cup Finals and winning three. They might've won more had they not been kicked out of their own arena every spring by the circus.

After 1940, well, that's a tale of doom and gloom you know all too well. But for those in need of a refresher:

From 1942 to 1967, the Rangers missed the playoffs 18 times. They made it to the Stanley Cup Finals once during that dark age, in 1950, only to lose in double-overtime of the seventh game.

They had the best record in the league in 1970 before their All-Star defenseman, Brad Park, tripped over the boards at the Olympia in Detroit and broke his ankle. With Park out, the team went into a tailspin and never fully recovered.

Two years later, leading scorer Jean Ratelle suffered a broken ankle in a game against the Golden Seals...off a shot from one of his own teammates! He returned to the lineup in time to face the Boston Bruins in the Stanley Cup Finals but was largely ineffective in a series the Rangers would lose in six games.

Another broken ankle, this one belonging to Ulf Nilsson, dashed the Rangers' Cup hopes in 1979.

And who can forget 1992 when Mike Richter surrendered a fluky, 65-footer to Pittsburgh's Ron Francis in the Patrick Division Finals, shifting momentum in the Penguins' favor. The Rangers, who had finished the regular season with the league's best record, went on to lose the game, the series, and most significantly, a very real chance to play for the Stanley Cup.

The Rangers found so many spectacularly epic ways to lose that to the superstitious, the team's plight took on an almost supernatural air. A curse became the easiest explanation/excuse for a phenomenon that, on the surface, defied logic. Folks who were willing to believe that mystical forces were conspiring to keep the Cup out of the Rangers' grasp went looking for the source of the jinx and usually traced it to one of two incidents.

The first stems from a desecration of the Stanley Cup that took place in February 1941 when Garden executives burned the arena's mortgage in the bowl of the Cup after making the final payment, as a sort of celebration. The legend goes that this symbolic gesture created all sorts of bad karma for the Rangers.

Another theory about the curse involves the first NHL team to play in New York, the Americans, who were also tenants of Madison Square Garden (read more about the Rangers-Americans rivalry in chapter 95). The Americans were run by coach and general manager Red Dutton, who was forced to suspend operations of the club during World War II. He had always intended to revive the Americans following the war, but when he attempted to do so in 1946, his plan was rebuffed by the NHL. Dutton believed the Rangers were behind the decision. Angered, he declared that the Rangers would never win the Stanley Cup again for as long as he lived.

But there never was a curse. There were, however, factors working against the Rangers—some well beyond their control, and others very much within their control.

Before the NHL expanded in 1967, every team had the rights to young players within its 50-mile territorial limits and could deny any other club from placing a minor league or amateur team on its turf. This meant that while the Canadiens and Maple Leafs had access to literally millions of potential hockey-playing kids, the Rangers had the rights to Queens, Staten Island, the Bronx, and Hoboken—great neighborhoods for discovering a new deli but not for discovering the next Maurice Richard.

The small number of teams and lack of free agency also severely limited player movement, making it even easier for the Canadiens, Red Wings, and Maple Leafs to perpetuate their dynasties. Between them, those three clubs accounted for 25 championships in 26 seasons.

After 1967, the playing field leveled a bit with the introduction of a universal amateur draft, but the Rangers still had to contend with a succession of corporate overlords who viewed the hockey club as just another revenue stream. Take Alan Cohen, the former chairman and CEO of Madison Square Garden who was once asked if it was more important to win a championship or earn profits for his shareholders. Cohen replied that his first priority was to shareholders, saying, "That's the bottom line." That earned him the nickname "Bottom Line" Cohen.

Phil Esposito received a harsh initiation into Garden politics after he became general manager in 1986. He claims to have negotiated a trade with the Edmonton Oilers for Mark Messier a full five seasons before Neil Smith. Esposito realized that Messier could be the knight in shining armor the Rangers had been searching decades for.

According to Espo, when Dick Evans, president and CEO of the Garden, and Jack Diller, president of the Rangers, found out that the deal would cost the team $5 million in cash, they nixed it.

And even when it would've made the most sense from a hockey standpoint to strip the club bare and rebuild through the draft, a succession of Ranger general managers instead pursued the low-lying fruit of aging veterans—"name" players who might put fannies in the seats but not banners in the rafters. That shortsighted strategy cost the Rangers a chance to draft the next Mario Lemieux, the next Steven Stamkos, or the next John Tavares. It's a vicious cycle that has repeated itself over and over and over again.

So there you have it. The most famous curse in hockey debunked, demystified, and thoroughly discredited.

Then again....

In 2010, Rangers captain Chris Drury broke a finger during training camp and missed three weeks of action. In his first game back, he broke the *same finger* in a collision with teammate Michal Rozsival and missed another two months. Can you imagine that happening to a player on any other team but the Rangers?

Neither can we.

3 Matteau! Matteau! Matteau!

Role players have a funny way of flying below the radar until a contest has entered its most critical phase. With everything riding on the next pitch, the next down, the next lucky bounce of a puck, they suddenly emerge—seemingly from out of nowhere—to make the big play and seal their place in history.

Aaron Boone's walk-off home run against the Red Sox. David Tyree's "helmet catch" in Super Bowl XLII. Those were big plays. But knowing what we know now about the course the 1994 NHL playoff season would follow, it's not a stretch to say that Stephane Matteau's double-overtime goal in Game 7 of the Eastern Conference Finals trumps them all.

By early spring, the 1993–94 Rangers had the best record in the league and were assured of a high playoff seed. But neither GM Neil Smith nor Coach Mike Keenan were satisfied. Regular season success had a vexing habit of not carrying over into the playoffs, and nobody wanted a repeat of 1992 when New York won the Presidents' Trophy then lost in the second round to Pittsburgh.

To win in the playoffs, Smith believed he needed a different kind of team—one with more grit and postseason experience. If that meant mortgaging the future to win now, he was prepared to do it.

On March 21, 1994, Smith traded New York's rising young star, Tony Amonte, to the Chicago Blackhawks for grinders Matteau and Brian Noonan. By his own admission, Smith had serious misgivings about the deal, but it gave the Rangers some veteran players that Keenan knew and liked.

A former second-round pick of the Calgary Flames, Matteau had good size and a willingness to play along the boards or drive to the net to score. The 24-year-old left winger wasn't soft, but he wasn't mean, either. Big men with mild dispositions almost always get a bad rap, and Matteau was no exception. Someone noticed that his name sounded an awful lot like "step on my toe," and the nickname stuck.

With 52 wins and 112 points, New York finished with the best record in the league. Division rival New Jersey (47–25–12, 106 points) finished second overall. When the teams met in the Conference Finals, the Rangers were seen as heavy favorites because they had swept the Devils 6–0 during the regular season.

Matteau shouldered at least some of the blame for the Rangers losing Game 1. It was his pass that was intercepted by ex-Ranger Bernie Nicholls—well, Matteau dished the puck right to him, actually—and it led to a goal by Bill Guerin that tied the score 2–2 in

Stephane Matteau (32) scrambles for a loose puck in front of New Jersey Devils goalie Martin Brodeur and Scott Niedermayer (27) on Thursday, May 19, 1994, in Game 3 of the Eastern Conference finals at Meadowlands Arena in East Rutherford, New Jersey. Matteau sent the puck into net to give the Rangers a 3–2 win in double overtime and a 2–1 lead in the series. (AP Photo/Ron Frehm)

the third period. The Devils went on to win in double-overtime 4–3 on a breakaway goal by Stephane Richer.

Matteau made amends for his Game 1 gaffe four nights later. He was at the end of a long shift in double-overtime of Game 3 when there was a scramble around Devils goalie Martin Brodeur.

The puck ended up at Matteau's feet—right place, right time—and he swept it into the net at 6:13 of the extra period to give the Rangers a 3–2 victory and a 2–1 lead in the series.

The Devils roared back to win the next two games, putting the Rangers on the brink until Mark Messier kept the season alive by scoring a natural hat trick in Game 6.

"We had beaten them every time we played them during the regular season," Mike Richter recalled, "and it made us feel like look, not that we had their number, but we knew we could do it. Heading into a Game 7, it's a good thing to have in your back pocket."

The Rangers had the series in the bag until 7.7 seconds left in regulation, when New Jersey winger Valeri Zelepukin beat Richter on a rebound of his own shot to tie the game at 1–1.

"There was so much drama when Zelepukin scored," Matteau said. "We were so quiet after that. But we didn't finish first during the regular season for nothing. All the experienced players who'd been through this before—Messier, Kevin Lowe, Craig MacTavish—they stood up and led the way."

They led the way by not panicking. They led the way by calmly, confidently reminding their teammates that they had played well for 60 minutes. What's the difference if they have to play another period to win it?

As it turned out, the Rangers would need more than an extra period. After the first overtime, the teams clomped off to their respective dressing rooms. Matteau describes what happened next: "Eddie Olczyk was in the room. For my game-winning goal in Game 3, he had touched my stick. Sure enough, I said to Eddie, 'Can you bring me some luck? Can you touch my stick?' He says, 'Sure thing, I can do it.' So he touches my stick, then he starts kissing it and making out with it. I told him, 'Look, don't go overboard.'"

About four and a half minutes into the second overtime, the puck went into the far corner in the Devils' zone to Brodeur's right. Matteau grabbed it and stickhandled behind the net to try a wrap-around shot from the other side. But with Devils defenseman Scott Niedermayer hooking him from behind, Matteau threw the puck in front of the net—possibly as a pass intended for Esa Tikkanen, who was tied up with Jim Dowd on the edge of the crease. It banked off someone and slipped past Brodeur.

WFAN play-by-play man Howie Rose nearly had a stroke delivering what would become the signature call of his career:

"Matteau swoops in to intercept. Matteau behind the net... swings it in front...he scores! Matteau! Matteau! Matteau! Stephane Matteau! And the Rangers have one more hill to climb, baby, but it's Mount Vancouver. The Rangers are headed to the Finals!"

As the goal horn sounded and a deafening roar filled the air, the Rangers poured off the bench to mob the hero of the hour.

Just like that, Matteau went from scrub to celebrity. Nothing he did before or after that goal mattered to Rangers fans. In their eyes, his entire career, his very existence, would forever be defined by that single play.

To his credit, he doesn't take offense. He knows there are worse things to be remembered for.

"They're passionate, the fans from New York," he said. "They always come sneaking up to me from behind to tell me how big that game was and how they were sitting in MSG that night. They always bring it up. They don't even say my first name anymore. They just keep saying 'Matteau, Matteau, Matteau.' It never gets old because when I'm back in Montreal, where I live, I never hear it. Only in New York. It's been 20 years, and I don't get tired of it."

4 The Trade

In the early 1970s, the success that New York's All-Star nucleus of Brad Park, Jean Ratelle, Rod Gilbert, and Ed Giacomin enjoyed during the regular season never culminated in a Stanley Cup. Fans and media started to get impatient so when the Rangers got off to their worst start in a decade to open the 1975–76 season, change was inevitable. Under pressure to make a deal—any deal—GM Emile Francis pulled the trigger on a trade that sent shockwaves through the hockey universe: Park, Ratelle, and minor-leaguer Joe Zanussi to the Boston Bruins for Phil Esposito and Carol Vadnais.

It was a blockbuster of the highest magnitude between two longtime rivals—the hockey equivalent of Joe DiMaggio being traded for Ted Williams (or, if you prefer a more contemporary baseball reference, Derek Jeter for David Ortiz). What possessed Francis to part with two of his most valuable and popular stars while still in their prime? Best to let The Cat explain it for himself:

"It was the most difficult decision I ever had to make in my life," he said. "Jean Ratelle was the best player that ever played for me and Brad Park, other than Bobby Orr, was the best defenseman in the NHL. But I'll tell you what happened—we were in a five-year period where we should have won, but we didn't. To win in the NHL, to win the Stanley Cup, you gotta be good, you gotta be lucky, and you have to stay free of injuries. We had a knack for getting the wrong guy hurt at the wrong time. It was always in March. In '72, we were playing the Seals when Ratelle passed the puck back to Dale Rolfe. Rolfe shoots the puck and guess what he hits? Ratelle's ankle. And Ratelle had the second-most points in the league at the time. Park got hurt two years in a row also. We seemed to be the unluckiest team going.

"I'll tell you why I made the deal. When we got beat out by Philadelphia in the '74 semifinals, the press really went off on our players. They called them 'fat cats,' meaning Brad Park and Jean Ratelle. These guys were the key to our team, so it hurt me to read that and it wasn't fair to them. But then we got off to a bad start in 1975. At one point, I got a call from the new chairman and CEO of the Madison Square Garden Corporation, Alan Cohen, telling me to fire our coach [Ron Stewart] and go back behind the bench myself. I told him, 'I've run this team for 16 years and I don't need you to tell me what to do now.' But I knew that our era was over. I knew that to protect Brad Park and Jean Ratelle, they should no longer be in New York because everyone was down on them. The media was down on all of us because we hadn't won.

"I got to talking with Harry Sinden, the Bruins' general manager. It started out as an innocent thing. We were at a GMs meeting and he said to me, 'Geez, your team is going bad and we're going bad. You want to talk about a deal?' I thought, why not? So I said, 'Harry, if we're going to make a deal, we can't deal the deuces and the threes. If we're going to make a deal, let's talk about a deal that is going to change our teams.' He asked me if I'd be willing to trade Park. I said yes. Then he wanted to know if I'd trade Ratelle. And I said yes. So he offered me Phil Esposito and Carol Vadnais. At first, I said no. I wanted Bobby Orr. I wanted Bobby Orr *and* Phil Esposito. He said, 'I wouldn't trade Orr until the day I died.' So we continued to talk for two or three weeks. The longer we talked, the worse our teams got. And I could tell that the new Garden CEO and I weren't going to get along. I knew that my time was limited. So I finally called Harry and we arranged to meet in Buffalo. That's when we made the deal. I knew what I was dealing. I knew what Park and Ratelle could do.

Who the (Bleep) Is Joe Zanussi?

He was the extra player in a trade featuring three future Hall of Famers—a throw-in by Rangers GM Emile Francis to sweeten the pot for his Boston-based counterpart, Harry Sinden.

Skating with the Rangers' minor league team, the Providence Reds, Joe Zanussi led the American Hockey League in scoring as a defenseman in 1974–75, earning him the Eddie Shore Award as the top defenseman in the AHL. That year, he also finished runner-up as the AHL's Most Valuable Player.

Still, when it came to making it in the NHL, Zanussi's size (5'9", 185 lbs.) and age (28) didn't work in his favor. He'd earned a few call-ups to New York but just couldn't stick with the varsity.

But then, virtually overnight, Zanussi went from being a minor leaguer to playing alongside Bobby Orr and Brad Park on the Bruins blueline. Don Cherry took an immediate liking to him.

"The guy's got good hockey sense," Cherry said of Zanussi. "It's beyond me why the Rangers didn't give him a shot when they could have."

Zanussi got his shot in Boston...and was traded a year later to the St. Louis Blues.

And I knew they'd help the Bruins. That was the toughest deal I ever had to make."

Don Cherry, Boston's effusive coach, was the one who had to break the bad news to Esposito. Then he tried to convince Phil not to report. "F--k them," he said, referring to Bruins management, Rangers management, and whomever else may have had a hand in the trade. "What are they going to do? Suspend you?"

Esposito, accepting the trade however reluctantly, flew immediately from Vancouver, where the Bruins were, to Oakland, where the Rangers were set to play the Seals on November 7, 1975—the same day as the trade. When he caught up with his new team, Esposito walked into the visitor's dressing room at the Oakland Coliseum and was stunned to find a captain's "C" stitched to his jersey. He felt awkward accepting such an honor without ever having played a game for the Rangers, believing Gilbert or Walt Tkaczuk—both career Blueshirts—to be more deserving.

But Esposito begrudgingly embraced his new leadership role and set out to change the attitude of a club that had plenty of talent but always faltered when the games mattered most. Coming from a close-knit group in Boston that exerted tremendous internal pressure to win, he was vocal about wanting to create a similar atmosphere on the Rangers. Self-expression was never a problem for the big centerman.

"Phil didn't like anything about anything that we did," recalled Pete Stemkowski. "He didn't like our hotels. He didn't like the trainer handing out the meal money. 'We didn't do it that way in Boston!' 'That's not the way we did it in Boston!' Hey, Phil, it wasn't Boston."

Vadnais' arrival with the Rangers, unlike Esposito's, was delayed for several days. Unknown to Francis, and inexcusably unknown to Harry Sinden, was the fact that Vadnais had a no-trade clause in his contract. He and his agent just sat tight. They wanted $100,000 to waive the no-trade clause.

Sinden and the notoriously frugal Bruins had no choice. They had to pay up, especially since Esposito immediately played his first game as a Ranger that very evening. Many hockey people joked that Sinden never would have made the deal in the first place if he knew it would cost him another $100,000.

Fan reaction to the trade was mixed, but the prevailing emotion felt by the roughly 150 people who called the Rangers front office (and the dozens more who rang NHL headquarters) was one of disbelief—they simply could not wrap their heads around it.

"We traded who?"

"Is this a joke?"

"We really got Esposito?"

"If Boston was willing to give him up, there must be something wrong with him, right?"

Fans weren't the only ones who felt blindsided. Park had been the Rangers' captain and thought he was the heart and soul of the team. Once the shock of the trade wore off, he broke down in tears. Sadness quickly turned to anger—anger at the team that traded him. He went to Boston highly motivated to show the Rangers they'd made a mistake.

Never one to mince words, Esposito said that getting traded to New York was the biggest hurt of his life, including the death of both of his parents. To this day, he's never completely forgiven Sinden or Bruins owner Jeremy Jacobs, the former for agreeing to the trade and the latter for being a "cheap bastard" who was probably relieved to be rid of his contract.

"As much as I admired Phil for his play with the Bruins and Team Canada when we were teammates in beating the Russians," Gilbert said, "his attitude was that he and Carol Vadnais had come to New York against their will. They did not want to leave Boston any more than Brad wanted to leave New York. They were different characters who were a little more outspoken about playing for the Rangers. When you're a veteran player on a team and you hear that two players are coming in who said, 'New York is the only place I didn't want to go,' we had to regroup. I don't think it ever developed into something exciting."

At least it didn't during Rod's time with the team. In 1979, a year after Gilbert was forced into early retirement by Emile Francis' replacement, John Ferguson, Espo and Vadnais helped lead the Rangers back to the Stanley Cup Finals. The Bruins made it to the finals twice with Park and Ratelle. Neither team won a championship.

So who won the trade?

"I don't think Esposito and Vadnais were ever accepted in New York the way Park and Ratelle were accepted in Boston," Francis concluded. "They never contributed to the New York Rangers like Park and Ratelle did for the Boston Bruins. No way."

5 The Guarantee

The greatest leader in professional sports earned that reputation by giving his all every night and demanding the same from his teammates. He did it with a glare that could burn a hole through lead and a smile that could melt the coldest glacier. He did it with his stick, his elbows, and the willingness to use either as a weapon.

Mark Messier was as complete a player as the league has ever seen—one who could pass, shoot, skate, hit, or fight his way to victory.

"He will make everybody believe that the New York Rangers can actually win," GM Neil Smith foretold, "and I'm not sure that there's ever been anybody yet in the last god-knows-how-many years that's been able to make the Rangers believe they can win."

Expectations reached the stratosphere in 1992 after a brilliant regular season saw Messier score 107 points, win his second Hart Trophy, and lead the Rangers to their first-ever Presidents' Trophy as the team with the league's best record. It made their gut-wrenching loss to Pittsburgh in the Patrick Division Finals that much harder to swallow and prompted some to wonder whether this Messier character, a five-time Stanley Cup winner with Edmonton, was man enough to rescue the Rangers from an eternity of "1940!" chants.

Hart Trophy Winners

The Hart Memorial Trophy is an annual award given to the NHL player determined to be the most valuable to his team. The winner is selected in a poll of the Professional Hockey Writers Association in all NHL cities at the end of the regular season.

Mark Messier was the fourth Ranger to win the award. The others were Buddy O'Connor (1948), Chuck Rayner (1950), and Andy Bathgate (1959).

Longtime linemate Adam Graves summed it up best. "People expect him to grab the puck, fly through the air, and drop the puck in the goal."

Graves was right. Messier couldn't work miracles by himself. He not only had to convince teammates that the impossible was possible, but also that it would require every man on the roster, from the stars to the role players, working toward the same objective.

Such was the message delivered during the 1994 Eastern Conference Finals against the New Jersey Devils. Here, if the Messier legend wasn't born, it was solidified.

With the Rangers a game away from elimination, Messier earned his place among New York's sporting icons when he delivered his famous "guarantee"—the promise that his team would triumph in Game 6 and extend the series to seven games.

"We're going to go in and win Game 6," Messier said following the morning skate at the Meadowlands, his comments intended as much for the small gathering of reporters as for his teammates. "We've done that all year—we've won all the games we've had to win. I know we're going to go in and win Game 6 and bring it back [to the Garden] for Game 7. We have enough talent and experience to turn the tide."

Had Messier dabbled in clairvoyance, or was it simply his way of rallying the troops at the season's most critical juncture? When it came to motivational tactics, the big, balding centerman had a knack for knowing which buttons to push.

"My first thought was 'Oh, no! What did I do?'" Messier recalled. "I forgot about the 14 million people who live [in New Jersey] and that Scott Stevens would be reading the paper. What I said was for my teammates. It certainly wasn't for Scott to put it up in the New Jersey dressing room. I was just trying to give our team confidence in a series where the momentum had swung New Jersey's way."

But he also knew that failure would result in the worst kind of embarrassment. So, despite having been stifled throughout the series by the Devils' smothering defensive system, a sore and exhausted Messier backed up his bold prediction by scoring a natural hat trick in the third period, helping the Rangers erase a two-goal deficit. Play-by-play man Mike "Doc" Emrick called Messier's signature performance "the stuff of legend," and it certainly has taken on an air of myth in the years since.

"Mess just kind of went along with a journalist's headline story," said Craig MacTavish, a teammate in Edmonton and New York. "I'll tell you one thing—it didn't make Mark play any harder. You knew he was going to play his rear end off in that game whether he made a guarantee or not."

6 Lester Saves the Day

Under normal circumstances, a team winning a championship in just its second year of existence would be big news. But the Rangers didn't win the Stanley Cup in 1928 under normal circumstances. The discovery of a most unexpected backup goaltender set this chapter of Stanley Cup lore apart from all others.

The Rangers had finished second overall in the standings that year behind Boston, then edged the Pittsburgh Pirates in a total-goals series before knocking off the Bruins in the semifinals. As it did every spring, the circus had taken over Madison Square Garden, cheating Rangers fans out of the chance to see their team battle the Montreal Maroons for hockey's ultimate prize live and in-person. So the entire Stanley Cup Finals were booked for Montreal.

The Maroons won the first game, and Game 2 was scoreless in the second period when Rangers goalie Lorne Chabot was badly hurt by a hard shot off the stick of Montreal winger Nels Stewart. Blood gushed from a wound directly above Chabot's left eye, and he had to be helped off the ice by teammates to await an ambulance. Needless to say, he was done for the night.

Crazy as it sounds, in that era, NHL teams didn't have backup goalies. Instead, rinks kept spare goalies around—usually from the home team's minor league club—sitting in the stands in case of emergency. On this night, however, no spares could be found. There were two goalies from other teams in attendance as spectators: Alex Connell of the Ottawa Senators and a minor leaguer named Hugh McCormick. Lester Patrick, coach and manager of the Rangers, asked if either man could be brought in to sub for Chabot, but the Maroons refused. Greed was likely behind the home team's disgraceful lack of sportsmanship—Montreal's ownership had promised each player a $3,000 bonus on top of their playoff pay for winning the Stanley Cup. They weren't going to do the Rangers any favors.

Patrick had to get a goalie somewhere, and quick. If he didn't, the Rangers would forfeit the match and fall behind 2–0 in the best-of-five series. He and his crew retreated to the visitors' dressing room to figure out their next move.

About a dozen well-wishers, among them Toronto manager Conn Smythe and Pittsburgh coach Odie Cleghorn, crammed themselves into the room to shout out suggestions and advice.

Smythe, the Rangers' original manager and the man responsible for putting most of those players in a Ranger uniform, marched around yelling that he'd gladly go in net. Nobody seemed quite sure if he was being serious.

An Ode to Lester's Gallant Stand

Sportswriter Jim Burchard of the *New York World Telegram* wrote this poem as a tribute to Lester Patrick. Eat your heart out, Robert Frost.

'Twas in the Spring of Twenty Eight
A golden Ranger page
That Lester got a summons
To guard the Blueshirt cage.
Chabot had stopped a fast one,
A bad break for our lads
The Cup at stake—and no one
To don the Ranger pads.
"We're cooked," lamented Patrick,
"This crisis I had feared."
He leaned upon his newest crutch
And wept inside his beard.
Then suddenly he came to life,
No longer halt or lame.
"Give me the pads," he bellowed,
"I used to play this game."
Then how the Rangers shouted
How Patrick was acclaimed.
Maroons stood sneering, gloating,
They should have been ashamed.
The final score was two to one,
Old Lester met the test.
The Rangers finally won the Cup,
But Les has since confessed.
"I just spoke up to cheer the boys,
"I must have been delirious.
"But now in reminiscence,
"I'm glad they took me serious."

Frank Boucher and his linemate, team captain Bill Cook, went off to a corner to exchange ideas. They agreed that putting another player in goal would leave them short-staffed at another position.

"Then my eye caught Lester," Boucher said, "standing in the middle of the room trying to restore some semblance of order, and I suggested to Bill that perhaps he was our solution."

Boucher and Cook took Patrick aside and asked if he'd be willing to go in net. He said no at first, but they persisted. Lester bowed his head in thought for a moment and then, quite dramatically, turned and called out for team trainer Harry Westerby.

Westerby came running, pushing himself through the crowd to find Patrick.

"Harry," Patrick said, "I want you to get me a dry set of underwear. I want you to strip off Lorne's skates and uniform, and I will use his equipment and go into the goaltender's position myself."

A stunned silence fell over the room which, just seconds earlier, had been a scene of absolute chaos.

"Check as you've never checked before," Lester reportedly told his players, "and help protect an old man."

But Lester was hardly old and not far removed from his playing days as a defenseman (in fact, he played one game on defense for the Rangers the prior season). The Silver Fox was only 44 but had an air of majesty about him and a head of gray hair that betrayed his true age.

After a lengthy delay, Patrick skated onto the Forum ice wearing Chabot's black cap and brown pads that fit like a baggy pair of pants. At first, fans didn't know how to react. Once they realized the Rangers' coach was in goal, they offered a smattering of bemused applause. Cleghorn, the Pirates coach, agreed to run the Rangers bench.

The Blueshirts were inspired by Lester that night, even if he milked the occasion for all it was worth. Suddenly full of confidence, he yelled to his players, "Make them shoot! Make them shoot!" while Cleghorn was screaming, "For God's sake, don't let them shoot!"

Perhaps because they thought they'd be able to score at will, the Maroons didn't press as hard as they should have when play resumed. They tested Patrick with a few long-distance shots that he easily stopped.

"Lester was in his glory," Boucher remembered. "He really seemed to be enjoying himself. Every time the puck came toward him, he'd drop to his knees and smother it."

By the second intermission, the game was still scoreless.

Thirty seconds into the third period, Bill Cook split the Montreal defense of Red Dutton and Dunc Munro to score New York's first goal of the series. Now the Maroons were behind, and they went on the attack. The Rangers, especially their top defensive pair of Taffy Abel and Ching Johnson, responded by hurling their bodies at anything in a red uniform, checking like fiends to protect their lead.

With less than 6:00 left to play, Nels Stewart struck again. This time, he sent a soft shot toward the Ranger net from out in the neutral zone. Patrick had time to prepare for it, and waited until the last moment to drop down to one knee to make the save, but the puck trickled through his legs. Tie game.

Exhausted from defending Lester, the Rangers knew as they prepared for overtime that the longer the game lasted, the more likely they were to give up the game-winning goal.

About seven minutes into the extra frame, the puck was deep in the Maroons' end, against the boards behind Montreal goalie Clint Benedict. Benedict came out of his crease to play the puck, but before he could get to it, Ching Johnson came barreling in, got his stick on it, and passed the disc out to Frank Boucher. As Benedict scrambled to get back into position, Boucher fired the puck into a wide-open net.

Any Rangers on the ice rushed toward Lester Patrick, and those on the bench immediately hopped over the boards to join in the celebration. His period-and-a-half turn as backup goalie became *the* storyline of the finals and, ultimately, the stuff of hockey lore.

Joe Miller, on loan from the New York Americans, started in goal for the Rangers for the remainder of the series. And Chabot, released from the hospital a week after his injury, sat in the stands during the fifth and decisive game wearing a black eye patch. With his one good eye, he watched the Rangers edge the Maroons 2–1 to win their first Stanley Cup.

Back in New York, the Blueshirts were welcomed home as champions on the steps of City Hall. Mayor Jimmy Walker, who never passed up an opportunity to be seen (and photographed) with heroes, was sure to position himself right next to Lester as flashbulbs popped.

7 The G-A-G Line

It is the Rangers' most famous line—a near-perfect balance of skill, speed, and toughness. The G-A-G Line of Jean Ratelle, Rod Gilbert, and Vic Hadfield was the vanguard of the Blueshirts' attack from the late 1960s to the early 1970s.

Contrary to Islander fan propaganda, G-A-G had nothing to do with the Rangers' propensity for choking in the postseason. The acronym stood for Goal-A-Game. The threesome scored so often that one season, 1971–72, team statistician Arthur "Art the Dart" Friedman changed the nickname to T-A-G Line for Two-A-Game.

Ratelle was the glue that held the unit together. It is not at all an overstatement to compare Ratty to a famous predecessor, Frank Boucher, or a famous successor, Wayne Gretzky. On the ice, he was

For One Fan, A Great Souvenir

With just less than five minutes remaining in Game 2 of the 1971 quarterfinals, Vic Hadfield and Maple Leafs center Jim Harrison decided to settle a game-long feud with their fists. Bernie Parent, the Leafs' goalie, rushed to Harrison's defense, prompting Ed Giacomin to bolt his cage. As the two goalies got tangled up, Hadfield spotted Parent's mask on the ice, picked it up, and tossed it into the stands. The Garden crowd loved it.

Once referee Lloyd Gilmour was finished handing out penalties, everyone readied themselves for play to resume...everyone except Parent. He wasn't going back into his net without his mask, and his spare was back in Toronto. As Garden security and Leafs exec King Clancy fanned through the stands looking for the mask, the crowd chanted, "Don't give it back! Don't give it back!" It was never recovered, so Toronto's backup, Jacques Plante, came in to play the final minutes of the game, which the Rangers won 4–1.

Parent's mask resurfaced at a 2006 auction, where it was purchased by a private collector who promised to give it to the Hockey Hall of Fame when he dies.

graceful, "as smooth as the ice itself," said Emile Francis, the club's long time coach and general manager, on many occasions.

"You always knew what you were going to get from Jean," Francis recalled. "He was always the same. It didn't matter if it was an exhibition game, a practice, or a playoff game. He was probably the most consistent player I ever had. He was our Beliveau, our Esposito. Plus, he never complained about anything."

Growing up in the suburbs of Montreal, Ratelle and Gilbert had played together since they were ten years old. The two future Hall of Famers could very easily have been snatched up at a young age by the Canadiens, but a Rangers scout named Yvan Prud'homme got them both out of Quebec to play for the Rangers' junior team in Guelph, Ontario.

"The Canadiens," Francis said, "had so many players, they overlooked them. They had too many."

A sharpshooting right winger who sailed across the ice with elegance and determination, Gilbert had been one of the top prospects in Canada and was tearing up the OHA in 1960 when he received word that he was being called up to New York. Before making his NHL debut, however, disaster struck in the form of a back injury that nearly destroyed his dreams of turning pro.

Doctors suspected a spasm, but X-rays told a different story: Gilbert had actually broken his fifth vertebra. So the Rangers put their star prospect on a 22-hour train ride to the Mayo Clinic in Minnesota, where doctors later removed bone from Gilbert's leg and used it in a spinal fusion operation. The prospects of Gilbert walking again were excellent. Whether he'd ever play hockey again, no one could say.

A few years and another operation later, Rod emerged as the face of the franchise—the Rangers' very own Mickey Mantle. And like New York's other No. 7, Gilbert's outgoing personality and love of the nightlife made him a natural fit in the Big Apple.

One of the reasons Gilbert and Ratelle had the freedom to perform their artistry in open ice is because they had a big guy riding shotgun. Hadfield was the G-A-G Line's muscle, complementing the Francophones' finesse with his size, physicality, and willingness to crash the net. Vic's metamorphosis from minor league tough guy to major league All-Star took much of the hockey world by surprise. Toiling for St. Catharines of the OHA and later the AHL's Buffalo Bisons, the blond and brawny left wing was adept at accumulating penalty minutes, not points, and he continued in an enforcer role for the Rangers after they claimed him from Chicago in the 1961 Intra-League draft. A decade later, he became the first Ranger to score 50 goals in a season.

"I was aggressive," Hadfield said, "and being aggressive for so long, I had more space on the ice because people stayed away from me. You have to stick with what got you there."

In 1971–72, the G-A-G Line became the first line in which all three players had at least 40 goals. They also finished third, fourth, and fifth in the NHL scoring race, trailing only Boston's Phil Esposito and Bobby Orr. Ratelle, despite a broken ankle that cost him the final month of the season, had 46 goals and 63 assists for 109 points, the best season of his career. The Rangers bolted to the Stanley Cup Finals that season and faced the Bruins. Ratelle tried a comeback from the ankle injury but was ineffective. The Bruins won four games to two.

The G-A-G Line remained largely intact until 1974 when the Rangers traded Hadfield to the Pittsburgh Penguins.

8 The Save: Richter vs. Bure

Pacific Coliseum, June 7, 1994, Game 4, Stanley Cup Finals
Mike Richter never led the league in goals against average, save percentage, or shutouts. He had a losing record in eight of his 14 seasons on Broadway. And when his career win total is matched against those of contemporaries Patrick Roy, Martin Brodeur, and Ed Belfour, 301 sounds small by comparison.

But there's a No. 35 banner with Richter's name on it hanging from the ceiling of Madison Square Garden because, until Henrik Lundqvist came along, those 301 victories were the most of any Ranger goalie. It's there because he never wore the uniform of another NHL team. It's there because he was one of the most focused and best prepared netminders of his generation. And, most importantly, it's there because he was the man guarding the crease when the Rangers won their fourth and most elusive Stanley Cup.

Did You Know?
The Mike Richter Award honors the top goaltender in NCAA men's hockey. In two seasons at the University of Wisconsin, Richter was named the 1986 WCHA Freshman of the Year and earned All-WCHA second team honors in 1987.

Richter's dazzling play throughout the 1994 playoffs was just one of many highlights from that storybook spring, but none were quite as dazzling as his groin-splitting stop on a Pavel Bure penalty shot in Game 4 of the finals.

Leading 2–1 in the second period on goals by Trevor Linden and Cliff Ronning, the Canucks badly needed to win the game to avoid falling behind 3–1 in the series.

With the Rangers chasing the tying goal, Vancouver was just as desperate to pad its lead. With about 6:30 remaining in the period, Bure had a breakaway from his own blue line but was pulled down by Brian Leetch just as he crossed into the Rangers' zone. Referee Terry Gregson blew his whistle and pointed to center ice.

One goalie. One skater. One shot. The Stanley Cup Finals.

"That's what you want as an athlete," Richter said. "You want to be up against the best in the world in an important moment. That's what you pretend in the driveway as a kid, right? A penalty shot in the Stanley Cup Finals. I felt very fortunate to be in that position."

In a team sport, here was a rare one-on-one competition between two stars in the prime of their careers.

Like his childhood idol, Flyers legend Bernie Parent, Richter was a great angles goalie who kept himself square to the shooter and just let the puck hit him. On the rare occasion when he was out of position, he was athletic enough to make what should have been a routine stop look downright spectacular.

"You look at Mike," Adam Graves said, "and he's a great athlete. He'd come in as the best-conditioned player. If you looked at him when he walked into the locker room you'd say, 'He *can't* be a goalie.'"

And Bure? He was simply one of the most dynamic players of the 1990s. His explosive speed earned him the nickname "The Russian Rocket," and in 1993–94 he led the league with 60 goals, 49 of which came in the season's last 51 games. His 16 playoff goals were tops that season, too.

"I've played with and against a lot of great players," former Canucks coach Rick Ley said, "but I've never seen a player like him, where you stand behind the bench, watch him, and just say 'Wow.'"

The decibel level at Pacific Coliseum soared as Bure readied himself at center ice to take the penalty shot. The crowd knew what was at stake. A goal would deflate the Rangers and swing the series' momentum in Vancouver's favor.

As soon as Bure's stick touched the puck, Richter came charging out of his crease to challenge the shooter but then had to retreat back into his net. He knew Bure would come in with speed and wanted to give him as little room to shoot as possible.

Employing a move he'd already used with success against Calgary's Mike Vernon in the first round of the playoffs, Bure feinted once to his backhand, returned to his forehand and then, as he closed in on Richter, tried to slide the puck under the goalie's right pad. But Richter was ready for it. With Gumby-like elasticity, he kicked his leg all the way out to touch the right post.

"Save by Richter!" screamed MSG Network play-by-play man Sam Rosen.

That save was arguably the biggest of Richter's career, and it was certainly the defining moment of the 1994 Stanley Cup Finals. And yet, years later, he sounded almost remorseful that his success in that crucial moment had come at Bure's expense.

"Poor Pav," Richter said. "He was such a great player. That whole playoff series, he was really lighting it up. Don't forget, he

*Goalie Mike Richter makes a save in the third period as the Vancouver
Canucks' Trevor Linden (16) skates away and Ranger Kevin Lowe (4) looks on
in Game 7 of the Stanley Cup Finals at New York's Madison Square Garden
on Tuesday, June 14, 1994. The Rangers won 3–2 to take the Stanley Cup for
the first time in 54 years.* (AP Photo/Ron Frehm)

scored plenty on me in that series. He had the whole arsenal. He scored on some breakaways, and he scored between my legs once. The guy could do anything, but that one time, I got him. It's sort of immortalized in that great picture. He's had to answer a lot of questions about that but nobody asks, 'Hey, what about the three you scored before that?' I always felt bad for Pav in that regard because he's a great guy and one hell of a player."

Emboldened by Richter's play and a four-point night from Brian Leetch, the Rangers came back to win Game 4 to take a commanding 3–1 series lead.

9 Visit the World's Most Famous Arena

Jews have the Temple Mount. Muslims have Mecca. Elvis impersonators have Graceland. But the capital of Ranger Nation is located in the heart of midtown Manhattan at 8 Pennsylvania Plaza, on Seventh Avenue between 31st and 33rd Streets.

Good evening, ladies and gentlemen, and welcome to Madison Square Garden, the world's most famous arena!

So how did a building named Madison Square Garden end up 10 blocks from Madison Square? The original Madison Square Garden built in 1874 was a converted railroad station at Madison Square, near the intersection of Madison Avenue and 26th Street. In 1890, a sports arena was built on the site. Primarily a boxing venue, it also hosted concerts, light operas, and the circus. But after only 35 years of use, the building was torn down to make way for a new corporate headquarters for the New York Life Insurance Company.

A new arena was built at Eighth Avenue and 50th Street. For branding purposes, it just made sense to keep the name Madison

Bending the Truth

"My favorite memory of Madison Square Garden was my first hockey game. I asked my roommate, who had an early morning check-in, to go with me. I told her it would only take an hour: three 20-minute periods."

Joanne Vickers, Aurora, Ontario
Wife of former Ranger Steve Vickers

Square Garden. It opened in 1925 and a year later, beneath a perpetual haze of cigar and cigarette smoke, the Rangers played their first home game.

The third Garden, like its predecessors, eventually outlived its usefulness. It was decided, and not without some controversy, that the original Pennsylvania Station—an architectural wonder inspired by the grand bath houses of ancient Rome—would be torn down and its facilities moved underground so that an arena could be built directly above it. Demolition of the terminal began in 1963 and construction of a fourth Madison Square Garden began three years later.

On the morning of February 12, 1968, workers flooded the arena floor of MSG IV for the first time. By nightfall, the liquid had frozen and Bob Nevin, the Ranger captain at the time, saw to it that his skates were the first to touch the quarter-inch-thick sheet of ice. Workmen and other onlookers clapped when he fired the puck into an empty net, unofficially christening the team's new home.

Encased in a shell of concrete and glass and shaped like a drum (or, if you prefer, a hockey puck), the current Garden has provided multiple generations of Rangers fans with a rich databank of memories bitter and sweet: Mike Milbury and Bruins teammates climbing into the stands to brawl with fans. Rangers pouring off the bench to celebrate beating the Islanders in the 1979 playoffs. Bob "The Chief" Comas running through the aisles in full Native headdress. The Matteau goal. The night a sheet of glass fell off the boards onto Wayne Gretzky's wife, Janet Jones, knocking her unconscious. John Amirante performing the National Anthem at the first Ranger game after 9/11. Mark Messier's 77-minute banner raising ceremony. And countless others, many of which are recalled on the pages that follow.

"I guess I didn't realize when I was playing there how great it was," former Rangers defenseman Tom Laidlaw said of returning to the Garden as an opponent. "There is no other building like it in the world. It's the atmosphere, even for a preseason game. It's the lighting, the sound, the history, the banners. Yeah, it's a special place."

What really makes the Garden special, setting it apart from every other pile of bricks, is the fans. They are the reason why it is said that winning a championship in New York is unlike winning anyplace else on earth. And there are no Rangers fans quite like the ones occupying that rowdy region known as the Blue Seats.

These denizens of the Garden's uppermost (and least expensive) tiers, the 400 level, are not unlike the Bleacher Creatures over at Yankee Stadium—mostly working-class folks from the outer boroughs who are there to watch a game, not entertain clients from out of town. They're fiercely loyal to the home team, unforgiving of any Ranger perceived to be soft or lazy, and merciless to visiting players and fans. They're a culture unto themselves, rich with their own rituals and traditions. This is where chants like "Potvin sucks!" "Beat your wife, Potvin!" "Shoot the puck, Barry!" and many others too racy to repeat were conceived, tested, and perfected. Even fellow Rangers fans—the ones sitting in the pricier sections below—have been targets of their heckling.

There's less illicit activity going on there these days, but the Blues have long been a neighborhood in need of a little extra policing. Back in the '70s and '80s, if one caught a whiff of pot smoke between periods, there's a pretty good chance it was coming from the corridors outside the Blues.

Construction at Madison Square Garden at 34th Street covered an area from Seventh Avenue to Eighth Avenue in Manhattan as shown in this photo dated September 13, 1964. This was the view looking west from the Empire State Building in New York City. (AP Photo)

Nick Fotiu: From Blue-Seater to Blueshirt

When he was a teenager, trekking from his home in Staten Island to find ice at Skateland in New Hyde Park, Nick Fotiu would tell anyone who would listen—his folks, buddies from the neighborhood, and even Rangers equipment manager Jimmy Young—that one day, he'd be the first fan to come down from the Blue Seats at Madison Square Garden and play for the Rangers.

Of course, nobody believed him.

But Nick, a brawling left winger, fought his way into the NHL and eventually joined the team he grew up cheering for. And he never forgot his roots.

It's common these days for players to gently toss souvenir pucks over the glass at Madison Square Garden, but Fotiu's habit of throwing them all the way up to the blue seats after pregame warm-ups endeared him to the crowd while greatly disturbing his coaches, who feared a shoulder injury, as well as Garden lawyers and security folks who feared for someone falling out of the balcony.

The time someone threw a trout at Islanders goalie Billy Smith? It came from the blues. Or when fans tore a Pelle Lindbergh Flyers jersey off a man and set it on fire? That happened in the blues, too. Or the time a pair of visitors unfamiliar with blue seat etiquette sat down and put their hats back on during the National Anthem and were nearly thrown over the railing? They escaped black-eyed and bleeding.

Although seats in the 400 level were changed to teal as part of a 1990 renovation of the Garden, they were still known as "the blues."

In 2009, it was announced that the arena would undergo a $500 million top-to-bottom facelift. The transformed Garden would have wider concourses with views of the city, new food and entertainment amenities, a new scoreboard, sound and LED video systems in high-def, new luxury suites, clubs and hospitality areas. The price tag for the renovations ballooned to almost $1 billion and took three years to complete.

Reviews have been mixed. Although the interior is brighter and concession offerings more plentiful, fans have railed against the higher ticket prices, a new floor plan that limits access between sections, new fan bridges that block views of the scoreboard in the 200 level, and cramped seating. All are valid concerns.

But here's the inescapable truth: there is something exhilarating about being in an arena with 18,000 fellow Rangers fans. It really hits you when that question you've silently asked yourself a million times, "Is there anybody else in the world who loves this team as much as I do?" is finally answered.

"Yes."

How long fans will get to experience that sensation at MSG's current address is in doubt. In July 2012, as construction crews finished the third and final phase of renovations, the New York City Council notified Cablevision CEO Jim Dolan and company that they have 10 years to vacate the 45-year-old premises and find a new home so that the city can demolish the building and begin a massive expansion of Penn Station.

Will the Rangers really have to pack their bags and move across town? Not only is it possible, it wouldn't be the first time.

10 Fish Sticks, Anyone?

An entire generation of Rangers fans has grown up only knowing the New York Islanders as a league laughingstock. It's hard to believe that a team that wasted first-round draft picks on Dave Chyzowski and Scott Scissons, traded away a franchise defenseman in Zdeno Chara, was briefly owned by a con man named John

Spano, and gave Rick DiPietro a 15-year contract is the same one that caused the Rangers and their fans so much heartache.

The Islanders owe their existence to the World Hockey Association. In 1972, the rogue league announced that its intended flagship franchise, the New York Raiders, was going to play at the new Nassau Coliseum in Uniondale with the ABA's New York Nets. But operators of the Coliseum weren't sold on the WHA and hastily lobbied the NHL to add a second New York team. Despite opposition from the Rangers, who didn't want or need competition from across the East River, the league granted an expansion team to Nets owner Roy Boe. The Battle of New York had begun.

The Islanders had to pay the Rangers a $4 million territorial fee. Eight years later, a powerhouse club led by Coach Al Arbour and stars Mike Bossy, Bryan Trottier, Billy Smith, and Denis Potvin accomplished what the establishment team from Manhattan had not in four decades. And then they had the nerve to do it four years in a row.

"In terms of building a fan base, the Islanders had to start from scratch," said Chris Botta, a former public relations exec who spent 15 years in the Islanders' front office. "It wasn't like they just attracted frustrated Rangers fans who couldn't get tickets at the Garden. No, the Islanders had to create their own fans, and they did it by being successful—not just by winning the Stanley Cup in year eight, but by beating the Rangers in the playoffs in year three. They had success as close to right away as I think you could possibly have had in that era."

That success gave rise to a chant that originated in the upper bowl of Nassau Coliseum and then gradually infected every other arena in the NHL.

"1940! 1940!"

"Playing against the Islanders was what I dreamt of as a kid growing up," said former Rangers captain Barry Beck. "Not the Islanders per se, but a rivalry at the highest level of hockey. They

Rangers All-Time Record vs. Islanders (1972–2014)

GP	W	L	T	OL
249	122	101	19	7

had great teams in that era with coaching and management to match. That's a pretty tough combination to beat. In those days, there was no free agency so your teams could stay together. They were a powerful group. We got close a few times, and I would like to think we pushed them to be their best."

Beck's Rangers lost to the Islanders in the playoffs four years in a row, from 1981 to 1984.

"The thing I remember most about games against the Rangers," former Islanders center and current MSG Network analyst Butch Goring recalled, "was that it was more about the fans and the media and the hype, particularly at Madison Square Garden. The fans there are crazy. It gave me more incentive to beat the Rangers to sort of quiet their fans. Even when we were in our own building, it always seemed like half the crowd was Rangers fans and half were Islander fans. We were always determined to beat the Rangers because I think most people felt we were the poor guys and they were the rich guys. I didn't hate their players but I enjoyed the rivalry."

"Games between these teams always meant something," Botta said. "I always took offense to the idea floated from time to time by some moronic broadcasters that somehow it was a bigger deal for the Islanders to beat the Rangers. It was a big deal for *both* teams. It's a true rivalry. I don't think it's any different than what goes on in other markets, but this is unique because of the geographic closeness and the fact that there are certainly a lot of Rangers fans on Long Island. It was something that served to inspire the Bob Nystroms and the Mike Bossys to the Zigmund Palffys to the players of today."

Highlights (and lowlights) of the Rangers-Islanders rivalry include:

April 11, 1975: The Islanders win their first playoff series, and eliminate the Rangers, on an overtime goal by veteran winger J.P. Parise. Prior to the decisive match, a pair of New York City police officers loyal to the Rangers had allegedly approached Rangers broadcaster Bill Chadwick and offered to close down the Whitestone Bridge or the Throgs Neck Bridge to delay the Islanders' team bus. Chadwick declined the offer, of course, but in hindsight, maybe he should have accepted.

February 25, 1979: Islanders captain Denis Potvin crushes the Rangers' brittle playmaker, Ulf Nilsson, against the boards. It's a clean hit, but Nilsson's right skate gets caught in a rut, and he crumples to the ice in agony. The resulting injury—a broken ankle that forces Nilsson to miss the rest of the season—ensures Potvin a seemingly permanent place of dishonor among the Blueshirt faithful, who have been chanting "Potvin sucks!" ever since.

May 8, 1979: With a 2–1 win at Madison Square Garden, the Rangers eliminate the favored Islanders in a classic semifinal series, four games to two.

May 24, 1980: The Islanders defeat the Philadelphia Flyers to win their first Stanley Cup.

May 5, 1981: The Islanders complete a sweep of the Rangers in the semifinals en route to winning their second Stanley Cup.

April 23, 1982: The Reign of Terror continues as the Islanders eliminate the Rangers in Game 6 of the Patrick Division Finals.

April 22, 1983: The Rangers, who spend another Expressway Series being serenaded with chants of "1940! 1940!" are defeated in Game 6 of the Patrick Division Finals. A month later, the Islanders win their fourth consecutive Stanley Cup.

April 8, 1984: Barry Beck suffers a dislocated left shoulder on a hit by Islanders winger Pat Flatley during Game 4 of the semifinals. Later, the Islanders' outspoken goalie, Billy Smith, admits in an

A "Piece" For Your Collection

"It was September 14, 1991, my 21st birthday. A preseason game between the Rangers and the Islanders at the Mausoleum. My friends and I were at the hotel across from the arena, having a few Long Island Iced Teas. We were in the lobby getting ready to head over to the game when we saw Billy Smith come through and head to the elevators. So we followed him upstairs and waited on his floor for him to come back down. When he got back into the elevator, we jumped in with him. I leaned over to him and I said, 'Hey Billy, I'm from Sears. I'm here to collect.' He was like, 'Excuse me?' And then I said, 'Yeah, I'm from Sears…and I'm here to collect the rug on your head.' So I grabbed his hairpiece right off his head and ran out of the elevator. I got about 20' before I dropped it. He was not happy."

Ricky Otazu, Lodi, New Jersey
Rangers fan since 1973

on-camera interview that while he never enjoys seeing an opponent get injured, he's glad that if someone on the Rangers had to get hurt, it was Beck.

April 10, 1984: The Islanders' Ken Morrow scores in overtime to eliminate the Rangers from the semifinals.

April 5, 1990: In Game 1 of the semifinals, Islanders star Pat LaFontaine suffers a concussion in a controversial, open-ice hit by Rangers defenseman James Patrick. LaFontaine falls on his head and lay unconscious until being taken off the ice on a stretcher. He is delayed en route to the hospital by Rangers fans who try to flip over his ambulance. Later, in the closing seconds of the game, Mick Vukota attacks Ranger defenseman Jeff Bloemberg, a Born-Again Christian who refuses to fight. Vukota receives a 10-game suspension and the Rangers go on to win the series in five games.

April 24, 1994: The Rangers complete a first round sweep of the Islanders, outscoring their longtime foes 22–3 in the series en route to winning their first Stanley Cup in 54 years. Added bonus:

watching a completely demoralized Ron Hextall try to save the Isles' season by himself.

June 22, 1995: Hoping to attract younger fans, the Islanders unveil new uniforms. The crest—a fisherman holding a hockey stick—is billed as an homage to Long Island's nautical history but bears an uncanny resemblance to the Gorton's Seafood fisherman logo. It inspires a new chant at Madison Square Garden: "We want fish sticks!"

April 4, 1998: During a brawl at Nassau Coliseum, Rangers backup goalie Dan Cloutier pounds the Islanders' Tommy Salo to the ice then skates over to the Islanders' bench and challenges the entire team. Order is eventually restored, and the Isles win 3–0.

November 8, 2001: Theo Fleury flaps his arms like a chicken at Islanders defenseman Dale Purinton, who earlier in the game turned down a challenge to fight Rangers enforcer Sandy McCarthy.

April 5, 2007: An Islanders Ice Girl—eye candy employed by the team to clean the ice during TV timeouts—claims to have been slashed by Henrik Lundqvist as she tried to tidy up the slush around Lundqvist's goal crease. Another Ice Girl accuses Rangers players of squirting water or spitting at her from the visitors' bench.

October 24, 2012: The Islanders announce that in 2015, they will move from aging, decrepit Nassau Coliseum to the Barclays Center in Brooklyn, historically Rangers territory.

April 13, 2013: In the most important (and hyped) regular season game between the teams in years, Dan Girardi's goal at 3:11 of overtime gives the Rangers a 1–0 win over the Isles at Nassau Coliseum. Both teams earn points in a tight playoff race.

Some have said that this rivalry isn't what it used to be—that it can't be a true rivalry with the Islanders often ranking among the league's worst teams. That's nonsense. As long as any game against the Rangers glows like a beacon on their schedule, and the

Islanders treat every contest against the city-dwellers like Game 7 of the Stanley Cup Finals, the Battle of New York will rage for years to come.

11 Brian Leetch: The Greatest Ranger

Defenseman; Inducted into Hockey Hall of Fame 2009; Number retired 2008

In 1994, Brian Leetch became the first American to win the Conn Smythe Trophy as the Most Valuable Player of the Stanley Cup Playoffs. But if Mike Keenan had his way, the award might have been handed to someone else: Chris Chelios.

In hindsight, it seems almost unimaginable. But Keenan had coached Chelios in Chicago and knew what the gritty blueliner could bring to a team with championship aspirations. An 11-year veteran, Chelios had been around the game long enough to know all the lines an NHL player should not cross, and how to cross those lines without getting caught. He played with a discernible snarl. And he'd been to the Stanley Cup Finals three times, winning a title in 1986 with Montreal.

Leetch, known more for his offensive flair than defensive prowess, was more artiste than warrior. Keenan wanted a warrior.

But Brian had two influential people in his corner: Mark Messier and Neil Smith. They realized how important Leetch was to the Rangers.

"I would never have allowed it," Smith recalled years later for the *Daily News*. "I never would have traded Brian. Mike Keenan's history was what it was. There was a fear there. I think Brian thought maybe Mike would go beyond me to get guys from

Chicago, and I'm sure Mike would've wanted Ed Belfour at the time instead of Mike Richter, Chelios at the time instead of Leetch, and all that. But it's up to the GM, and I never once questioned trading Brian in 11 years."

He may not have realized it at the time, but Keenan didn't need Chelios because he had already succeeded in molding Leetch into a better all-around defenseman. There were benchings throughout the season—a tactic found in every coach's little bag of tricks—and other mind games designed to get Leetch to commit himself to being more responsible in his own zone.

Altering his style to gamble less on offense so he'd have more energy to help shut down opposing teams' top forwards, Leetch still managed to tie a personal best with 23 goals during the regular season then lead all players in postseason scoring with 34 points in 23 games.

For Leetch, the 1993–94 season was full of career highlights, but there were plenty of others: a Calder Trophy as Rookie of the Year, two Norris Trophies as the league's top defenseman, nine All-Star Game appearances, six team MVP awards, and a World Cup title in 1996 with Team USA. No homegrown Ranger can touch Leetch's resume.

He was also one of the few valuable assets the team had left as it limped into the twenty-first century.

With the Rangers poised to miss the playoffs for the seventh straight year, Neil Smith's replacement, Glen Sather, saw an opportunity to build for the future. On March 3, 2004, he traded Leetch to the Maple Leafs for Jarkko Immonen, Maxim

Did You Know?

Six future Rangers played on the 1988 U.S. Olympic Team in Calgary. Team captain Brian Leetch was joined by Tony Granato, Corey Millen, Kevin Miller, Mike Richter, and Kevin Stevens. The Americans finished seventh.

Brian Leetch, fresh from competition on the U.S. Olympic hockey team, takes the ice for the New York Rangers at Madison Square Garden on February 29, 1988. It was Leetch's first pro game for the Rangers. (AP Photo/Ron Frehm)

Calder Trophy Winners

Named for former NHL president Frank Calder, the Calder Memorial Trophy is awarded to the league's best rookie. The winner is selected in a poll by the Professional Hockey Writers Association at the end of the regular season.

The trophy—a silver cup mounted on a wooden base—is dotted with the names of promising Ranger newbies. Most went on to have solid, and in some cases, spectacular NHL careers:

Player	Year	Legacy
Kilby MacDonald	1940	Played only 151 NHL games. Career interrupted by war.
Grant Warwick	1942	Seven seasons with Rangers. All-Star in 1947.
Edgar Laprade	1946	Four-time All-Star. Hockey Hall of Fame, 1993.
Pentti Lund	1949	After three years with Rangers, traded to Boston.
Lorne Worsley	1953	Hall of Fame career included four Stanley Cups.
Camille Henry	1954	Three-time All-Star played 12 seasons with Rangers.
Steve Vickers	1973	Holds club record for most career points by a left winger.
Brian Leetch	1989	Nine-time All-Star. Hockey Hall of Fame, 2009.

Kondratiev, a first-round pick in 2004 (No. 24, later traded to Calgary, who selected Kris Chucko), and a second-round pick in 2005 (No. 40, Michael Sauer).

"When we traded Brian to Toronto," Sather said, "he didn't want to go. A great player at the end of his career, he wanted to stay where he was, but he didn't have a no-trade clause. It was a real key piece for us to be able to retool our team. But I know Brian was upset."

"I was devastated," Leetch recalled of the trade that capped his run on Broadway at 1,129 games and 981 points. "No question about it. I was led to believe that I was going to be in New York for my career and if that was going to change, I thought I would've heard about it beforehand. I actually got traded on my birthday. I flew back to New York that night from Boston, grabbed my stuff, jumped on a plane the next morning to Toronto, and played the Islanders the next night. It was a whirlwind of emotions and it definitely hurt. It still hurts. That'll probably never go away."

And yet, Leetch gave serious consideration to going back to the Rangers in 2006.

"The Rangers weren't interested in me after the lockout. But it was the following year, after I'd played in Boston, that [Rangers coach] Tom Renney reached out to me and said, 'If you're interested, we think you could help out.' I just wasn't sure. I'd played on some teams in New York that hadn't made the playoffs for a number of years, and after missing the playoffs again in Boston, I was getting tired out mentally. I wasn't sure the Rangers were ready to make the playoffs again and I didn't want to go back and go through it all again. And I wasn't sure that I should be playing anymore."

The idea of going back to New York City—*especially* New York City—and being anything less than 100 percent of the player he had once been, in that building, in front of those fans, held little appeal for Leetch.

And so we are left to remember him as he was in his prime.

"He's never wanted to be in the spotlight or to be singled out individually," Messier once said. "That's just not his style. But he deserves to be noticed as one of the greatest Rangers ever, if not *the* greatest Ranger ever."

12 Thanks, Tex

There are no statues, plaques, or banners commemorating George "Tex" Rickard's role in founding the Rangers. Indeed, the extent to which the influential boxing promoter enjoyed or even understood pro hockey is subject to debate.

This much is known: Rickard developed the new Madison Square Garden at 49th Street and Eighth Avenue with an eye toward making it a top boxing venue and only agreed to bring in the expansion New York Americans as an ancillary attraction (along with indoor bicycle races and the circus) to fill vacant dates on the schedule. When the Americans, which were owned by mobster "Big Bill" Dwyer, performed better at the gate than expected, Rickard decided the Garden needed a team of its own.

At the urging of hockey man and longtime business partner Col. John S. Hammond, Rickard acquired an expansion team to open the 1926–27 NHL season. It was George Daley, sports editor of the *New York Herald Tribune*, who first referred to the new club as "Tex's Rangers"—a play on Rickard's nickname—and it stuck. There's some evidence that Tex grew to like hockey because the physicality of the sport reminded him of boxing, though that didn't stop Rickard from kicking the Rangers out of the Garden every spring to accommodate the circus.

A tall man with small, twinkling eyes and an infectious, boyish smile, Rickard was often seen about town sporting his trademark fedora and carrying a straight, gold-handled Malacca cane and cigar. He dressed like a proper Manhattanite because he wanted to be accepted as part of the upper crust, but he had an air of the West about him that was unmistakable.

Conn Smythe: The Rangers' First GM

Lester Patrick is often thought of as the father of the Rangers, having guided the team as coach and manager during its glory years of the 1920s and '30s. But Patrick's predecessor, Conn Smythe, deserves some credit for the Rangers' early success. It was Smythe who built the expansion Rangers into an instant Stanley Cup contender.

After serving in World War I, Smythe returned to his native Toronto and opened a sand and gravel business. At night, he coached the University of Toronto varsity hockey team. It was through his coaching of this team that he caught the attention of NHL executives. Smythe and his team of collegians traveled regularly to Boston for games against schools in the area, with great success. In 1926, Boston Bruins owner Charles Adams recommended Smythe to John Hammond, and Smythe was hired to construct a team from scratch and then manage it. It was Smythe who recruited Frank Boucher, Bill Cook, Ching Johnson, and other players who would go on to star for the Rangers.

But in October 1926, before the Rangers had played a regular season game, Hammond fired Smythe after he refused to sign two-time NHL scoring champ Babe Dye.

Tex Rickard tried to lure Smythe back to the Rangers with the promise of a different front office job, but a dispute over back pay Smythe felt he was owed signaled the end of his time in New York. He went on to become the hugely successful owner and manager of the Toronto Maple Leafs, and the NHL trophy awarded to the Most Valuable Player in the Stanley Cup playoffs still bears his name.

Born in 1871 in Kansas City, Missouri, but raised on the frontier plains of Texas, Rickard grew up herding cattle on his family's ranch. At 23, he took a job as marshal of Henrietta, a little town about 100 miles northwest of Dallas. He was known to be a tolerant and honest lawman...and an expert poker player.

In 1894, he married Leona Bittick. The girl's parents were opposed to the wedding, given her poor health. Leona was battling tuberculosis and within a year both she and the couple's infant child would be dead. Some reports indicate they had died due to complications of the birth. Soon after Leona's death, Rickard resigned as marshal and left for Alaska and the gold rush.

Up in the Klondike, he staked a mining claim, struck gold, flipped it for a handsome profit, then poured his money into a gambling hall and saloon called The Northern. From there, he moved on to California, Nevada, and New York, running gambling halls and building up his reputation as a skillful fight promoter.

In his travels, Rickard became acquainted with John Ringling of the Ringling Bros. and Barnum & Bailey Circus. Ringling recommended Tex to the New York Life Insurance Company, which owned Madison Square Garden. In 1925, Rickard was hired to promote all events at the arena.

A natural politician and compromiser, Rickard was not above the occasional bribe or making secret deals to obtain a promoter's license, a contract, or a stadium. It's not that he was dishonest—he just had a businessman's sense of when and how to bend the rules to get what he wanted. He was always a gambler at heart, but he knew how to balance a gambler's odds with sound business acumen.

Despite his many professional triumphs, tragedy and controversy seemed to plague Rickard in his personal life. He was once accused of drugging, kidnapping, and sexually assaulting an underage girl but was acquitted after the prosecutors' case against him unraveled. Reports from the day suggest the entire affair may have been staged as part of an extortion plot.

In October 1925, Rickard's second wife (or third, if you count the saloon singer he's believed to have married and divorced in Alaska) passed away from a heart ailment. Months later, he announced his engagement to a former actress named Maxine Hodges. Salacious rumors and innuendo followed the couple, including a story that they'd already married in secret and, more disturbingly, that the bride was only 16 at the time of the nuptials. Rickard, 56, dismissed it all as hearsay.

"She will be 25 years old on her next birthday," an indignant Rickard told a reporter. "I have known her for eight years. We have been engaged and intend to marry in the fall. This ridiculous rumor of a secret marriage has followed me since last winter."

In December 1928, while in Miami Beach making final preparations for a heavyweight bout between Jack Sharkey and Young Stribling, Rickard was rushed to a local hospital with acute appendicitis. Doctors performed an emergency appendectomy and initially expected him to make a quick recovery, but he developed an infection and a high fever.

As Rickard clung to life, legendary boxer Jack Dempsey flew in to be by his friend's side. But Rickard's condition never improved, and he died on January 6, 1929. His body was returned to New York by train in a $15,000 bronze casket and placed in Madison Square Garden, where Rickard lay in state for mourners to pay their final respects. It was the kind of extravagant send-off reserved for heads of state.

Rickard was buried in Woodlawn Cemetery in the Bronx. The large headstone at his gravesite is the only monument to the person most directly responsible for the birth of the New York Rangers.

13 The "Hex" of 1940

Long before it became a vexing reminder of futility, "1940" was an achievement—a cause for celebration and a reason for the Rangers and their fans to hold their heads high. That was the year the team won its third Stanley Cup, and thanks to Bryan Hextall, it happened in dramatic fashion.

Managed by Lester Patrick and coached by former Rangers star Frank Boucher, the 1939–40 Blueshirts were solid from top to bottom.

"It took us four years to build up the present organization," Patrick remarked as he admired his handiwork, "and I don't think that there is a single weak link in the group."

If there was, it wasn't in goal, where Dave Kerr was in Vezina Trophy form. Nor was it on defense, where Art Coulter, Babe Pratt, Ott Heller, and Muzz Patrick could outmuscle most attackers. And it certainly wasn't up front, where Boucher was able to roll three balanced, productive lines.

"It was," Boucher would later conclude, "the best hockey team I ever saw."

Leading the way was Hextall, the durable, tough-as-nails right winger with the left-hand shot and, according to one ex-teammate, "bones like spears." A man of few words, he preferred to let his play do the talking. And in that way, friends and foes heard him loud and clear.

"I always dreaded playing Detroit," Boucher said, "because the Wings had a body-thumper on defense named Black Jack Stewart. Every time they met, Hex and Black Jack belted each other. Neither would give ground, so it was a succession of hammerings which could be heard all over the arena. Surprisingly enough, neither ever seemed to lose his temper. They simply reveled in the bumping."

That Hextall, center Phil Watson, and left wing Lynn Patrick comprised the number two line—the Powerhouse Line, as it was known—was a testament to the strength of that Rangers team.

In an era when scoring 20 goals was like getting 50 today, Hex led the league with 24 in 48 games. But the biggest goal of his season—indeed, of his entire career—occurred on April 13, 1940, a Saturday night in Toronto. The Rangers were leading the Maple Leafs three games to two when Game 6, tied at 2–2, went to sudden death overtime.

The winning play began with Leafs Gordon Drillon and Jack Church colliding with each other and falling to the ice. Dutch Hiller of the Rangers swooped in to retrieve the loose puck and immediately passed it up to Watson. "Fiery Phil" took it behind the Leafs' net then passed it out front, blindly, hoping a teammate would be there. He didn't even see Hextall waiting between the faceoff circles. From that distance, Hex was a sure shot. He beat

Bryan Hextall shown here in the 1930s. (AP Photo)

> ## The 1939–40 Rangers: Stanley Cup Champions
> Dave Kerr, Mac Colville, Neil Colville, Art Coulter, Ott Heller, Bryan Hextall, Dutch Hiller, Kilby MacDonald, Lynn Patrick, Muzz Patrick, Alf Pike, Babe Pratt, Alex Shibicky, Clint Smith, Sanford Smith, Phil Watson, Lester Patrick (manager), Frank Boucher (coach), Harry Westerby (trainer)

Toronto goalie Turk Broda with a high backhander 2:07 into the extra session, and the visitors' bench exploded with cheers.

"That goal," Hextall's widow, Gertrude, recalled many years later, "was the highlight of his life."

Hextall would wear the Blueshirt for 10 glorious seasons and 449 games, never playing for another team. He led the NHL in goals again with 26 in 1940–41. The following year, he led the NHL in scoring and toted home the Art Ross Trophy. He was also named to the first All-Star Team three times from 1940 to 1942. His Hall of Fame resume, impressive as it is, would've been even more so had he not missed all of 1944–45 and all but three games of 1945–46 due to wartime border restrictions that prevented many players from entering the United States. It's a pity since Hex was at his peak when the war broke out.

Retiring from hockey in 1949, Hextall retreated to tiny Poplar Point, Manitoba, where he grew up. There, surrounded by wheat fields, he and Gertrude raised four sons and a daughter. Two of his boys, Dennis and Bryan Jr., would go on to play for the Rangers (a grandson, Ron, also played in the NHL. Maybe you've heard of him). He also ran a lumber business and a hunting lodge. An outdoorsy fellow, he could often be found prowling the marshes for waterfowl. Even after circulatory problems led to Hextall having both of his legs amputated, he would climb into his canoe on two artificial legs and shoot ducks.

With Gertrude at his side, Hextall returned to New York only once, in 1968, to see the closing of the old Garden and the opening of the new one. But he continued to follow his former team from afar, in part out of curiosity to see if anyone would break his record of being the last Ranger to score a Cup-winning goal. Three times before his passing in July 1984, the Rangers made it to the Stanley Cup Finals. Three times, they failed.

"I think it was after that series with Boston [in 1972]," Gertrude said, "we were watching it on television. When the Rangers finally lost, he got up to go to bed and said, 'Well, my record still holds.'"

14 Battle of the Hudson

Devils fans' resentment of the Rangers and the attention lavished upon them by the tri-state media is bolstered by the pervasive inferiority complex many New Jerseyians have toward New York and New Yorkers in general—Rangers fans living in New Jersey being the exception, of course.

Geographically, only seven miles separate the Rangers and Devils—the shortest distance between any two clubs in the NHL—but it might as well be 700, so different are the worlds they inhabit. The Rangers celebrated their Stanley Cup in 1994 with a glorious parade down the Canyon of Heroes in Manhattan. A year later, the Devils celebrated their first championship in a parking lot surrounded by swampland.

Despite playing in the shadow of the New York skyline, the Devils went on to establish a degree of consistency and success enjoyed by few pro sports teams: nine division titles, five conference championships, and three Stanley Cups since 1995. The club's transformation from what Wayne Gretzky once called a "Mickey Mouse organization" to one of the NHL's model franchises was orchestrated by GM Lou Lamoriello, an obsessive micromanager and unabashed skinflint who spent years playing contract hardball with his own players then broke the bank (and circumvented the salary cap) for Ilya Kovalchuk. Lou's right-hand man, scouting director and draft guru David Conte, has provided the club with a steady stream of NHL-ready prospects, ensuring that the Battle of the Hudson is never a one-sided affair.

The 1993–94 season was the high-water mark of the rivalry, of course, when the Rangers and Devils finished first and second overall respectively before facing off in an epic Eastern Conference Final. But there's more to this story than just "Matteau! Matteau! Matteau!"

Ftorek's Phantom Goal

Long before he became coach of the Devils, Robbie Ftorek was a scrappy little Rangers center who wore a bubble-shaped helmet so big and round that he looked like the BIC Pens logo (we'll wait while you Google that).

On January 6, 1985, a Sunday night at Madison Square Garden, the Devils were leading the Rangers 4–3 late in the third period when Ftorek scored a controversial game-tying goal. Just more than a minute into overtime, rookie Tomas Sandstrom won it for New York on a short wrist shot.

As the teams were leaving the ice, an unhinged Devils coach Doug Carpenter had to be restrained by both linesmen from going after referee Bryan Lewis. Lewis had been trailing the play when Ftorek took a backhanded shot that hit goalie Chico Resch then deflected off the crossbar and fell to the ice *outside* the red goal

Rangers All-Time Record vs. Devils (1982–2014)				
GP	W	L	T	OL
227	106	87	27	7

Zing!

"I haven't gotten *NHL 14* yet, but I hear as soon as you turn it on for the first time, Ilya Kovalchuk leaves for *KHL 14*."

Jim Schmiedeberg, Mesa, Arizona
Rangers fan since 1977

line. But from Lewis' vantage point, the puck went in the net. He allowed the goal even though the goal judge never turned on the red light to indicate a score.

"I let in enough goals on my own," an angry Resch said afterward. "I don't need a ref letting one in for me."

Escape to New York

Many a New Jersey Devil has played for less than he thought he was worth. That's why some, upon reaching free agency, have raced across the river to cash in at 4 Penn Plaza. But when it comes to signing ex-Devils, the Rangers' track record is pretty poor.

There was Bruce Driver, the puck-moving defenseman who spent 12 seasons in New Jersey before signing with the Rangers in 1995. Driver's birth certificate said he was 33, but in a Rangers uniform, he looked closer to 53.

In 2002, the Rangers signed center Bobby Holik to a five-year deal worth $45 million. Holik, a fine two-way player in New Jersey, struggled to perform in New York under increased media pressure and a huge contract, scoring 41 goals and 91 points over the course of three seasons in which the Rangers failed to make the playoffs. In 2005, the team bought out the final two years on Holik's contract.

Slick playmaker Scott Gomez failed to live up to the expectations that accompanied the seven-year, $51.5 million pact he signed with the Rangers in 2007, but at least Glen Sather didn't have to buy out that contract. He let the Montreal Canadiens do it.

The Snub

It is a long-standing hockey tradition—a great one, really—that when a playoff series ends, both teams put their differences aside and line up to shake hands as a sign of good sportsmanship. But Martin Brodeur, still seething over Sean Avery's antics and trash talking throughout the 2008 quarterfinals, passed Avery on the line and refused to shake his hand. This prompted Avery to later say in an interview, when referring to the Devils goalie, that "fatso forgot to shake my hand."

The Line Brawl

The final regular season meeting between the teams on March 19, 2012 made headlines, created social media buzz, and fueled debate about the value of staged fights after it began with three bouts at the opening faceoff. Both teams put their tough guys on the Madison Square Garden ice to start the game, clearly indicating a melee was coming.

As soon as the puck dropped, Brandon Prust dropped his gloves with Cam Janssen, Michael Rupp took on Eric Boulton, and Stu Bickel squared off with Ryan Carter.

Did the Bride Wear Blue?

"Donna and I met at a Rangers game, so it was only fitting that we get engaged at a Rangers game, too. I didn't want her to be distracted so I picked a meaningless preseason game: September 30, 1990, Devils at Rangers. I arranged for the Garden to play Eric Clapton's 'Wonderful Tonight' over the PA system at 6:45 PM. While we were watching warm-ups, I took out the ring and proposed. We spent the rest of the game on the Garden pay phones calling all of our friends and family to tell them the good news."

Mark Rubin, Bronxville, New York
Rangers fan since 1979

Even coaches John Tortorella and Peter DeBoer got into it, jawing at each other from their respective benches.

After all the combatants were sent off to their respective penalty boxes, the game was briefly delayed as the Garden maintenance crew scraped Carter's blood off the ice. It was like a scene right out of *Slap Shot*, and fight fans loved it.

Henrique Beats Henrik

Just 63 seconds into overtime of Game 6 in the 2012 Eastern Conference Finals, New Jersey rookie Adam Henrique found himself parked in the crease behind Henrik Lundqvist. Although Ilya Kovalchuk and Alexei Ponikarovsky were nearby, jabbing their sticks at a loose puck, it was Henrique's stick that found the rubber and he swept it past the Rangers goalie to give the Devils a 3–2 win.

Henrique's goal eliminated the Rangers, coming off their best season since 1993–94, and propelled the Devils into the Stanley Cup Finals.

Who's Your Daddy?

It's the rivalry within the rivalry: Henrik Lundqvist versus Martin Brodeur.

"Marty Brodeur loves tweaking Henrik Lundqvist," said Blueshirt United's Jim Cerny. "He really doesn't like giving Henrik his due. In Marty's mind, he's thinking, 'Wait a minute, I'm the no-doubt Hall of Famer and the guy who's won the three Cups. This guy's the King? What has he won?' Clearly, there's something about Henrik that gets under his skin."

Lundqvist has dominated Brodeur in head-to-head meetings, winning 26-of-38 regular season games through 2014. Brodeur held a slight advantage in the playoffs, though, winning eight of 14 games against Lundqvist.

"To Henrik's credit," Cerny said, "he is deferential and very respectful of what Marty Brodeur has accomplished in his career. But maybe what bothers Marty is the whole bigger picture. He's been a Devil for 20 years, and it doesn't matter what they do over there because the Rangers are always the bigger story. And I'm sure that just drives Marty crazy."

1972

Boston Bruins Defeat New York Rangers in the Stanley Cup Finals

No discussion about the greatest Rangers teams would be complete without mentioning the 1971–72 squad that won 48 games and fell just two victories short of a Stanley Cup.

The 1972 Stanley Cup Finals saw the Blueshirts reach the championship round for the eighth time in their history but just the second since winning their last title in 1940. Powered by future Hall of Famers Rod Gilbert, Ed Giacomin, Brad Park, and Jean Ratelle, the Rangers had already knocked off the defending champs from Montreal in the first round, four games to two, in what many observers considered a Ranger upset. Then in the semis, New York avenged its heartbreaking Game 7 loss to Chicago the previous spring by sweeping the West Division champion Black Hawks to earn a meeting with the rival Bruins in the finals.

New York and Boston followed similar paths from league cellar-dwellers to Cup contenders, spending much of the 1950s and '60s fighting over the NHL's table scraps.

"Few championships in any sport could offer such contrasting teams," Mark Mulvoy recounted for the readers of *Sports Illustrated*.

"The Bruins frivolous and cocky, the Rangers quiet and serious. The Bruins practice when the mood sets in; the Rangers work six days a week and sometimes seven. The Bruins have a loose rapport with their coach, Tom Johnson, and usually call him Tommy; the Rangers stiffen at the sight or mention of Emile Francis, and out of respect for his unchallenged authority, they always call him Mister."

This clash of opposites also represented the first time in more than a decade that the league's two top regular season finishers had made it to the championship round. The matchups were everything a hockey fan could dream of:

Boston's Phil Esposito led the NHL in scoring that season with 66 goals and 133 points. John Bucyk, John McKenzie, Derek Sanderson, and Fred Stanfield were solid complementary scorers on an attack that was tops in the league. Gerry Cheevers was solid in goal and the Bruins rolled to a 54–13–11 regular season record, then lost only once in the opening two playoff rounds as they blew through Toronto and St. Louis to reach the finals.

The Rangers had plenty of star power, too, their offense second only to Boston's. Ratelle led the way with 109 points and actually scored more even-strength goals than Esposito, who padded his stats on the power play. Ratelle's wingers, Gilbert and Vic Hadfield, also had career years with 43 and 50 goals, respectively. Walt Tkaczuk, Bill Fairbairn, and Bobby Rousseau supplied the second and third lines with some scoring punch. Giacomin and Gilles Villemure, who'd shared the Vezina Trophy a year earlier, each won 24 games.

"The Rangers were on par with the Boston Bruins," said Boston's longtime general manager, Harry Sinden. "The difference between the Rangers and Bruins was Bobby Orr."

Park, Orr's counterpart on the Rangers, was a dominant defenseman in his own right, but there's a reason he finished runner-up for the Norris Trophy five times. Orr was simply that much better than every other blueliner in the league. There are quite a few hockey aficionados who insist he was the best to ever play the game, period.

The finals opened on April 30 at storied Boston Garden with New York defenseman Dale Rolfe scoring the first goal of the series just 3:52 into the opening period. The Bruins then took over, however, as they exploded for four goals against Giacomin before the first intermission.

While the Rangers eventually tied the game at 5–5 with a three-goal rally against Cheevers in the third period, Bruins winger Garnet "Ace" Bailey tallied with just more than 2:00 left in regulation to give Boston a 6–5 victory.

After watching their teams surrender a combined 11 goals in the opening game, both coaches switched netminders for Game 2, with Gilles Villemure going in for New York and Eddie Johnston taking over for Boston. Again, the Bruins came out on top 2–1 on a third-period goal by Ken Hodge.

With their move four years earlier to the far more versatile "new" Madison Square Garden, which could accommodate both a circus performance *and* a hockey game within hours of each other (imagine that!), the Rangers could look forward to getting some late-round playoff dates on home ice. With Giacomin back in net, they dominated Game 3, scoring three power-play goals in the first period—two from Park and one from Gilbert—en route to a 5–2 win.

After losing Game 4 3–2, New York staved off elimination in Game 5 in Boston with a pair of third-period goals in a come-from-behind 3–2 road victory to set up the sixth game at Madison Square Garden on May 11.

Villemure was back in net for the Rangers, facing Cheevers at the opposite end. With Tkaczuk in the box for hooking midway through the opening period, Orr collected his fifth goal and 23rd point of the playoffs. Wayne Cashman added a pair of third-period insurance goals, and Cheevers preserved the 3–0 shutout.

Even if the sight of Bucyk, Boston's captain, carrying the Stanley Cup around Garden ice made them want to retch, Rangers fans managed polite applause for the invaders. A few threw garbage. Others tried to flip the Bruins' bus as they were getting ready to leave.

As much as Orr had factored in the Bruins' triumph, Ratelle was equally a non-factor for the Rangers. The smooth playmaker suffered a broken ankle two months earlier, missed the end of the regular season, and came back in time for the finals but was largely ineffective, managing just one assist in six games.

For many New York players, the 1972 finals marked their last, best shot at a Stanley Cup ring. Although the Rangers of that era were solid in so many areas—seasons of 49, 48, and 47 wins confirmed their regular season dominance—the playoffs would continue to be an annual source of frustration and disappointment.

"With Brad Park and Vic and Ratelle, we all wanted to be successful," Gilbert said. "But we were only as strong as our weakest link. I recall that the bigger the game was in the playoffs, some players didn't play hard, they didn't come up big. Some of the players didn't play to their fullest capability and it happened four or five years in a row. Yes, Ratelle broke his ankle that year, but four or five years in a row we could have won the Cup. We had the better team. We *supposedly* had the better team. It didn't work out that way."

16 The King of New York

He is the Rangers' most marketable star—the rare hockey player recognizable even to non-hockey fans. There he is in a *Page Six Magazine* spread heralded as "The Sexist Ice Man" (which he must be, because nobody else can make a velvet blazer look good). There he is in a "This is Sports Center" commercial on ESPN, translating for the Muppets' Swedish Chef. There he is with his electric guitar playing "Sweet Child O' Mine" on *Late Night With Jimmy Fallon*. There he is making an apple crostata on the *Martha Stewart Show*.

But you know you've reached the top of your profession when the slightest blemish on your record is cause for panic in the blogosphere. Welcome to Henrik Lundqvist's world.

"I'll bet he's hurt. It must be his wrist."

"He's tired from the Olympics."

"Looks like a rotator cuff to me."

"It's his contract. It has to be his contract."

And so on and so forth. Maybe the bar is set so high for New York's All-Star goaltender because he has spent so much of his career having to be almost perfect in order to give the Rangers a chance to win.

It may seem like Lundqvist has got it all—a mountain of money, thousands of adoring fans, and the looks of a Benetton model—but there's still one achievement missing from his resume: a Stanley Cup. He came heartbreakingly close in 2014, backstopping the

Vezina Trophy Winners

The Vezina Trophy was donated to the NHL in 1926-27 in memory of Georges Vezina, the great goaltender who died of tuberculosis the previous spring. Originally, the trophy was given to the goaltender(s) of the team allowing the fewest number of goals during the regular season. Since 1981-82, the trophy has been awarded to the goalie determined to be the best at his position as voted on by the general managers of all NHL clubs. Five Rangers have won or shared the Vezina Trophy:

Dave Kerr (1940)
Ed Giacomin and Gilles Villemure (1971)
John Vanbiesbrouck (1986)
Henrik Lundqvist (2012)

Goalie Henrik Lundqvist (30) looks to cover up the puck during the game between the New York Rangers and Philadelphia Flyers at Wells Fargo Center in Philadelphia, Pennsylvania. The New York Rangers beat the Philadelphia Flyers 5–3. (Cal Sport Media via AP Images)

Blueshirts to the finals to cap off a season in which he moved ahead of Mike Richter to become the winningest goalie in club history and collected his record 50th career shutout, passing Ed Giacomin on the team's all-time list.

The 205th overall pick in the 2000 draft (and 20th goalie, if you can believe it), Lundqvist was another great late-round find by European scout Christer Rockstrom, the man who discovered Alexei Kovalev, Fedor Tyutin, and Sergei Zubov, among others. The attributes that first caught Rockstrom's eye—world-class skills and a competitive fire that burns white-hot—are the same ones that have endeared Henrik to the Rangers faithful.

The Puck Goes In-ski

If Henrik Lundqvist makes a compelling case as the greatest Ranger goaltender ever, who was the worst? That distinction, made with the utmost respect and affection, probably belongs to Steve Buzinski, a scrawny, bowlegged little fellow brought into training camp by Lester Patrick in 1942 because the team had nobody else to put in goal.

Frank Boucher, the Rangers' coach, had his doubts about Buzinski from the get-go, but Patrick was high on him. "A very good goaltender, Frank, an excellent goaltender," Patrick said. "I think you'll be pleasantly surprised."

Buzinski looked sharp in scrimmages, but it quickly became obvious that he wasn't an NHL goalie. He played nine games for the Rangers, going 2–6–1 with a goals against average of nearly 6.00.

The most memorable moment of Buzinski's brief NHL career occurred one night during a game against the Maple Leafs. Toronto scored a goal but Buzinski seemed to have been knocked unconscious on the play. Players from both teams argued with the referee over whether Buzinski was hit by the puck or an errant stick from a Leaf player in the crease, which would have disallowed the goal. When it seemed like the Leafs had convinced the officials that the puck knocked Buzinski out, the goalie sat up, opened his eyes, and yelled, "That's a damn lie. He high-sticked me." Then he dropped back to the ice and closed his eyes.

As a rookie in 2005-06, Lundqvist was in the spotlight early and often. With lightning-quick reflexes, a great glove hand, and all the poise of a ten-year veteran, he wrestled the starting job from Kevin Weekes, went on to set a franchise record for victories by a rookie (30), and helped the Rangers earn their first postseason berth since 1997. Along the way, he found time to win a Gold Medal for Sweden at the Olympics in Torino, Italy.

Fans spoiled by a decade of Richter's acrobatics had a new masked marvel to support, and they voiced their approval virtually every home game with chants of "HEN-RIK! HEN-RIK!"

In 2009, he became the first NHL goalie to win at least 30 games in each of his first four years in the league, a record he extended to seven seasons until the lockout-shortened 2012–13 season limited him to 43 appearances (he still won 24 of them). In 2012, he won his first Vezina Trophy, having been a finalist for the award on four other occasions.

Everything that has transpired so far may have been just a warm-up for the man teammates call "Hank" and "Henke" but who fans have crowned "King Henrik." He's acutely aware of the expectations that come with his job—it's hard not to be in a building where reminders of the Rangers' last championship are never far from view—and a new long-term contract that made him the highest-paid player on the team and the richest goaltender in the game.

"I really want to win the Cup here in New York," Lundqvist said shortly after signing a seven-year contract extension that would keep him with the Rangers through 2021. "It's my biggest goal and my biggest dream. Secondly, I want to be a Ranger for life. To picture myself anywhere else was just wrong. It was never an option."

17 The A-Line

For the first decade of the team's existence, a stretch in which they appeared in five Stanley Cup Finals (winning twice), the Rangers were led by the inseparable trio of Frank Boucher and brothers Bill Cook and Bun Cook. They were called the A-Line, named for the A subway line that was under construction beneath the third Madison Square Garden, and because there was nobody ahead of them on the team depth chart.

"Back in those days, all teams were built around the first line," recalled Murray Murdoch, an original Ranger and, at the time of his death in 2001 at age 96, the last surviving member of that first Rangers team. "The first line did exactly as they pleased. The second line did exactly as they were told. The third line was just so happy to be there that they never said a word."

Murdoch wasn't exaggerating. During practices, it wasn't uncommon for Boucher and the Cooks to be at one end of the rink, trying out different plays, while Coach Lester Patrick would be at the other end, working with the rest of the team.

Often confused with the 1940-era Bread Line of Mac Colville, Neil Colville, and Alex Shibicky, the A-Line was a perfect mix of scoring power first, but also finesse and defensive ability. And they really were inseparable. Bill and Bun moved with their families (and their mom!) into the same apartment building out in Flatbush, and Boucher and his wife, Agnes, joined them there a short time later.

"We'd come home after games and open some beers," Boucher recalled, "and we'd work plays in comfort while our wives talked together across the room. We never put diagrams on paper. Somehow, just in describing our ideas, we'd all grasp it."

It was in one of those brainstorming sessions that the trio supposedly came up with the drop pass (somebody had to invent it, right?).

Boucher was the elegant playmaker often compared, physically and stylistically, to Wayne Gretzky. Like Gretzky, Frank was a left-handed shot and extremely adept at avoiding opposition checks. He was also one of the cleanest players in NHL history. He had, in fact, only one major penalty during his 13-plus NHL seasons: a fight with Bill Phillips of the Montreal Maroons in the Rangers' very first game. Boucher went on to win the Lady Byng Trophy for clean and effective play *seven times*, prompting the league to give him the trophy permanently before commissioning a new one.

Bill, team captain and elder of the two brothers, was the strong, silent type who never went looking for trouble but found his share anyway. "In a way," his brother Bun said, "Bill's presence on the

Lady Byng Trophy Winners

Named for Marie Evelyn Byng, the wife of a former Governor General of Canada, the Lady Byng Trophy is given to the player determined to have exhibited the highest level of sportsmanship and gentlemanly conduct (i.e., low penalty minute total) combined with a high standard of playing ability. Finalists are chosen at the end of the regular season by a vote of the members of the Professional Hockey Writers Association. The following Rangers have won the award:

Player	Position	Year(s)
Frank Boucher	Center	1928–31, 1933–35
Clint Smith	Center	1939
Buddy O'Connor	Center	1948
Edgar Laprade	Center	1950
Andy Hebenton	Right wing	1957
Camille Henry	Left wing	1958
Jean Ratelle	Center	1972
Wayne Gretzky	Center	1999

ice took a lot of the pressure off me and Frank. We were finesse players primarily, and the other teams left us alone. That was fine with me."

Joe Primeau, the outstanding Toronto Maple Leafs center, played many memorable games against the Cook brothers and Boucher. He held Bill in the highest regard. "He was a terrific hockey player," Primeau recalled. "Nobody fooled around with Bill Cook because he was tough, *real* tough."

Cook was also the team's most dangerous goal scorer. He won the NHL scoring championship with 37 points (33 of them goals) in his first season in the league, which at the time played a 44-game schedule. He added another scoring crown in 1933 at the ripe age of 36.

Frederick Joseph Cook—the nickname "Bun" sprang from his habit of hopping like a bunny to gain momentum on his skates—has been credited as the first NHL player to utilize the slap shot, years and years ahead of Bernie "Boom Boom" Geoffrion and Bobby Hull. For some reason, he only employed the maneuver in practice.

Gifted with natural talent, Bun was a superb skater and stick-handler but he sometimes struggled with consistency. On the occasion when Bun's head wasn't completely in a game, Bill would skate over and give his younger sibling an earful. That was usually enough to put the junior Cook back on track.

Bun was elected to the Hockey Hall of Fame in 1995, long after brother Bill and Boucher were enshrined. To this day, they are the only complete line in Rangers history to make the Hall of Fame.

"Some people say we were the best line ever," Boucher once remarked. "Why should I argue?"

18 Meet Adam Graves

New Yorkers can smell a phony from a mile away...or at least the distance from Port Authority to Penn Station. So if there was a single disingenuous bone in Adam Graves' body, it would've been detected long ago. Spend five minutes with him, and he will make you believe that pro athletes really can be heroes.

The son of a Toronto police officer, "Gravy" earned respect throughout the NHL and the entire New York area for his team-first attitude, goal-scoring ability, and tough work in the corners and the slot. But what set this absurdly modest player apart from other stars was his selflessness off the ice. Growing up in a house full of foster children taught Graves the importance of helping those less fortunate, and as an adult, he's never shied away from the humanitarian responsibilities that often accompany such a high-profile occupation...even at the least opportune times.

"Adam is a completely generous person without an ounce of phoniness," said Donna Rubin, a longtime Rangers season ticket holder and co-owner of the American Legends collectibles shop in Scarsdale. "We've had him in the store for many signings, and he is just great. He looks everyone in the eye when he talks to them and takes a genuine interest in their lives and what they have to say. We're still amazed that he did a signing at our store ten days after one of his twin boys passed away. We told him we would understand if he wanted to cancel but he said he made the commitment and would still do the signing, which was to benefit someone in need. I think that just about sums him up. My husband and I always say that Adam Graves is not just the nicest person in sports, but one of the nicest people we've ever met, period."

But woe to the opposing player who mistook his soft side for weakness. If Mark Messier was the man to lead your team into battle, then Graves was surely the one you wanted watching your back. He didn't have the fleetest feet in the world, but nobody moved to the aid of a teammate in trouble faster than No. 9.

Graves signed with the Rangers as a free agent in 1991 after brief tours with the Red Wings and Oilers. Although the rugged left winger blossomed into one of the game's more versatile forwards, earning the trust of coaches to play in almost every situation, there was nothing especially fancy about Graves' style. He was an awkward skater, and his slap shot was almost nonexistent.

Still, one doesn't become the third-highest goal scorer in team history without some ability. Graves managed 280 goals during his ten Rangers seasons, with the majority of those scored on rebounds and tip-ins off shots from the point.

Together with Messier, Brian Leetch, and Mike Richter, Graves helped form the tight-knit nucleus of a surging Rangers team with championship aspirations, and in 1993–94 he broke out

Masterton Trophy Winners

The Bill Masterton Memorial Trophy is presented annually by the Professional Hockey Writers Association to the NHL player who best exemplifies the qualities of perseverance, sportsmanship, and dedication to hockey. The winner is selected in a poll of all chapters of the PHWA at the end of the regular season. The trophy was first awarded in 1968 to commemorate the late Bill Masterton, a player for the Minnesota North Stars who died on January 15, 1968, as a result of an injury sustained during a game.

The following Rangers have won the Masterton Trophy: Jean Ratelle (1971), Rod Gilbert (1976), Anders Hedberg (1985), Adam Graves (2001), and Dominic Moore (2014).

with a franchise-record 52 goals—a mark since eclipsed by Jaromir Jagr—then added ten more in the playoffs to help the Blueshirts win their first Stanley Cup since 1940.

As the 1990s came to a close, so too did Graves' time with the Rangers. In 2001, he signed with the San Jose Sharks as a free agent and played two more seasons before retiring in April 2004.

Graves returned to the Rangers a year later to work with prospects and serve as a team ambassador. In that role, he's continued to do what he does best: make every person he meets feel special.

"I was at a Steiner Sports signing event at Iona College in New Rochelle," Marc Weissman recalled, "and when I approached Adam to have him autograph my jersey, I shared with him that I was strongly considering becoming a foster parent. I knew that his parents had taken in more than 40 foster kids over the course of Adam's childhood. A lot of people, myself included, believe that's why he is who he is. Well, all of a sudden, he put down his pen, stood straight up, held out his hand to shake mine, and said [quite convincingly], 'Best thing you'll ever do.' I was so overwhelmed by that gesture that I could barely speak and was literally brought to tears."

"When my son, George, was younger, he attended the Rangers Youth Hockey Camp in Tarrytown," Karen Ann Hopkins said. "One of the mornings I brought George to camp, he realized that he'd forgotten his stick tape. He was so upset because he prides himself on always being prepared. We were outside the Training Center and Adam was there. He saw how upset George was, so he walked over and told him that it happens and that he could use some of his tape. I found out when I picked George up at the end of the day that Adam had not only helped him tape up his stick, but he also brought George into all the 'No Campers Allowed' areas for a tour and sat with him at lunch. The smile on my son's face that day is one that I will never forget and will treasure in my memory always."

19 Andy Bathgate

Right wing; Inducted into Hockey Hall of Fame 1978; Number retired 2009

As much as Henrik Lundqvist has been the face of the Rangers since the end of the 2004–05 lockout, or Mark Messier in the 1990s, Andy Bathgate *was* the Rangers from the mid-1950s to the early 1960s. A strapping right wing who spent time at every forward position, Bathgate was the Rangers' first superstar since before World War II—a hero to Rangers fans in an era that produced a few highs but many more disappointments. It's no wonder that writers of the day called him "The Lone Ranger."

Bathgate's career produced so many memorable highlights, among them the penalty-shot goal he scored against Detroit's Hank

Bassen on March 14, 1962. Some who were there insist the Garden actually shook.

Coming into that game, the Rangers were mired in a bad slump and dead-even in the standings with the Red Wings at 57 points apiece, though Detroit had a slight edge in the playoff race with six games remaining to the Rangers' five.

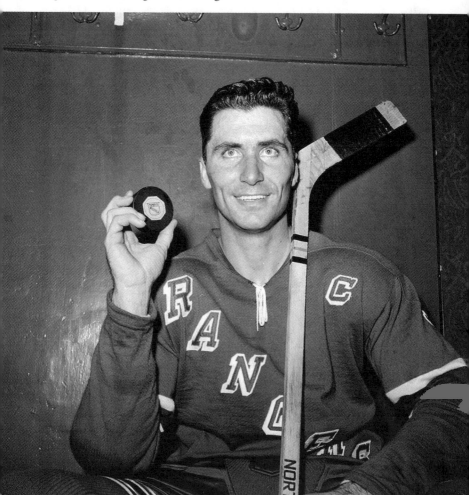

Forward Andy Bathgate poses in the locker room at New York's Madison Square Garden on November 12, 1961. He is holding the puck that accounted for the 200th goal of his career, which he scored against the Chicago Black Hawks. (AP Photo)

With the game tied 2–2 in the second period, Dean Prentice took a pass from Bathgate and skated in on Bassen. Before Prentice could get a shot off, the Detroit goalie threw his stick at him, and Prentice crashed hard into the boards. Referee Eddie Powers came over and called for a penalty shot, but awarded it to Bathgate in error.

Andy didn't say a word. He just skated to center ice, waited for a signal from the ref, then carried the puck into the Detroit zone. Bassen came way out to poke check him but fell down. Andy skated around the prone netminder and easily tapped the puck into a wide-open net.

Bathgate's goal not only turned out to be the game-winner, it gave the Rangers the emotional lift they needed to finish the season strong and qualify for the playoffs.

That year also saw him battle with Chicago's Bobby Hull for the scoring title, a season-long affair that came down to the 70th and final game of the season on March 25, 1962, with the Rangers hosting the Black Hawks before a Garden crowd of 15,618.

The Hawks assigned their two top checkers, Eric Nesterenko and Reggie Fleming, to shadow Bathgate. The Rangers had Pat Hannigan following Hull.

Hull struck first, his 50th goal of the season, at 4:58 of the first period. About five minutes later, Bathgate tied the game with a wrist shot that beat Chicago's Glenn Hall. The pace slowed down a bit after that but then picked up again in the third period when it seemed that Hull and Bathgate were playing every shift.

NHL rules dictate that no matter how many penalties a team takes, it can never be short more than two players. So with two minutes left in the game, and nothing to lose, Chicago players took advantage of that loophole by leaning on, hooking, pushing, and grabbing Bathgate virtually every second he was on the ice.

"Hull was hoping just to sit on the 50 goals," Bathgate recalled. "They weren't worrying about him scoring—they were worrying about keeping me off the sheet. In the last five minutes, we got two goals at least, but the Chicago guys were shooting the puck and trying to hit me with it. I was trying to get around the net and even then they were wrestling me to the ice or hanging onto me. The fans were stunned. They couldn't understand what the hell was going on. They had never seen anything like this. They were booing. I was trying all game to get something going, but it was tight all the way."

Hull and Bathgate finished tied with 84 points, but Hull won the Art Ross Trophy by virtue of scoring 50 goals to Bathgate's 28. Bathgate never complained, especially not after the league announced that both men would receive a $1,000 bonus (usually, that prize only went to the scoring champ).

Four times the Rangers' Most Valuable Player, Bathgate was a star who knew how to take care of himself when the game got rough.

The former Ranger captain rarely started a fight but ended his fair share. He learned how to throw jabs and hooks from his father, a boxer who would have represented Scotland in the 1940 Olympics had the games not been canceled due to the outbreak of World War II. He'd encourage each of his five children—Andy being the youngest and one of three boys—to settle their differences in a makeshift boxing ring in the backyard of their Manitoba home.

"Well," Bathgate conceded, "it was hardly a ring, but it had ropes and boxing gloves hanging in the corner. We'd be out in the rain whacking away at each other and my father, in a very gruff voice, would say, 'Get in there, get in there!' or 'Don't do this roundhouse thing!' or 'Hit straight on, straight on!'"

Andy was careful to follow that last bit of advice as he moved up through the junior hockey ranks to the NHL.

"In a fight," he said, "I would grab the fella by the sweater as tight as I could. Knowing that his chin was right above my hand, I'd tuck my head down and try to hit him as hard as I could in the solar plexus—that area right above his stomach. I'd give him one shot and when I heard, 'Ooooh,' I knew that I had him. Then I'd give him one shot in the jaw, and that was it.

"Sometimes, if I really disliked the guy, or if I thought he was trying to hurt me, I would hit him in the top of his ear. Not the eardrum, mind you, but just above it. I'd give him a real smackin'. It would hurt my hand but, 20 or 30 years later, there were guys who still remembered that I did it to them. I had one guy walk up to me at a meeting about our NHL pensions and say, 'You son of a bitch, did you try to hit me in the ear? Every time I comb my hair, I think of you.'"

Bathgate began to develop an unwanted reputation for his fighting ability. His preference—and his duty—was to be on the ice helping his team win hockey games, not accepting challenges from every punk who wanted to goad the Rangers' best player into trading blows and then spend the next five minutes in the penalty box.

But that combination of skill and toughness helped Andy become one of the top right-wingers in hockey. In the late 1950s and early 1960s, there really wasn't anyone better, save for perhaps Rocket Richard in Montreal or Detroit's Gordie Howe, the latter of whom often used his elbows and stick as weapons.

That didn't endear him to Bathgate, who was so disgusted by a perceived proliferation of spearing in hockey that he blasted the practice—and its worst offenders—in a controversial article for a men's magazine.

Sure enough, during a game between the Rangers and Red Wings, the butt end of Howe's stick found its way into Bathgate's gut. If intimidation was Howe's *modus operandi*, he picked on the wrong Ranger.

"If you spear me again," hissed Bathgate, remembering that Howe had suffered a fractured skull earlier in his career, "I'll move that plate in your head!"

In fact, Howe's head injury had not required the insertion of a plate. But why let facts get in the way of a good threat?

20 Ed-die! Ed-die!

It's unfortunate that the most memorable game Rangers legend Ed Giacomin ever played at Madison Square Garden was in the uniform of the Detroit Red Wings.

After one of the most stellar decades a Ranger goalie has ever known, Giacomin began to show signs of age and his play declined. The end came without warning on Halloween night 1975. Emile Francis, in full rebuilding mode, put Giacomin on waivers, and the Red Wings (and only the Red Wings) bit, for a paltry $2,500.

Alex Delvecchio, Detroit's general manager, knew Eddie was upset and wondered if the goalie would even report. As luck would have it, the Red Wings were scheduled to be in New York just two days later, on November 2. Would Eddie play?

"The New York Ranger fans knew Eddie Giacomin better than Eddie Giacomin knew himself," the goaltender recalled. "They knew I was going to play that game, but I didn't. Until 5:30 the night of the game, I was sitting in the hotel room waiting for Detroit to come to town just to have a word with them. I found out that they already had me penciled out, that I was not going to play. What happened that evening when I came onto the ice was unbelievable."

For anyone who was there—and there were more than 17,000 witnesses—it was a surreal scene they will never forget. Eddie Giacomin, after ten seasons in Ranger blue and white, was looking mighty uncomfortable as he faced the Seventh Avenue end of

Ed Giacomin: Comedian

"One Sunday morning during practice, I was sitting upstairs at Rye Playland with assistant coaches Wayne Cashman and Eddie Giacomin. Bob Froese was in goal during a scrimmage. All of a sudden, he starts singing, 'Eddie Giacomin has no friends, do da, do da. Eddie Giacomin has no friends, oh de do da day.' Then Eddie replies, 'Bob Froese blocks like a girl, do da, do da, Bob Froese lets the easy ones in, and that is why he does not play.' Priceless."

Tracy J. Paulet, Lagrangeville, New York
Rangers fan since 1977

Madison Square Garden in the bright red uniform of the visitors from Motown.

The fans cheered Giacomin's first name ("ED-DIE! ED-DIE!") and virtually drowned out the National Anthem. Tears flowed freely down the goaltender's face as the stunning tribute continued for the man who had been sent away just two days earlier. Rangers fans, as loyal a group as there is in all of sports, were going to be cheering for the Red Wings that eerie night. It was one of the strangest and most emotional games in Rangers history.

As a kid, Ranger fan Tony Kono idolized Giacomin. At the summer hockey school the Rangers held at Skateland in New Hyde Park, players served as instructors and Eddie taught Tony the right way to tape a knob onto his goalie stick.

"I was only 14 at the time," Kono said. "I had a shared season ticket plan and sat in Section 339. The night Giacomin came back as a Red Wing was unreal. The chants of 'ED-DIE! ED-DIE!' were as loud as the night they won the Cup in 1994."

The fans continued to chant Giacomin's name throughout the game. They roared with every save he made and cheered every Red Wings goal. Final score: Detroit 6, New York 4. The Rangers just didn't have their hearts in that particular game. Giacomin surely did.

Heeeeeeere's Eddie!

In 1966, Giacomin appeared with new Rangers teammate Bernie Geoffrion on *The Tonight Show* to demonstrate for host Johnny Carson how to stop a slapshot. Rehearsal went fine, but on live TV, Geoffrion drilled a shot into Giacomin's throat, leaving the goalie unable to talk for a week.

"Our players wouldn't shoot at him," Francis recalled. "They didn't want to embarrass him. It was a great night for Eddie and he deserved that because he was our franchise for ten years. Then, with five minutes to go in the game, guess what they were chanting: 'Kill the Cat!' We had the best security people in MSG, and when they heard that they came down at the end of the game and said, 'We need to give you protection. They're going to kill you.' And I said, 'Hey, I walked in here and I'm going to walk out. They may get me, but I guarantee you I will take a couple of them with me.'"

The feisty Rangers GM, of course, made it out of the Garden that night unscathed and was surely as proud as anyone when Giacomin was elected to the Hockey Hall of Fame in 1987.

21 Broadway vs. Broad Street

Rangers vs. Flyers is cheesecake vs. cheesesteak. It's the Statue of Liberty vs. the Liberty Bell. It's Original Six vs. Expansion Six. It's hating Dan Carcillo like he kicked your dog...and the strange twinge you feel in your stomach upon learning he just became a Ranger.

Brad Park's mother was once asked if she would invite any members of the Flyers to dinner. She replied, "I wouldn't invite them to my garage." That just about sums up the feeling most Rangers fans and quite a few players have had about the organization that helped usher in the NHL's blood-soaked goon image in the 1970s.

The Flyers were the first expansion team to win the Stanley Cup. Intimidation was a major ingredient in their back-to-back championships in 1974 and 1975 though their coach, Fred Shero, insisted he never instructed his players to hop over the boards and start fights. He simply encouraged them to play with passion.

"They were like a pack of wolves," former Rangers star Ron Duguay said. "You knew that if you picked on one guy, the rest would come after you. It worked for them and I respect the way they played. They scared the heck out of a lot of players and a lot of teams. They were good at it. They brought the best out of me because I knew going in there that if I wasn't awake and ready to go, I was going to get a beating."

Today, the Flyers are still very much a team of and for blue-collar Philadelphians, whose loathing of all New York sports teams comes from someplace primal and instinctive, like the way an animal urinates on a rock or a tree to mark its territory. The animal analogy is harsh but not misplaced. This is, after all, the city where Phillies fans threw D-batteries at centerfielder J.D. Drew, the Eagles had to build a courtroom and jail to house all the drunken thugs at Veterans Stadium, and off-duty New Jersey cop Neal Auricchio Jr., in town to root for the Rangers at the Winter Classic, was brutally beaten outside a South Philly cheesesteak shop.

"Before that incident," Auricchio said, "I knew Philadelphia fans had a bad reputation, but I'd never experienced it. As a Mets fan, I'd been to Phillies games plenty of times and never had an issue. Although there are some bad fans down in Philly, it's an epidemic that happens in a lot of cities. I heard from countless Flyers fans who were appalled by what happened to me, but I can't see myself going back there for a game anytime soon."

Here are some of the rivalry's most famous episodes:

The Dale Rolfe Incident

Game 7 of the 1974 semifinals might have been the biggest playoff game New York and Philadelphia have ever played. The winner would advance to face Boston in the Stanley Cup Finals.

Having already knocked off mighty Montreal in the opening round, the Rangers needed to win a road game, something neither team had yet to do in the series. Philadelphia's 4–3 win in the decisive match reinforced the New Yorkers' reputation as postseason chokers.

Steve Vickers, who still holds the Rangers record for most career points by a left winger, took the loss especially hard.

"I didn't mind taking a bit of a beating in the crease," he said, "especially if I got to play against guys like Eddie Van Impe and Moose Dupont. That 1974 team was the best that I ever played on, and to lose that way was disheartening. I think we had the team to go all the way but we couldn't win in Philly. That hurt us."

The final score of the game might have caused less long-term damage to the Rangers' collective psyche than the first period beating defenseman Dale Rolfe took from Flyers enforcer Dave "The Hammer" Schultz. While Schultz pounded away at Rolfe like he was tenderizing a raw piece of tenderloin, Ranger teammates just stood and watched. Over the years, their inaction has been misconstrued as cowardice or indifference. It's a black mark on the club that is undeserved.

"Let's get it straight once and for all," Brad Park told the *New York Post*. "We did not meekly stand by; we were forced to stand by. It was Game 7 and [the league] had brought the third-man-in rule, so someone would have gotten thrown out of the game. So who did you want to lose: Rod Gilbert, Jean Ratelle, Vic Hadfield, or myself? I did finally decide to intervene, but Dale looked me in the eye and said to stay out of it."

Beat Philly, Comrade!

"How much do I hate the Flyers? During the height of the Cold War, when they played an exhibition game against the Soviets, I rooted for the Commies."

Mario Morgado, Greenwich, Connecticut
Rangers fan since 1970

Bye Bye, Bernie

On February 17, 1979, Flyers goalie Bernie Parent suffered a career-ending eye injury in a game against the Rangers when an errant stick entered the right eyehole of his mask, causing permanent damage to his vision. It was a major setback for the Flyers, who turned to backup Wayne Stephenson to salvage their season. But Stephenson was no Parent.

When the teams met a few months later in the second round of the playoffs, the Rangers carved up the Flyers like a Thanksgiving turkey. After dropping Game 1 in overtime, New York rattled off four straight wins by a combined score of 26–5.

Revenge of the Smurfs

The Rangers and Flyers met in the playoffs six times in the 1980s, with each team winning three series. The most satisfying Rangers victory occurred in 1983.

In the days leading up to the Patrick Division Semifinals, the coach of the favored Flyers, Bob McCammon, dismissed as "Smurfs" the diminutive Rangers line of Rob McClanahan, Mark Pavelich, and Anders Hedberg, all of them well under 6' tall. But they weren't the only vertically challenged Rangers. Robbie Ftorek, Eddie Johnstone, Mike Rogers, and Reijo Ruotsalainen were pretty Smurfy, too.

McCammon soon came to regret the characterization. The Rangers won two close games on the road and on April 9 at Madison Square Garden, they completed the sweep by routing Philadelphia

9–3. The McClanahan-Pavelich-Hedberg line accounted for four goals.

Writer Stuart Miller described what happened next: "Up in the blue seats, the most rabid of Ranger fans waved a huge, inflated Smurf, turning the Flyers' taunt into a salute to the Rangers' grit and determination."

A New Low

In November 1985, Flyers goalie Pelle Lindbergh died after crashing his Porsche 930 Turbo into a concrete wall next to an elementary school in Somerdale, New Jersey.

Lindbergh's successor in goal, rookie Ron Hextall, received no quarter from the blue seat crew—not even after they learned that his grandfather, Bryan Hextall, scored the Cup-winning goal in 1940. His father, Bryan Jr., also played for the Rangers.

For years, Ron was serenaded with chants of "Buy a Porsche, Hextall, buy a Porsche!"

When it comes to loyalty, Rangers fans are beyond compare. But this was not their finest hour.

Targeting Tomas

Because he didn't mind wearing a bull's-eye on his back, Rangers winger Tomas Sandstrom made his share of enemies. Quite a few of those enemies wore orange and black.

During a game in November 1987, Sandstrom speared Philadelphia's Mark Howe in the gut. Before Howe could enact revenge, Flyers enforcer (and future Rangers scout) Dave Brown jumped in and broke Sandstrom's jaw with a crosscheck to the face.

Rangers All-Time Record vs. Flyers (1967–2014)

GP	W	L	T	OL
276	121	111	37	7

Brown, who only weeks earlier drew a five-game ban for jamming his stick into Sandstrom's head, was slapped with a 15-game suspension which, at the time, was the second-longest ban by the NHL for an on-ice incident.

You Must Be Jokinen!

On April 11, 2010, the Flyers and Rangers were part of perhaps the most cliffhanging conclusion to an NHL regular season. Playing in Game No. 82 on their respective schedules, the winner would make the playoffs while the loser would not.

After a period of overtime failed to break a 1–1 deadlock, the game went to a shootout. The season came down to New York's Olli Jokinen after Erik Christensen was stopped by Flyers goalie Brian Boucher and Claude Giroux scored against Henrik Lundqvist. Jokinen tried to slip the puck between Boucher's legs, but Boucher made the stop that put the Flyers, not the Rangers, into the postseason.

The choice of Jokinen, who had scored only four goals in 26 regular season games as a Ranger, raised some eyebrows. Rangers coach John Tortorella wouldn't say why he didn't pick 40-goal scorer Marian Gaborik to be one of his first three shooters, though Gabby expected to go fourth.

In the dressing room after the game, a disgusted Jokinen took off his Ranger jersey for the last time and threw it into a laundry cart. He signed with Calgary as a free agent that summer, much to Rangers fans' relief.

22 The Cat

Hall of Fame Coach and General Manager Emile Francis

Although the Rangers failed to win a Stanley Cup during the dozen-year reign of Emile Francis, they regained respectability for the first time since before World War II. For a team that often finished fifth or sixth in a six-team league, respectability was a big deal.

Francis was himself a former goaltender with Chicago and the Rangers. He earned the nickname "The Cat" from his slight frame and lightning-quick reflexes. He was also an avid baseball player and is credited with developing the modern catching glove used by goalies. He began experimenting with a first baseman's glove by adding a cuff to protect the rest of his hand and wrist.

After he retired as a player, Francis received calls from every team in the NHL to talk about coaching in their organizations. He credits baseball for earning him a shot at a new career in hockey.

"In the off-seasons," he said, "I'd been a ballplayer all my life and I also managed from the time I was 24. I managed in the old Canadian-American Baseball League. I managed against big league players, and we won a bunch of championships. That's why teams offered me a job in hockey—not so much because of what I did in hockey but because they knew what I did in baseball. In the end, I chose the New York Rangers because I'd been with them as a player longer than anybody."

The Rangers gave Emile a choice of running one of their junior teams in Kitchener or Guelph, Ontario. He chose the latter and inherited hot prospects Rod Gilbert and Jean Ratelle, both of whom would later star for him in New York.

In 1964, he succeeded Muzz Patrick as general manager of the Rangers, a team that had missed the playoffs five of the previous

Emile Francis, the general manager and coach of the New York Rangers, fields questions at a press conference held at Madison Square Garden in New York on April 28, 1972. (AP Photo/Harry Harris)

six seasons. His first order of business? Making the Rangers bigger and meaner.

"We'd start the season playing well," he recalled, "then fold by Thanksgiving. We'd do pretty well on Saturday night, then get clobbered early Sunday at home. We needed bodies. Big, tough bodies."

After addressing the need for size with players like Orland "K.O." Kurtenbach, Reg Fleming, and Vic Hadfield, Francis got to work on adding skill. He made Gilbert and Ratelle a focal point of the offense, drafted Brad Park, and practically stole a young goalie named Ed Giacomin from the minor league Providence Reds.

Francis proposed a package of four minor league players for Giacomin and presented the offer to Lou Pieri, the Reds owner. Pieri believed that good-looking, helmetless players would sell tickets, so Francis brought along 8x10 glossy publicity photos of the players he was offering.

"I slid the pictures, one by one, across Pieri's desk," Francis recalled, "and I saved Jim Mikol for last. Now, Jim was a pretty good-looking guy. Pieri smiled, and I had myself a goalkeeper."

He was crafty, this wiry little man of no more than 145 lbs. And feisty, too. During games, Francis would pace back and forth behind the Ranger bench, cursing up a storm and barking out commands in a voice as coarse as 80-grit sandpaper. He had quite a few run-ins with the officials over the years, most memorably on November 21, 1965.

It was a Sunday afternoon in New York as the Rangers hosted the Red Wings. Midway through the third period, Detroit's Floyd Smith beat Giacomin with a shot that seemed to hit the back of the net and bounce back out in an instant. Goal judge Arthur Reichert flipped on the red light to signal a goal. Francis went berserk, bounding from his box seat to challenge Reichert's call.

Fans seated nearby, no doubt emboldened by having had one too many beers, started taunting Francis. Tempers flared and fists started flying. The Cat got in a few good licks but was quickly overmatched. Rangers players led by Vic Hadfield scaled the glass to rescue their scrappy GM.

It was an embarrassing episode for Francis and for Madison Square Garden. The three fans involved in the melee originally said they didn't want to file assault charges, then changed their minds two days later. Court proceedings dragged on for years, and the trio was eventually awarded $80,000 in damages.

The Rangers won only 20 games in Emile's first year as GM and 18 in his second, during which he also took over behind the bench (for the first of three coaching stints) by replacing Red Sullivan in December 1965. He worked tirelessly—and tinkered compulsively—to transform the Rangers into a Stanley Cup contender, going so far as to suggest the team do all of its training and practices in Kitchener, far away from the distractions of

For Love of the Game

At 15, Brian Mullen landed a job as stick boy for the Rangers, putting the rink rat from Hell's Kitchen closer than ever to his favorite team. But a chance encounter with Emile Francis really helped his hockey dreams take off.

"The schoolyard across from my apartment building was sunken in and about one story down," Mullen said. "When you walked by it, you could only see the tops of people's heads. Emile Francis was walking past the schoolyard one day, before a Rangers game, and he went over to the fence and peeked his head in and saw all of these kids playing hockey. He watched for a while and he thought there could be a way to get these kids on the ice. He wound up starting the Metropolitan Junior Hockey Association, and that's where me and all of my brothers played their ice hockey."

Mullen would go on to play 11 seasons in the NHL, including four with the Rangers.

In 2007–08, the Rangers established the Emile Francis Award to honor outstanding supporters of youth hockey in the metropolitan area.

Manhattan, and come back only for games (Garden management shot that idea down).

Francis coached the Rangers to the 1972 Stanley Cup Finals, where they were defeated in six games by the Bruins. To keep the nucleus of that team together, and prevent defections to the rival WHA, he (against his better judgment) signed a number of veterans to lucrative long-term contracts. Critics started calling them "Fat Cats."

After disappointing playoff results in 1973 and 1974, Francis began to sense that his core group had gone as far as it could. He unloaded popular stars like Hadfield, Ratelle, Park, and Giacomin in a series of moves that were roundly criticized, especially after they didn't immediately put the Rangers back on track. Emile knew his days at MSG were numbered.

His firing on January 6, 1976, took much of the league by surprise. Francis had been a fixture on the New York hockey scene for so long that friends and foes alike couldn't imagine the Rangers without him.

"I think it's a bloody shame," grumbled a sympathetic Fred Shero, coach of the Flyers who previously worked under Francis in the Rangers' farm system. "He is definitely a scapegoat. He brought New York from nothing to world prominence. Just because his team didn't win the Stanley Cup means nothing."

It certainly didn't prevent Francis from finding work. Right after being given his walking papers by the Rangers, he walked right into a job running the St. Louis Blues. He'd made so many deals with St. Louis over the years that he already knew most of their players.

23 Harry the Horse

Unlike the Boston Celtics, who have retired so many uniform numbers they may eventually need to switch to Roman numerals, the Rangers waited more than 50 years before taking a number out of circulation...probably out of fears that celebrating anything short of a Stanley Cup would lead to backlash from fans and the press. As a result, some very special players never got the recognition they deserved, or they had to wait an inordinate length of time to receive it.

Harry Howell's long overdue moment in the limelight, shared with former teammate Andy Bathgate, came on February 22, 2009. That night, Howell's No. 3 joined Bathgate's No. 9 in the Garden rafters where it belongs.

"Harry Howell Night in 1967, when they gave Dad a car and all sorts of other gifts, and his Hall of Fame induction in 1979 were very exciting," said Harry's daughter, Cheryl, "but retiring his jersey was fantastic. I am so grateful that the Rangers did it while Dad was healthy. It was a great honor for him. My kids were amazed that so many people in New York still recognized him. So many of them gave Dad a 'Hi Harry' as we were walking down the street."

He was known as Harry the Horse, this remarkably durable athlete who played a club-record 1,160 games and missed only 20 in his first 16 years with the team. Starting early in the 1952–53 season, when he arrived in New York from the championship Guelph Biltmores of the Ontario Hockey Association, Howell went about his business with a quiet efficiency. The 6'1", 195-lb. defenseman played with a smooth, almost matter-of-fact style that emphasized precision and accuracy over brute strength. Mostly, he left the jarring bodychecks to others, like longtime defense partner Lou Fontinato. It was a style that sometimes led to catcalls from the Garden crowd but Harry, ever the pro, took it in stride.

Thanks to an off-season job with Texaco lifting heavy oil drums, he was always in shape in time for training camp. Like many players, he was also an instructor at hockey clinics.

Never a great offensive talent, it's somewhat ironic that Howell scored his first NHL goal on his very first shift. It was Saturday, October 18, 1952, during a 4–3 loss to the Toronto Maple Leafs. A Ranger career like no other was launched that night.

Howell's play with the Blueshirts, especially early in his career, was so impressive that team management, perhaps somewhat hastily, made him the club's ninth captain for the start of the 1955–56 season. At just 22, the youngest captain in team history up to that point, Howell was not overly comfortable in his new role.

Two years later, he chose to resign the captaincy. "It was the right thing to do," he recalled. "I had played two bad seasons in a row, and I knew it. I wanted to be free to concentrate on improving

Daddy Was a Ranger

"One of my favorite childhood memories is getting to do the oh-so-serious job of being Dad's nurse. He was always getting stitches in his face during games. When they'd start to itch, we'd go into the bathroom and I would stand on the toilet seat and hand him the rubbing alcohol, scissors, and tweezers so he could take his stitches out. It was always a big deal for me, and Dad always made me feel important. I am very proud of my father. He's always been very humble. We knew growing up that he had a different job than most dads, but it was never a big deal. We just had to be quiet in the afternoons on game days so he could nap."

Cheryl Howell
Hamilton, Ontario

Norris Trophy Winners

Named for the former owner of the Detroit Red Wings, the James Norris Memorial Trophy is an annual award given to the league's best all-around defenseman. The winner is selected in a poll of the Professional Hockey Writers Association at the end of the regular season. The following Rangers have won the award: Doug Harvey (1962), Harry Howell (1967), and Brian Leetch (1992 and 1997).

my play." And improve he did, leading the Rangers defensively on the ice and by example in the dressing room.

The NHL was awash in great defensemen at the time, Doug Harvey, Pierre Pilote, and Tim Horton among them, so Harry was sometimes overlooked when it came to postseason honors. Howell did win the Norris Trophy as the league's top defenseman and made the first All-Star Team in 1967, just as Boston's budding superstar, Bobby Orr, was coming onto the scene. He also represented the Blueshirts at six All-Star Games.

Off the ice, Howell was a public relations godsend for the Rangers, rarely saying no when public appearances were needed. He was—and still is—one of the good guys.

"Harry is really unique," ace sportswriter Mel Woody of *The Newark News* wrote many years ago. "It seems like he is friends with everyone, and everyone wants to be friends with him."

Harry scouted for the Edmonton Oilers for many years, picking up a Stanley Cup ring in 1990 before returning to his ancestral home to scout for the Rangers from 2000 to 2004. Then quietly, as is his way, he retired at the age of 71, following the 2003–04 season.

24 2014

Los Angeles Kings Defeat Rangers in 2014 Stanley Cup Finals

How best to describe the 2013–14 season for future generations of Rangers fans? Perhaps like this: it was like taking the world's most awesome rollercoaster ride—thrilling, chilling, and suspenseful. But instead of ending on a joyous note, the ride stops abruptly. Then, as you're walking away wondering, "What the hell just happened?" you get punched in the stomach by a carny. That's how it feels to lose three overtime games in the Stanley Cup Finals.

The campaign opened with Henrik Lundqvist distracted by stalled negotiations on a contract extension, and it showed in his play. In response, new coach Alain Vigneault gave a heavier workload to backup Cam Talbot, who replaced the recently retired Martin Biron. Talbot gave the team an unexpected lift by winning six of his first seven starts.

Lundqvist, one of seven Rangers who participated in the Winter Olympic Games at Sochi, Russia, returned to form after New Year's, helping the Rangers distance themselves from the pack in an extremely tight playoff race. Declining offensive production from veterans Rick Nash and Brad Richards was offset by breakout performances from Mats Zuccarello (team-leading 59 points), Chris Kreider (career-high 17 goals), and Ryan McDonagh (career-high 14 goals).

At the trade deadline, the Rangers made the difficult decision to deal team captain Ryan Callahan, an impending free agent, to the Tampa Bay Lightning for two-time scoring champ Martin St. Louis.

The Rangers finished second in their division with a 45–31–6 record, earning home ice advantage for a first-round meeting with the Philadelphia Flyers. After a bumpy transition period, St. Louis broke out of his scoring slump with two goals and six points in the series, which the Rangers won in seven games.

New York's semifinal series against Pittsburgh also went the distance and included an historic comeback from a 3–1 deficit. Lundqvist was fined a whopping $5,000 for squirting his water bottle at Sidney Crosby, but the death of St. Louis' mother prior to Game 5, and the galvanizing effect it seemed to have on the club, would prove to be the dominant storyline.

A 7–2 blowout in Game 1 of the Eastern Conference Finals confirmed that Montreal's Bell Centre was no longer a "house of horrors" for Lundqvist and the Rangers. That afternoon, the Canadiens also lost their best player, goalie Carey Price, for the remainder of the playoffs after he suffered a knee injury in a collision with Kreider. Minor leaguer Dustin Tokarski stepped in for Price for the rest of the series and was strong in relief. But Lundqvist was just a bit better in Game 2, stopping 40-of-41 shots to lift the visitors to a 3–1 victory. Brandon Prust's jaw-breaking hit on Derek Stepan in Game 3 earned the ex-Ranger a suspension, as did Dan Carcillo's shoving of linesman Scott Driscoll. Montreal won that game in overtime, but then the Rangers answered with an overtime win of their own in Game 4, courtesy of St. Louis' snap shot from the right circle at 6:02 of the extra session. Lundqvist was chased from the net in Game 5, a 7–4 Montreal rout, but bounced back to blank the Habs 1–0 in Game 6, becoming the Rangers' all-time playoff wins leader in the process. Dominic Moore, the gritty fourth-liner who'd combined with Brian Boyle to form one of the league's top penalty-killing duos, scored the series-clinching goal for New York.

For the first time in 20 years, the Rangers were headed back to the Stanley Cup Finals. Their opponents, the Los Angeles Kings, were heavy favorites. Hollywood's hockey team was bigger, deeper, and more physical than the Rangers. They were the highest scoring team in the playoffs and getting timely goals from a suddenly hot ex-Blueshirt, Marian Gaborik. Their goalie, Jonathan Quick, was on par with Lundqvist and made a compelling case as the best in the game. L.A. also had a vexing habit of not knowing when to quit. Of his club's resiliency, Kings defenseman Alec Martinez said, "We never say die. Someone described us as a bunch of cockroaches. We don't go away."

Sure enough, the Rangers had a two-goal lead early in Game 1 but the Kings battled back to tie the score. In overtime, a Dan Girardi clearing attempt put the puck right on the stick of Kings center Mike Richards, who found Justin Williams alone in the slot. Williams beat Lundqvist at 4:36 of the extra period. It was a tough break for Girardi, a top-pairing defenseman valued for his ability to log a ridiculous amount of ice time while blocking shots and absorbing hits from the other team's top forwards.

Twice the Rangers led by two goals in Game 2 but couldn't put the Kings away. Gaborik's wrist shot at 7:36 of the third period tied the game 4–4 before Kings captain Dustin Brown deflected a Willie Mitchell shot under Lundqvist's left arm at 10:26 of the second overtime.

Even if the Rangers had played better than they did in Game 1, there was a growing sense of frustration in their dressing room. No one was more disappointed than Lundqvist, who knew the Rangers had squandered a golden chance—two chances, really—to steal a game on the road.

The series moved back to Madison Square Garden, where ticket prices for the finals made even the team's most zealous supporters question their priorities ("Hmmm, go to a game or pay my rent?"). Secondary market prices for Game 3 were so high that most fans couldn't get into the arena for less than $1,000, with many seats in the lower bowl selling for double or triple that amount.

The Kings spoiled the Rangers' homecoming by scoring the first goal of the game with less than a second remaining in the first

Rangers in the 2014 Winter Olympics

Player	Country	Medal finish
Ryan Callahan	USA	—
Carl Hagelin	Sweden	Silver
Henrik Lundqvist	Sweden	Silver
Ryan McDonagh	USA	—
Rick Nash	Canada	Gold
Derek Stepan	USA	—
Mats Zuccarello	Norway	—

period, sucking the life out of a building that had been absolutely riotous 20 minutes earlier. The Rangers never found their groove after that, losing 3–0. Rangerstown was now Heartbreak City.

As they had throughout the postseason when facing elimination, the Rangers dug deep and found a way to win in Game 4. Goals from St. Louis and Benoit Pouliot and a 40-save performance by Lundqvist were enough to prevent an L.A. sweep and have the Cup awarded to the visitors on Garden ice. New York's goaltender was simply spectacular late in the game when the Kings pressed to score the tying goal. On two occasions, the puck trickled past Lundqvist but stopped short of crossing the slush-covered goal line ("Thank God for soft ice now and then," Vigneault quipped). Defenseman Anton Stralman cleared the puck away in the first period, and Stepan did it with his hand with just 1:11 remaining in regulation.

Game 5, played on Friday the 13th beneath a full moon, offered no good omens that the Rangers would be the first team since the 1942 Maple Leafs to climb out of a 3–0 hole in the finals to win the Stanley Cup.

Justin Williams gave L.A. the lead in the first period, and a Kreider power play goal made it 1–1 late in the second. About four minutes later, Brian Boyle put New York ahead with a beautiful shorthanded goal, skating around Drew Doughty to beat Jonathan Quick gloveside. In the third period, with the Kings on a power

The Wager

Honoring their end of a bet with *Tonight Show* host Jimmy Fallon, the Canadiens had to change their Twitter avatar to a photo of Fallon's choosing after they lost to the Rangers in the Conference Finals. Fallon selected a shot of Henrik Lundqvist playing guitar. Then the Habs had to tweet 10 pictures of team mascot Youppi walking around Montreal in a Rangers jersey. If they had won, Fallon would have had to wear a Canadiens jersey during one monologue.

play following an atrocious tripping call on Zuccarello, Gaborik scored his league-best 14th goal of the playoffs. Smelling blood, the Kings outshot the Rangers 12–3 in the final frame, but Lundqvist kept the game tied through the end of regulation.

Both teams traded chances in the first overtime, and each team hit a post (McDonagh for New York, Tyler Toffoli for Los Angeles), and shots were 13–10 Los Angeles. The period also featured two other near-misses: Tanner Pearson nearly beat Lundqvist with a wraparound attempt, and Kreider missed the net on a breakaway. No matter which team you happened to be rooting for that night, it was excruciating to watch.

It was the early morning of June 14 back on the East Coast—the 20th anniversary of the Rangers' last Stanley Cup—when Alec Martinez led a rush into the Rangers' zone and slid the puck to Toffoli who fired a shot on goal. Lundqvist stopped it, but the rebound came right back to Martinez, and he scored with a wrist shot at 14:43 of the second overtime.

And just like that, New York's rollercoaster ride was over.

While the Kings celebrated their second Stanley Cup in three years, the Rangers retreated to the visitors' dressing room empty-handed. Some players choked back tears during postgame interviews. Others sat silently and stared into the distance, no doubt replaying the game in their heads. An exhausted Lundqvist, the man who'd given his all (and then some) to extend the

Rangers' season, collapsed into his stall and buried his head in his hands.

There's an old cliché that nobody remembers who finished second. But a generation of Rangers fans will always remember with a bittersweet mix of pride and nagging regret how close their team came to winning it all in 2014. Truth is, for better or worse, they couldn't forget if they tried.

25 Stemmer's Big Goal

Think fast—where were you on the evening of April 29, 1971? In your friend's basement listening to *Led Zeppelin III?* Cruising around town in dad's Buick? Gnawing on the edge of your crib? Or were you watching Pete Stemkowski and the Rangers play Chicago in Game 6 of the semifinals? That's a night Stemmer will never forget.

The Rangers, on the brink of elimination in the series, rallied from a 2–0 deficit to tie the score. The teams played two scoreless overtime frames in a warm and humid Madison Square Garden. Exhaustion set in on both sides and, between periods, an oxygen tank was wheeled into the Rangers' dressing room for anyone who needed a whiff.

Just more than a minute into the third extra period, there was a mad scramble in front of the Chicago net. Ted Irvine of New York emerged with the puck, skated to the right side of the crease, and fired a shot from a sharp angle. Tony Esposito, the acrobatic Blackhawks goalie, kicked out the disk but it skipped right to Stemkowski. With Esposito flat on the ice in front of him, Stemmer lifted the puck into the net, giving the Rangers a 3–2 win

Can You Wait Until I'm Finished?

"One day, before a Rangers game, my son and I stopped into Penn Station to use the bathroom. I was at the urinal and next to me was Pete Stemkowski. I said, 'Hey, aren't you Pete Stemkowski?' Then I asked for his autograph…while we were both peeing. So he gave me his autograph, right there in the men's room. When we ran into each other years later, he laughed when I reminded him how we first met. We're really good friends now."

Adam Guntmacher, Lawrence, New York
Rangers fan since 1970

and ending one of the longest NHL games ever at four hours and 23 minutes. It was Stemkowski's second OT winner of the series and for his feat he was promised a summer's supply of Polish sausages or, as he called them, "the breakfast of champions."

Although the Blackhawks rebounded to win Game 7 in Chicago two days later—a detail conveniently swept under the rug of history by some Rangers fans—Stemmer's tally was certainly the biggest of his 15-year NHL career and one of the most dramatic playoff goals on record.

A big, lumbering center who could also play left wing, Stemkowski broke into the NHL with Toronto and helped the Maple Leafs win the Stanley Cup in 1967. He was eventually traded to Detroit, settling in as one of the Red Wings' more consistent two-way players. After three seasons in Motown, he was dealt once again, this time to the Rangers.

When the 6', 200-lb. Winnipegger arrived a few days later, he immediately became the Rangers' biggest forward. Emile Francis initially had Stemmer center a line with Bob Nevin at right wing and Irvine on the left, giving the Blueshirts greater depth.

Stemkowski's NHL career spanned more than 1,000 combined regular season and playoff games with Toronto, Detroit, New York, and Los Angeles, but his clutch performance in the 1971 playoffs is the highlight most fans want to chat about when they meet him. He doesn't mind.

"I must've had a couple hundred guys say they were at home in bed with a transistor radio in their ear because their parents wouldn't let them stay up late or their son or daughter was born on that night," he said. "It's not winning a Cup or winning a Game 7—it just prolonged the series. But a lot of people still remind me about it and that's nice."

26 The Avery Rule

As popular as he was polarizing, no player has inspired such heated debate between Rangers fans as Sean Avery.

To some, he was a shameless self-promoter who put his own brand ahead of the teams for which he played. To others, he was "the spark"—an abrasive, antagonistic presence that could throw the other team off its game. To the suits at NHL headquarters, Avery was a problem child who tarnished the image of their business with his big mouth and rebellious behavior. He saw himself as the victim of a double standard that sometimes punished rude words more harshly than acts of physical violence.

What made Avery such a compelling character, and his story so engaging, is that he was all of those things.

Since breaking into the NHL in 2001 as an undrafted free agent with the Red Wings, controversy seemed to follow the product of Pickering, Ontario, who once complained that he despised "hockey-obsessed Canadians." It certainly followed him to Los Angeles where, owing to the broken filter between his brain and his mouth, Avery once dismissed all French-Canadian players who wear visors as cheap-shot artists who "run around and play tough but can't back anything up."

To say that Avery made enemies in hockey is kind of like saying that Duff (*Ace of Cakes*) Goldman has cracked his share of eggs. Avery wasn't the first pest on the scene, but his willingness to say and do just about anything to get under an opponent's skin set him apart from the Esa Tikkanens and Darcy Tuckers of the world. In a 2007 poll conducted by *The Hockey News*, a majority of NHL players listed Avery as the most hated *and* overrated player in the league.

In February of that year, the Kings traded Avery to the Rangers. His impact was immediate. With Avery in the lineup, the Rangers went 33–14–10. Without him, 9–13–3.

But his lasting legacy in hockey may be that he has a rule named after him...unofficially.

In Game 3 of the 2008 quarterfinals against the Devils, Avery turned his back on the play in order to face and screen goalie Martin Brodeur during a five-on-three Rangers power play. Ignoring the puck, Avery waved his hands and stick in front of Brodeur's face in an attempt to distract the goalie and block his view. The puck was later cleared out of the Devils' end zone, but on the second Rangers offensive attack, Avery scored a power play goal.

Screening is a common tactic employed by attacking players, especially on the power play, but nobody had ever seen anything like this. While it was not an explicit rules violation at the time of the game, many NHL commentators, executives, and players regarded Avery's actions as unsportsmanlike—not the first time that word had been used in reference to the Ranger agitator.

"It was childish," New Jersey's John Madden said. "We're trying to sell this game and you see stuff like that going on."

The NHL's director of hockey operations, former Rangers coach Colin Campbell, moved quickly to discourage any copycats by issuing a so-called "interpretation" of the league's unsportsmanlike

A Timeline of Turmoil

February 2007: The Los Angeles Kings trade Avery to the Rangers.

March 2008: Avery's name and private cell phone number are found in the "little black book" of a New York prostitute. Avery laughs it off as someone's idea of a practical joke.

April 2008: During a playoff game against the Penguins, Avery suffers a lacerated spleen and misses the rest of the season.

May 2008: Avery parlays his love of fashion into a summer internship at *Vogue*.

July 2008: Avery signs a free agent contract with the Dallas Stars.

December 2008: Avery is suspended indefinitely for making comments "detrimental to the league."

March 2009: The Rangers claim Avery off waivers.

May 2009: Warren 77, Avery's Tribeca bar/restaurant, opens to mostly positive reviews (try the BLT!).

May 2011: Avery tapes a public service announcement for the Human Rights Campaign in support of same-sex marriage in New York. He is roundly praised for being one of the few pro athletes to speak out in defense of gay rights.

August 2011: Avery is arrested after shoving a cop who was trying to break up a loud party at his home in Los Angeles. Police later drop the charges.

September 2011: Avery accuses Philadelphia's Wayne Simmonds of using a homophobic slur against him during a preseason game.

December 2011: For the second time in as many months, Avery is placed on waivers.

March 2012: Avery is released by the Rangers. A short time later, he appears on Bravo's *Watch What Happens Live* to chat about his favorite hobby, fashion, and announces his retirement from hockey, stating, "I threw my skates in the Hudson."

March 2013: Hours after the Rangers are shut out in Montreal, Avery takes to Twitter to fire a shot at John Tortorella: "Fire this CLOWN, his players hate him and won't play for his BS."

May 2013: Avery delights in the firing of Tortorella. He tells the *New York Post*, "I had a huge smile on my face."

conduct rule to cover actions such as the one employed by Avery, which would now result in a minor penalty. It became known as "The Avery Rule."

Rangers backup Steve Valiquette admitted that he would have reacted differently to a player doing to him what Avery did to Brodeur.

"Sean," Valiquette said, "would've been picking his teeth up off the ice if it was me."

The Rangers lost that game 4–3 on an overtime goal by Madden but eventually won the series in five games. Avery, the man about whom commentator Don Cherry said "once a jerk, always a jerk," was the difference-maker. He'd drawn multiple power plays and scored goals in each of the first three games.

His stock on the rise, Avery sought a big raise when his contract expired in July 2008. As much as he loved living and playing in New York City, he chased the money to Dallas, where the Stars offered him a four-year deal worth $15.5 million—far more than the Rangers were willing to spend. It was a decision he would come to regret.

Avery brought plenty of baggage with him to Dallas but had yet to give his detractors much ammunition. That is, until he stepped in front of TV cameras in Calgary and delivered his infamous "sloppy seconds" crack, a crude potshot at Flames defenseman Dion Phaneuf, who at the time was dating Avery's ex-girlfriend, actress Elisha Cuthbert. The sexy star of *The Girl Next Door* had also been linked to former Habs defenseman Mike Komisarek.

Avery later claimed he'd only been trying to generate interest in the game. But since Gary Bettman has never really embraced the notion that any publicity is good publicity, he immediately suspended Avery six games and ordered him into counseling. The Stars not only backed the commissioner's ruling but took the additional step of making Avery's suspension indefinite. He never played for Dallas again.

When his suspension was lifted a few months later, Avery was waived by the Stars and then assigned to Hartford of the American Hockey League so the Rangers could claim him on re-entry waivers. It wasn't long before the one-man sideshow was back on Broadway.

John Tortorella, who'd eviscerated Avery on-air while working as an analyst for TSN, had since replaced Tom Renney behind the Ranger bench. Everyone wondered how a no-nonsense coach and a player with the magical ability to conjure nonsense out of thin air would respond to this shotgun wedding orchestrated by GM Glen Sather.

"[John] doesn't have the history with Sean that we do," Sather assured. "Over time you learn to love him, just like I do."

But that was never going to happen. Not with all the time in the world.

Ironically, it wasn't Avery's bad-boy shtick that doomed his relationship with Tortorella and, ultimately, his NHL career. It was that he couldn't figure out how to play with consistent intensity without becoming a liability. Feeling like a marked man who'd never get a fair shake from the league, the refs, or his own coach, Avery became a marginal player, ineffective and expendable.

It's a shame, really, since Avery was a better hockey player than perhaps even he or his many critics realized. He had good speed, soft hands, an accurate shot, and underrated playmaking ability— skills too often overshadowed by all his theatrics.

Cut loose by the Rangers in 2012, Avery initially vowed to work his way back to the NHL and reward some lucky team for taking a chance on him. But finding no takers, he retreated from public life to work for *Playboy* and appear on ABC's *Dancing With the Stars*.

27 Worst. Trade. Ever.

May 26, 1976: Rangers trade Rick Middleton to Boston for Ken Hodge.

When it comes to trades, declaring one team the winner and another the loser is a highly subjective business—unless, of course, one party gets taken to the cleaners so thoroughly as to ensure that deal's permanent place on every hockey expert's list of the most lopsided trades of all-time.

This is the story behind one such trade.

In November 1975, the Rangers acquired Phil Esposito from the Boston Bruins. One of the reasons New York fans were so slow to embrace Espo, apart from all the nights he'd victimized them as an opponent, is that he was unable to put up the same gaudy numbers that made him a scoring champ in Boston. Without his former linemate, the brawny right winger Ken Hodge, to barrel into the corners, dig out the puck, and feed him waiting in the slot, Esposito was just another big, slow center in a turtleneck.

The Rangers' new coach and general manager, John Ferguson, didn't bring Espo to New York—his predecessor, Emile Francis, did—but Ferguson had to live with the fallout and the burden of proving to fans and media that the blockbuster trade, which cost the Rangers Brad Park and Jean Ratelle, hadn't been made in vain.

Fergie believed that reuniting Hodge and Esposito might be the key to reigniting both players. And he knew Hodge was available—the 32-year-old winger's numbers were down and he was on the outs with Bruins coach Don Cherry. The price? Rick Middleton, a 22-year-old left wing brimming with potential. The former first rounder had great hands and could skate like the wind.

Six More Stinkers

July 2, 2008: Rangers trade Fedor Tyutin and Christian Backman to the Columbus Blue Jackets for Nikolai Zherdev and Dan Fritsche.

March 10, 2000: Rangers trade Mike Knuble to the Boston Bruins for Rob DiMaio.

March 14, 1996: Rangers trade Mattias Norstrom, Ray Ferraro, Ian Laperriere, Nathan LaFayette, and New York's fourth choice (Sean Blanchard) in 1997 to the Los Angeles Kings for Marty McSorley, Jari Kurri, and Shane Churla.

August 31, 1995: Rangers trade Petr Nedved and Sergei Zubov to the Pittsburgh Penguins for Luc Robitaille and Ulf Samuelsson.

January 1, 1987: Rangers trade Kelly Miller, Mike Ridley, and Bob Crawford to the Washington Capitals for Bobby Carpenter and a second-round pick (Jason Prosofsky) in 1989.

February 6, 1963: Rangers trade Dean Prentice to the Boston Bruins for Don McKenney.

He'd already scored more than 20 goals in each of his first two seasons and seemed to have a *very* bright future in the NHL.

The party line at 4 Penn Plaza was that the Rangers could afford to give up a young, fast player like Middleton because they had lots of youth and speed to spare. Unofficially, Ferguson felt he needed to get Middleton out of New York and away from whatever bad influences were contributing to his hard-partying lifestyle.

It turned out to be a colossal miscalculation by the Rangers boss and an absolute steal for his Boston-based counterpart, Harry Sinden.

As much as Esposito was approaching the downslope of his career, Ferguson would learn the hard way that Hodge was already there. He lasted just more than a season in New York, scoring 23 goals in 96 games. Hodge's play deteriorated so rapidly that he was sent down to the Rangers' minor league team in New Haven, and he retired following the 1979–80 season.

And Middleton, who scored a hat trick in his first-ever game with Boston, went on to become one of the top-scoring Bruins of all time.

28 Visit the Hockey Hall of Fame

Would the Hockey Hall of Fame be a good attraction in New York City? Absolutely. But would New York be the *right* place? Arguably not. Clarence Campbell and other NHL power brokers felt very strongly that the Hall of Fame belonged in Canada, given that country's obsessive (in a good way) love affair with the sport.

But don't be a jaded New Yorker and dismiss the Hall as just some Canadian tourist trap. If you love hockey, you simply must gas up the old Wagon Queen Family Truckster and head to Toronto.

"Even though we're in Toronto," said Craig Campbell, manager of the Hockey Hall of Fame's Resource Center & Archives, "our philosophy is that we're *everyone's* Hall of Fame. It's global. Maybe that perception isn't shared by some hockey fans because they're tucked away in St. Louis or someplace. But we've got it all: all leagues, all levels, worldwide. If that doesn't encompass enough, I'm not sure what does."

When most hockey fans enter the Hall for the first time, they're blown away. Even marginal fans are impressed by the scope of the sport and how it's presented.

"They realize, 'Wow, you guys care about *everything*,'" Campbell said. "Here's Mark Messier's jersey from when he played for the Cincinnati Stingers and an old club jersey from some team in Hungary, and everything in between. There's so much here that you expect to see, but a lot more that you don't."

The Hall's collection is too big to show all at once, so anything not on display is stored at a secure, climate-controled facility on the other side of town. Curators try to preserve and display at least one item from every one of their honored members, a list that at last count included 55 former Rangers players, coaches, and executives.

"We know it's going to be difficult," Campbell said, "but when possible, we'd like to have six to 12 items so that we can do a showcase on that person. Say we have a stick from Boom Boom Geoffrion's last NHL game when he was playing for the Rangers. That's nice, but it would be even better to show that player's entire career—include some photos from his years in juniors and minor pro, too. You want the visitor to get a real sense of what that player's achievements were, other than just the one thing you might remember about them."

The Hall is held in very high regard throughout the hockey community, but it only exists thanks to the generosity of individuals. Lacking the resources to buy up massive collections of artifacts, the Hall relies on donations from players, friends, and families of players, fans, and collectors from all over the world. A perfect example is the equipment Wayne Gretzky used in his last game on April 18, 1999.

Wayne was and still is a big fan of the Hall of Fame. His father, Walter, would bring him to the Hall when he was a young boy. Word has it that Lefty Reid, a former curator, would let Wayne and his dad in when the building was closed. Wayne loved looking at Gordie Howe's Detroit Red Wings sweater. He's always had a kind heart toward the Hall and appreciates the history of the game. When Wayne announced in 1999 that he would be retiring, curator Phil Pritchard—the white-gloved "Keeper of the Cup" you may have seen carrying the trophy—put in a formal request to Gretzky that he donate his final game equipment.

Gretzky never gave the request a second thought. After he undressed and changed into his street clothes, he zipped up his equipment bag and said, "That's for the Hall."

That bag found its way to Craig Campbell's desk.

"I remember the day it came to my office," Campbell said. "My wife still remembers me phoning to say, 'You'll never believe what's in here.' Obviously, the guy is a wonderful player, arguably the greatest, hence his nickname. Those are special, special artifacts that come in, and the fact that it was *all* of Wayne's equipment from that last game, made it even more special."

Campbell's been immersed in this world of old jerseys and pucks for much of his adult life, but any day he gets to add a new or unique piece to the collection is like Christmas morning.

"But that's not exclusive to me," he said. "The people who work here are all pretty passionate. And it doesn't have to be an artifact from one particular league or even from the world's best player. It's just a thrill to know that someone has been so generous to donate this item to the Hall, and it's sent to us personally. It's rewarding to be able, during our time as caretakers of the game, to take in these items and then share them with everyone. That's the beauty of it, the beauty of our collection, and that's why museums are important. Its strength is in the number of eyes that get a chance to see it and experience it."

Touring the Hall

Rangers fans who brave the long drive up the interstate through a seemingly endless stretch of cow pastures and rusted-out tractors will be rewarded for their endurance once they reach their destination.

The Hockey Hall of Fame is full of displays celebrating the careers of the game's biggest stars as well as cases and cases full of artifacts from every team and every era of NHL hockey. A full-scale reproduction of the Montreal Canadiens dressing room in the Montreal Forum is accurate down to the last roll of stick tape. There are displays detailing the history of the WHA and other defunct minor-pro leagues and teams. National jerseys from Israel, Japan, Australia, and elsewhere give the visitor an idea of just how

Rangers in the Hockey Hall of Fame

Inductee	Year	Inductee	Year
Brendan Shanahan	2013	Gump Worsley	1980
Fred Shero*	2013	Lynn Patrick	1980
Pavel Bure	2012	Harry Howell	1979
Brian Leetch	2009	Jacques Plante	1978
Luc Robitaille	2009	Andy Bathgate	1978
Glenn Anderson	2008	William Jennings*	1975
Mark Messier	2007	Art Coulter	1974
Herb Brooks*	2006	Chuck Rayner	1973
Dick Duff	2006	Doug Harvey	1973
Pat LaFontaine	2003	Bernie Geoffrion	1972
Roger Neilson*	2002	Terry Sawchuk	1971
Mike Gartner	2001	Bill Gadsby	1970
Jari Kurri	2001	Bryan Hextall	1969
Craig Patrick*	2001	Neil Colville	1967
Wayne Gretzky	1999	Babe Pratt	1966
Glen Sather*	1997	Max Bentley	1966
Fred "Bun" Cook	1995	Doug Bentley	1964
Edgar Laprade	1993	Earl Seibert	1963
Marcel Dionne	1992	Babe Siebert	1961
Clint Smith	1991	John Kilpatrick*	1960
Bud Poile*	1990	Ching Johnson	1958
Brad Park	1988	Frank Boucher	1958
Buddy O'Connor	1988	Conn Smythe*	1958
Guy Lafleur	1988	Bill Cook	1952
Ed Giacomin	1987	Lester Patrick	1945
Jean Ratelle	1985	Howie Morenz	1945
Phil Esposito	1984		
Emile Francis*	1982	* Enshrined as builder	
Rod Gilbert	1982		

global the game of hockey has become. There are interactive exhibits like the NHLPA Be A Player Zone, where you can test your shot against a life-sized, computer-simulated goaltender. Or put on a glove and blocker and try to stop video images of Mark Messier and Wayne Gretzky, who fire weighted sponge pucks at you at speeds of up to 70 mph.

Once you've navigated the labyrinth of memorabilia and other attractions, walk up a short flight of steps to the Esso Great Hall. Renovated in 2012, this breathtaking structure is the former Bank of Montreal building. Standing in this lavishly designed room, beneath a 45' stained glass dome and surrounded by some of hockey's most revered treasures, one has the sensation of having entered a sacred space. It houses portraits of all the honored members as well as every major NHL trophy (the Art Ross, the Norris, the Vezina, etc.). In the center of the room is a replica Stanley Cup that you can pose next to while a friend takes your picture. The original bowl—the one forged in Sheffield, England, more than 120 years ago and donated by Lord Stanley of Preston as a prize for the top amateur club in Canada—is stored in the old bank vault a few steps away.

Helpful Tips

Canadian winters can be harsh. If you decide to take a road trip to the Hockey Hall of Fame during hockey season but want to avoid getting stuck in a blizzard—as the authors did in late March—consider making your trip in early fall or mid-late spring.

If possible, book a hotel downtown near the Hall. The nightlife in this part of the city can be a bit, well, lifeless, but the further away you stay, the likelier it is that you'll take a wrong turn and end up in Mississauga.

Be sure to bring a functional GPS navigation system or, at the very least, someone good at reading maps. Canadians are, by and large, a gracious and friendly people but nothing disappears faster than a Torontonian who has been asked for directions.

You won't be prepared for the amount of hockey clothing, collectibles, trinkets, and *tchotchkes* available for purchase everywhere in Toronto, so budget accordingly. The retail store at the Hall, the Spirit of Hockey, is particularly dangerous.

The Hockey Hall of Fame is open 362 days a year, closing only for Induction Day (typically a Monday in November), Christmas Day, and New Year's Day. To plan your visit, go to www.hhof.com.

29 A Wicked Awesome Rivalry

Writing for the *New York Times* in 1928, the venerable John Kieran had this to say about the charged atmosphere of a typical Rangers-Bruins game:

"Listening to the booing the Boston players get at the Garden when they spill one of Lester Patrick's fast forwards, one might think they were a horde of criminal malefactors specializing in beating up honest citizens but, of course, that's a mere matter of uniform."

Kieran wrote those words more than 50 years before Bruins players famously climbed over the glass at the Garden to slug it out with some "honest citizens." Would that episode have escalated so quickly if the Rangers' opponents were the Hartford Whalers? Arguably not.

The Rangers-Bruins rivalry is one of the oldest in the National Hockey League. For many years, they were the only NHL teams in the Northeastern U.S., glaring at each other across a wasteland of cul-de-sacs that the locals call Connecticut.

"Harry Sinden said it himself, and he was probably one of the first—before the Montreal Canadiens, the Boston Bruins' number-one rival was the New York Rangers," said Mick Colageo, a sportswriter who covers the Bruins for the *New Bedford Standard-Times*. "There was nobody else. It was just them and us—two big, American cities. But they're bigger than us and in some ways better than us. Boston's the Prudential Building but New York is the Empire State Building. That said, I always felt the rivalry between the Rangers and Bruins was driven by the personalities, by the players involved. As a fan growing up, I respected Jean Ratelle but I hated Brad Park. I hated Walt Tkaczuk. I hated Rod Gilbert. It was and still is a great rivalry, and of course it's even better when both teams are good."

Battle for the Cup, Part I

When the defending champion Rangers met the Bruins in the 1929 Stanley Cup Finals, it marked the first time two American teams clashed head-on for the trophy. Typical of the time, it wasn't a given that the Blueshirts would even get a home game in this best-of-three series until team president John Hammond announced Game 2 would be played at Madison Square Garden.

The Bruins won the first game 2–0, then both teams hopped on a midnight train from Boston to New York to play Game 2 the next night.

Already facing elimination, the Rangers had to regroup quickly. They finally put one past Boston's fabulous rookie goalie, Cecil "Tiny" Thompson, at 6:48 of the third period, tying the game at 1–1. But with less than 2:00 to play, Bill Carson put the Bruins ahead 2–1, which turned out to be the game and Cup-clinching goal.

Two games, two losses, season over. What a crummy way to lose the Stanley Cup.

Rangers All-Time Record vs. Bruins (1926–2014)

GP	W	L	T	OL
634	249	286	97	2

Patrick vs. Shore

During the 1939 playoffs, the Rangers faced the Bruins in the semi-finals. Boston's Eddie Shore, the NHL's resident tough guy, was working over Phil Watson particularly hard one night at Madison Square Garden. Muzz Patrick came to Watson's rescue, pummeling Shore mercilessly and leaving him with a bloodied face and a busted nose. It was the worst beating Shore had ever endured, and his battered mug made the pages of *LIFE* magazine.

More importantly, Boston won the seven-game series.

Battle for the Cup, Part II

Despite Bobby Orr's ailing knee and Phil Esposito having Rangers defensemen draped all over him for much of the series, the two Bruins superstars led Boston to a six-game conquest over New York in the 1972 Stanley Cup Finals.

Many years later, former Boston goalie Gerry Cheevers was at a Connecticut bookstore to schmooze with fans and autograph copies of the Bruins' 75th anniversary book. A young Rangers fan approached him and asked him to share his recollections of the 1972 finals.

"They couldn't beat us in a year full of Sundays," Cheevers said, playfully tweaking the young fan. "Do you know what some of their players said? 'The only reason the Bruins beat us is because they had Bobby Orr.' Well, no shit!"

Park's Poison Pen

A franchise defenseman with world-class skills and toughness to spare, Brad Park had a transformative effect on the Rangers when he came up in the late 1960s. He was so good, in fact, that his play drew frequent comparisons to Orr, which, naturally, did nothing to boost his popularity in Boston.

"Brad was in a class above everybody as an offensive defenseman," said Ted Irvine, Park's teammate in New York for six seasons. "Superstar that he was, he took a lot of punishment in other teams' buildings. He had a bull's eye on his back if we went to Boston or Montreal. In both places, they wanted him badly. But Brad handled himself very well and didn't back down, didn't ask for anything. He just stood up and held his own and that's why he got so much respect."

The Bruins had no respect for Park after he ripped them in his 1972 book *Play the Man*. In it, he called the Bruins "a bunch of bloodthirsty animals" (only partly true) and accused them of taking cheap shots when the referees weren't looking (absolutely true).

But then, three years later, a funny thing happened: Park got traded to Boston, and almost overnight, their mutual animosity melted away.

"I was so hated in Boston before the trade, I got mail from someone threatening my wife and I," Park recalled for NHL.com. "For a year and a half, the FBI escorted us when we were in Boston. To this day, people tell me they hated me when I was with New York, but they loved me in Boston."

Bounty Hunters

Placing a bounty on the head of an opponent is serious business. The Rangers have been accused of doing it at least twice (that we know of), and in each instance, a Bruin was the alleged target of retribution.

On December 26, 1965, Phil Goyette suffered damage to his spleen when he was speared in the stomach by Boston defenseman Ted Green. A savvy playmaker who centered the "Old Smoothies" line with Donnie Marshall and Bob Nevin, Goyette missed about a month of the season but recovered.

Green, a hard-hitting, shot-blocking blueliner known around the league as "Terrible Ted," later offered what sounded like a sincere apology for injuring Goyette, claiming it had been an accident. But Rangers fans weren't buying it, and from that moment on, they chanted "Get Green! Get Green!" whenever the Bruins came to town. Bill Jennings, the Rangers team president, fanned the flames by telling a reporter that he "felt like putting a bounty on Green's head."

NHL president Clarence Campbell wasn't thrilled that Jennings' incendiary comments were made on the record, but the Garden exec escaped punishment by the league.

Five years later, in the third game of a bloody quarterfinal series Boston would win in six games, the Rangers came out determined to prove that they were just as tough as the "Big, Bad Bruins." Early in the first period, Rangers goalie Ed Giacomin left his net before a faceoff to tell Derek Sanderson, Boston's pugnacious provocateur, to keep his head up.

Sanderson remembered the exchange a little differently: "[Giacomin] told me, 'We're getting paid to get you and we're going to.'"

Fans too young to have seen Sanderson play should imagine Sean Avery, only better. Trash-talk spewed from his mouth like raw sewage gushing out of an open valve, but he was also a skilled and hard-working player who could be used in virtually any game situation: up a goal or down a goal, even-strength or shorthanded. He was, to use an old sports cliché, the S.O.B. you hated when he played against you but loved when he played for you.

Hand-painted banners hung from the balconies of Madison Square Garden instructed the Rangers to "KILL DEREK." Another said "SANDERSON IS A CHICKEN." "DEREK WANTED DEAD OR ALIVE" read another. No wonder he thought there was a bounty on his head.

Sanderson and New York's Dave Balon were ejected for their roles in a first period brawl. Derek figured it was all part of Emile Francis' master plan to get him off the ice. He seemed almost flattered.

"That's the greatest compliment anyone ever paid me," Sanderson cracked. "Using 15 guys to get one out. They never even did that to Rocket Richard."

Over the Glass We Go

The Rangers-Bruins rivalry began to decline in 1974 when realignment placed the teams into different divisions. Five years later, though, there was still plenty of bad blood between them. The darkest chapter of the rivalry involves an infamous athlete-spectator confrontation that took place on December 23, 1979, at Madison Square Garden.

It began with Phil Esposito of the Rangers smashing his stick on the ice in frustration and skating off to the locker room after failing to score on a breakaway in the waning seconds of a game the Bruins would win 4–3.

When the final buzzer sounded, Al Secord, Boston's rugged left wing, decked the Rangers' Ulf Nilsson. It was retaliation, Secord claimed, for a sucker punch Nilsson had given him earlier in the game.

As a scrum of players exchanged words, a Ranger fan named John Kaptain reached over the low glass panel and hit Stan Jonathan, a Bruins enforcer, with a rolled-up program, drawing blood beneath Jonathan's eyes. Then he grabbed Jonathan's stick and made off with it.

Seeing this, Boston winger Terry O'Reilly climbed over the glass to go after Kaptain.

"There was no way he was going to strike one of my teammates and steal his stick, wield it like a weapon, and then disappear into the crowd and go to a local bar with a souvenir and a great story,"

O'Reilly said. "As soon as I got him into a bear hug, I felt like I was being pummeled by multiple people."

Bruins Max McNab and Mike Milbury were the next ones over the glass, ostensibly to help out O'Reilly. More Bruins followed—18 in all—as the stunned Rangers watched the melee unfold from ice level.

When Kaptain broke free of O'Reilly, McNab and Milbury chased him a few rows up and pinned him across a seat. That's when Milbury pulled off Kaptain's shoe, smacked him across the leg with it, and threw it onto the ice.

Garden security guards eventually separated the combatants, none of whom were seriously injured. Kaptain, his brother, his father, and another man were all charged with disorderly conduct.

After the game, a crowd of about 300 Rangers fans rocked the Bruins' bus and had to be dispersed by eight mounted police officers.

In the decades since, the incident has come to be remembered fondly by Bruins fans, but the NHL did not look kindly upon it at the time. Milbury, McNab, and O'Reilly were fined and suspended by the league. The rest of the Bruins received fines as well, except for Gerry Cheevers, who was in the locker room having a beer when the brawl broke out.

The Kaptain family filed a lawsuit to clear its name, though nothing came of it. Charges against them were eventually dropped and authorities opted not to press charges against the players.

To prevent episodes like this from occurring again, the NHL mandated that higher glass be installed in all of its arenas to better separate the players from the fans.

A Rivalry Renewed

You are no doubt familiar with the classic paradox that occurs when an unstoppable force meets an immovable object. When that unstoppable force is Zdeno Chara and the immovable object is Henrik Lundqvist, you get a lot of one-goal games.

New York and Boston have found success playing a hard-nosed, blue-collar brand of hockey. It resulted in a Stanley Cup championship for the Bruins in 2011 and a Conference Finals appearance for the Rangers the following year.

As evenly matched as the clubs seemed to be, the Rangers had no answer for Chara, the hulking defenseman known for his thunderous hits and blistering shot, while the Bruins had no answer for Lundqvist—that is, until the 2013 playoffs.

In the first postseason meeting between the teams in 40 years, the Bruins exploited the Rangers' relative lack of depth, atrocious power play, and banged up blueline to win the second-round series in five games. Lundqvist played well, but not well enough to beat Boston by himself.

"For the longest time," Colageo said, "Henrik Lundqvist owned the Bruins, and it's only recently that Boston has started to gain an edge. You don't ever want to get on the wrong side of that rivalry again."

30 The Swedes

Anders Hedberg and Ulf Nilsson Bolt the WHA for the Bright Lights of Broadway

Every team in the National Hockey League lined up to lure Anders Hedberg and Ulf Nilsson away from the rival World Hockey Association when they exercised an escape clause in their contracts to become free agents in the summer of 1978. It was a courtship that would end with the Rangers making the two Swedish stars the highest-paid players in all of hockey.

"It came down to three teams I think: the Flyers, the Blackhawks, and the Rangers," Nilsson recalled. "It was a strange thing that happened. Because the Jets had the right to match any offer we received, they could have kept us in Winnipeg. The Flyers suggested we sign two contracts—one we'd show the Jets and one we'd actually play for. We didn't want to get involved in that sort of business, so now it was down to two teams."

In the end, there was no way the Rangers were going to be outbid by the Blackhawks—not with Chicago's purse strings held in a vice grip by owner "Dollar Bill" Wirtz, and certainly not with Sonny Werblin running Madison Square Garden. Werblin, the former owner of the New York Jets who made quarterback Joe Namath a household name, understood that sports was more than just sports. It was also entertainment, and to entertain, one needs star power. Sonny sensed that the Swedes had it.

"Can these guys play hockey?" Werblin asked Rangers GM John Ferguson. "No question," was the reply. And with that, Werblin authorized the Rangers to increase their offer from a combined $1.9 million over two years to $2.4 million to make sure Winnipeg didn't match.

What did the Rangers get for their investment? Two of the most intelligent and offensively creative players in North America and an immediate morale boost.

Hedberg, a right wing with wavy golden locks and the kind of Scandinavian good looks that would've earned him a fortune in endorsement deals had he played in a different era, first achieved fame as a member of the Swedish national team in 1970 when his inspired play earned him the nickname "the new Tumba" after 1950s Swedish hockey star Sven "Tumba" Johansson. Not an honor to be taken lightly; in Sweden it was roughly akin to dubbing someone "the new Gretzky."

Unlucky 11?

Ulf Nilsson spent so much of his time in New York on the IR that in 1982, frustrated and out of ideas about how to change his fortunes, he changed his uniform number from 11 to 19.

"I got a letter from a man who said he was a longtime Ranger fan," Ulfie explained, "and he remembered that a coach from years ago, Phil Watson, said no Ranger should wear No. 11 because on this team it was a bad luck number. The letter had a list of Rangers who had that number and got traded or injured. As the guy said in the letter, it doesn't make any logical sense, but what do I have to lose?"

Nilsson, a crafty playmaker who topped 100 points every year he played in the WHA, displayed a Gretzky-like sense of timing that resulted in pinpoint passes and an uncanny knack for knowing where the puck would go next.

Arriving with as much fanfare as they did could've bruised some egos in the Rangers dressing room, but Hedberg and Nilsson fit in because they were completely team-oriented and, as former captain Dave Maloney noted, "They weren't coming in here trying to get a candy bar named after them."

If they had, it might have been sold under the unpalatable label "True Grit." That was the term Ron Greschner used to describe the Swedes, who didn't let off-color remarks, cheap shots, and other intimidation tactics throw them off their game.

"Guys were going to run the Europeans right back over the Atlantic so they wouldn't take any more jobs," Hedberg said. "But we had already seen it all, done it all, and had experienced the most discrimination and prejudice playing in Winnipeg by the time we arrived in New York. It wasn't that bad there. And I felt that if you're going to survive, you can't play it by the rules of your opponent who wants you to fight, because you're going to lose. So I had to beat them in other ways."

Like on the scoreboard, where the Swedes' impact was felt immediately. Hedberg paced the Blueshirts with 78 points in 80 games in his first season. After the team suffered a pair of bitter overtime losses to the Islanders in the 1979 semifinals, he scored the game-winning goal in the closing minutes of Game 5 to shift momentum in the Rangers' favor and they went on to win the series.

Nilsson gave his all for the Rangers, too, averaging a point-per-game and winning the Player's Player award in 1978–79. Team president Bill Jennings thought Nilsson was one of the best centers the Rangers ever had, and he might have been…when he was healthy. His three-plus seasons with the club were marked by serious injuries, the worst being a shattered right ankle resulting from a clean check by the Islanders' Denis Potvin. A major knee injury suffered during the 1981 Canada Cup kept Nilsson out of NHL action completely in 1981–82, and he managed to play only 10 more games before retiring in 1983.

Even without Nilsson as his set-up man, Anders continued to rank among New York's top scorers. And with the influx of younger European players, he emerged as a leader who could be the bridge between different groups on the team. The Swedes and the Finns stuck so close to Hedberg that on one Father's Day, they actually sent him flowers.

The 1984–85 season was Hedberg's last as a player. Although he declined a hero's sendoff that would have included a ceremony on Garden ice, preferring to go out with less fanfare than what accompanied his headline-grabbing debut, he did accept the 1985 Masterton Trophy for perseverance, sportsmanship, and dedication to ice hockey.

Hedberg and Nilsson's success in New York proved a great many things, not the least of which was that Europeans had what it took to be stars in the NHL. They were the forerunners of an international explosion that forever changed the face of the league.

31 The Patricks

It is the most influential hockey family of all-time, predating the Howes, the Sutters, the Staals, and all the rest. Although the Patrick family tree has many, many branches, these are the ones that yielded fruit for the Rangers:

Lester Patrick

The son of a lumber tycoon, Lester Patrick grew up in Quebec but as a young man moved with the family to British Columbia. By then, he was already an accomplished hockey player, having first starred on defense at McGill University before dropping out to pursue a pro career that would land him in the Hockey Hall of Fame.

Backed by father Joe Patrick's lumber fortune, Lester and brother, Frank, started the Pacific Coast Hockey Association, which was intended to be an alternative to the biggest pro league operating at the time, the National Hockey Association. Frank and Lester have been credited for introducing many innovations to the game that are still in use today, including numbered jerseys, penalty shots, allowing goalies to leave their feet to make a save, rewarding assists on goals, and on-the-fly line changes.

The PCHA eventually folded, with the Patricks selling the league and all of its players' rights to the NHL in 1926. This is how Lester came to the attention of Madison Square Garden management. After Garden executive John Hammond had a falling out with the Rangers' original manager, Conn Smythe, Hammond sent Lester a telegram offering him a job to run the team.

A short time later, Lester was in New York addressing his players, and he didn't mince words. "Gentlemen," he said, "when we start playing in the National Hockey League, you're going to win some games and you're going to lose some. I just want to stress this: if you lose more than you win, you won't be around."

Frank Boucher, who played for Lester for a decade before being tabbed to succeed him as coach, regarded Patrick as the most knowledgeable hockey man he had ever met—a great intellect with an extensive vocabulary.

Lester Patrick (center), the old "Silver Fox," enjoys a laugh as sons Murray (left) and Lynn, general managers respectively of the New York Rangers and Boston Bruins, playfully challenge each other with sticks after a November 23, 1955, game in New York. (AP Photo/Matt Zimmerman)

"Lester definitely had a way with words," Murray Murdoch commented. "What he said was nice, but he wasn't nearly as generous when it came time to talk contract."

Indeed, the way Lester handled negotiations with his players, you'd think he was paying them out of his own pocket.

"I wouldn't say that Lester was cheap," Babe Pratt said, "but he certainly was adjacent to cheap."

After the Rangers won the Stanley Cup in 1928, a party was thrown in the team's honor. John Hammond took it upon himself to introduce Lester to one of the high society debutantes in attendance.

Hammond proudly recalled for the woman how the Rangers' goaltender had been injured during the finals, and how Lester had courageously slipped into a uniform, strapped on some pads, and saved the game.

"How marvelous!" the woman exclaimed. And then, in all earnestness, she asked, "And had you ever played hockey before, Mr. Patrick?" The handful of Rangers standing close enough to hear the exchange just about died laughing.

Lester coached the Rangers to a second Stanley Cup in 1933. Six years later, he passed the coaching reins to Boucher but continued in the role of general manager as the team won its third title in 1940. Patrick retired as GM in 1946 but stayed on as vice president of Madison Square Garden until 1950.

Lynn Patrick

At 6' and 200 lbs., Lynn had a bigger-than-average hockey frame, plus a sterling athletic reputation tracing to his roots in British Columbia. It was his style that brought him criticism. He was a finesse player, preferring to dazzle on his skates and with his stick instead of playing the body like his rollicking, hard-checking younger brother, Muzz.

Did You Know?

Lester Patrick had his own board game. Released in 1939 by Toy Creations, *Lester Patrick's Official Hockey Game* came with a board representing a rink, special dice (or a spinner), two metal nets, and a little wooden puck. Players took turns rolling the dice to see where on the board the puck would go, all the while praying that someone would hurry up and invent the video game.

Hecklers at Madison Square Garden called Lynn "Twinkletoes" or "Sonja," the latter a reference to the world-famous figure skater Sonja Henie. Lynn did his best to shrug it off, much as he had the criticism and doubt that came from his own father.

As great as Lynn's athleticism was, Lester simply didn't think Lynn could make it in the NHL. A few of the Ranger veterans who'd seen Lynn play convinced Lester otherwise, and he finally signed his eldest son to a contract in 1934.

Lynn was a key contributor to the Rangers' Stanley Cup championship in 1940, scored a career-high 32 goals in 1942, and earned First Team All-Star honors that year. In all, he'd play ten seasons for the Blueshirts, scoring 145 goals and 190 assists for 335 points.

In retrospect, Lester had to admit that signing Lynn "was one of the best things I ever did. Nothing has given me the flush of satisfaction that came with the realization that my bumbling but persistent redheaded son had made the grade to hockey stardom."

Lynn followed his dad into coaching, first running the minor league New Haven Ramblers before being called up to coach the Rangers in 1948. The following season, he led the team to a surprising fourth-place finish and all the way to the seventh game of the Stanley Cup Finals.

"The coach who got the most out of me," Edgar Laprade recalled, "was Lynn Patrick. When we went out to Detroit, he got six or seven of us—key players—into a room before each game and gave us a strategy on how he wanted to play that game. He was the only coach I ever had who did that."

But even if the Rangers had won the Cup, Lynn wanted out of the Rangers organization. In fact, he wanted out of New York City, period. He hoped to move his growing family some place with more open space and fresh air…some place like Boston. So when the Bruins telephoned him that off-season with a lucrative offer to be their next head coach, Lynn bid *adieu* to Broadway.

Muzz Patrick

Like his brother Lynn, Frederick Murray "Muzz" Patrick was a fantastic all-around athlete, excelling at boxing, basketball, football, and track in addition to hockey.

But Muzz's playing style couldn't have been more different than Lynn's. With his 6'2", 205-lb. frame, Muzz struck an imposing figure on the Ranger blueline and he had no qualms about throwing his weight around. He loved to hit.

Patrick's career was interrupted in midstream in 1941 when he joined the U.S. Army. His military service wiped out what would have been prime years of his hockey career. After the war, he returned to the Rangers for one more season before retiring as a player in 1946. But his life was committed to hockey, and he pursued it as a coach and manager in minor league outposts before returning to Madison Square Garden in 1954, first as coach of the Rangers and then as the team's general manager—jobs his brother and father had held before him.

Craig Patrick

Frustrated by the Rangers' disappointing 1979–80 season, in which the club lost in the quarterfinals a year after reaching the Stanley Cup Finals, Garden president Sonny Werblin overhauled team management by hiring Craig Patrick as director of

Lester Patrick Trophy Winners

The Lester Patrick Trophy was presented by the Rangers in 1966. Players, coaches, referees, and executives are eligible to receive the award, which recognizes outstanding service to hockey in the United States. Winners are chosen by a committee of officials from throughout the sport, including representatives from the NHL, the Rangers, the Hockey Hall of Fame, the U.S. Hockey Hall of Fame, the NHL Broadcasters' Association, and the Professional Hockey Writers Association.

Many recipients of the Lester Patrick Trophy have had some connection to the Rangers, either as a player, coach, general manager, front office executive, or broadcaster.

Recipient	Year	Role with Rangers
Mike Richter	2009	Player
Mark Messier	2009	Player
John Halligan	2007	Executive
Brian Leetch	2007	Player
Glen Sonmor	2006	Player
Marcel Dionne	2006	Player
Red Berenson	2006	Player
John Davidson	2004	Player and broadcaster
Larry Pleau	2002	Executive
Herb Brooks	2002	Coach
Craig Patrick	2000	Executive, GM, and coach
Pat LaFontaine	1997	Player
Brian Mullen	1995	Player
Wayne Gretzky	1994	Player
Frank Boucher	1993	Player, coach, and GM
Rod Gilbert	1991	Player
Lynn Patrick	1989	Player and coach
Emile Francis	1982	GM and coach
Fred Shero	1980	Player and coach
Phil Esposito	1978	Player, broadcaster, GM, and coach
Bill Chadwick	1975	Broadcaster
Murray Murdoch	1974	Player
Terry Sawchuk	1971	Player
William M. Jennings	1971	Executive

operations (in effect, the general manager) and telling Fred Shero to forget the "general manager" in his dual title and concentrate on coaching.

Lynn Patrick's oldest son had extensive international experience as a player with the U.S. National Team (1969–71) and at numerous other tournaments before becoming assistant general manager and assistant coach under Herb Brooks for the 1980 U.S. Olympic team. Craig was front and center when a band of collegians defeated the heavily favored Soviet Union squad en route to winning the gold medal in what became known as the "Miracle on Ice."

In 1980, at age 34, he officially became the youngest general manager in club history and held the post until 1986. Craig led the Rangers to playoff berths in each of his five seasons and served as head coach for parts of two (1980–81 and 1984–85).

And boy, did he have an eye for young talent. James Patrick (no relation), Jan Erixon, John Vanbiesbrouck, Tony Granato, Tomas Sandstrom, Ulf Dahlen, Darren Turcotte, Brian Leetch, and Mike Richter were all Patrick draft picks.

It's true that Craig was long gone by the time Neil Smith was accepting congratulations for assembling the first Stanley Cup winner in New York since 1940, but where would the Rangers have been without Leetch and Richter?

In 2001, Craig was inducted into the Hockey Hall of Fame, becoming the fourth member and third generation of his family to enter the Hall, joining grandfather Lester, father Lynn, and great-uncle Frank.

32 Test Your Rangers IQ

1. In 1970, this Hall of Famer married his first cousin.
    A. Jean Ratelle
    B. Brad Park
    C. Ed Giacomin
    D. Rod Gilbert

2. Who surrendered J.T. Miller's first and second career NHL goals?
    A. Ilya Bryzgalov
    B. Martin Brodeur
    C. Tuukka Rask
    D. Evgeni Nabokov

3. All of these players scored at least 100 points in a single season as a Ranger *except*:
    A. Rod Gilbert
    B. Mark Messier
    C. Mike Rogers
    D. Vic Hadfield

4. This goaltender suffered nerve damage in his left hand when he fell through a glass coffee table.
    A. Henrik Lundqvist
    B. John Vanbiesbrouck
    C. John Davidson
    D. Ed Giacomin

5. During the 2012 playoffs, he was suspended three games for elbowing Ottawa's Daniel Alfredsson in the head.
   A. Artem Anisimov
   B. Carl Hagelin
   C. Stu Bickel
   D. Anton Stralman

6. All of these Rangers scored their first NHL goal during the playoffs *except*:
   A. Tony Amonte
   B. George McPhee
   C. Chris Kreider
   D. Lauri Korpikoski

7. All of these Ranger coaches also played for the Rangers *except*:
   A. Fred Shero
   B. Emile Francis
   C. Phil Watson
   D. Mike Keenan

8. He is the only Ranger to win the club's Most Valuable Player award for seven consecutive seasons.
   A. Mark Messier
   B. Rod Gilbert
   C. Henrik Lundqvist
   D. Andy Bathgate

9. This Ranger defenseman led the NHL in plus-minus (not turn-overs!) for the 2005–06 season:
   A. Fedor Tyutin
   B. Tom Poti
   C. Michal Rozsival
   D. Marek Malek

10. He is the only player to have won a Stanley Cup with the Islanders *and* Rangers.
    A. Phil Bourque
    B. Greg Gilbert
    C. Mike Hudson
    D. Glenn Healy

11. They were the first Rangers to appear on the cover of an EA Sports video game.
    A. Mark Messier and Alexei Kovalev
    B. Mike Richter and Randy Moller
    C. Brian Leetch and Paul Broten
    D. Adam Graves and Jeff Bloemberg

12. When he was only 12 years old, this future Ranger was aboard a steamship in the Irish Sea that was sunk by a German torpedo.
    A. Bill Gadsby
    B. Harry Howell
    C. Jack Evans
    D. Dean Prentice

13. This player joined Walt Tkaczuk and Bill Fairbairn on the original Bulldog Line, a checking unit assembled in 1968 by Emile Francis.
    A. Dave Balon
    B. Orland Kurtenbach
    C. Don Marshall
    D. Bob Nevin

14. All of these brother combinations have played for the Rangers *except*:
    A. James and Steve Patrick
    B. Henrik and Joel Lundqvist
    C. Chris and Peter Ferraro
    D. Andy and Frank Bathgate

15. After retiring from hockey, this former Rangers goalie became a pastor.
    A. Bob Froese
    B. Glen Hanlon
    C. Ed Mio
    D. Doug Soetaert

16. Citing his poor record in the tie-breaker, this Rangers star once asked not to be used in a shootout.
    A. Marcus Naslund
    B. Brendan Shanahan
    C. Scott Gomez
    D. Jaromir Jagr

17. After their Stanley Cup victory in 1994, the Rangers lobbied the NHL to have these two additional names engraved onto the trophy.
    A. Greg Gilbert and Alexander Karpovtsev
    B. Nick Kypreos and Peter Andersson
    C. Mike Folga and Bruce Lifrieri
    D. Mike Hartman and Ed Olczyk

18. This player had three tours of duty with the Rangers.
    A. Lucien DeBlois
    B. Esa Tikkanen
    C. Ron Duguay
    D. Petr Nedved

19. Each of these Rangers was voted the team's most valuable player *except*:
    A. Eric Lindros
    B. Bobby Holik
    C. John Ogrodnick
    D. Walt Poddubny

20. During the team's trip to Europe to open the 2011–12 season, he purchased the Broadway Hat, the black fedora handed out to the Rangers' player of the game after each Broadway Blueshirt victory.
    A. Sean Avery
    B. Brandon Prust
    C. Brad Richards
    D. Henrik Lundqvist

21. This Ranger had an odd pregame ritual of watching Three Stooges videos.
    A. Tomas Sandstrom
    B. Don Maloney
    C. Walt Poddubny
    D. Jan Erixon

22. Who played on the Rangers' FLY Line?
    A. Theo Fleury, Eric Lindros, and Mike York
    B. Robbie Ftorek, Pierre Larouche, and Tom Younghans
    C. Scott Fraser, Eric Lacroix, and Harry York
    D. None of the above

23. Who holds the Rangers' single-season plus-minus record?
    A. Jaromir Jagr
    B. Brian Leetch
    C. Phil Esposito
    D. Brad Park

24. Who was the first active Ranger to appear on the cover of *TIME* magazine?
    A. Frank Boucher
    B. Camille Henry
    C. Gump Worsley
    D. Davey Kerr

25. He was named Most Valuable Player of the 1993 NHL All-Star Game.
    A. Tony Amonte
    B. Mike Gartner
    C. Mark Messier
    D. Mike Richter

Answers:

1. B, Brad Park. It's true—Park married Gerry George, a cousin from his mother's side of the family. Although he and Gerry rarely saw each other growing up, they became reacquainted while he was playing for the Rangers and she was a stewardess working New York–Toronto flights for Air Canada. "My mother called me and asked if I would be willing to show Gerry around New York and give her a place to stay," Park recalled in *Straight Shooter: The Brad Park Story*. "So, we spent time together, got along well, and I showed her the bright lights of New York. Well, one thing lead to another. Shortly after we got engaged, I went back to Toronto and my mother picked me up from the airport. We were driving back to my parents' home when she mentioned that she hoped Gerry might find a nice guy to date. I told my mother that she already had, and my mother asked, 'Really? Who?' I told her, 'Me.' In a state of shock, she almost drove off the highway. That surprise lasted for quite a while in our family."

2. D, Evgeni Nabokov. Playing in his second NHL game, J.T. Miller scored twice in a 4–1 win over the Islanders on February 7, 2013.

3. A, Rod Gilbert. The team's all-time scoring leader had a career-high 97 points in 1971–72 and then matched his output in 1974–75.

4. B, John Vanbiesbrouck. On June 13, 1988, Vanbiesbrouck suffered nerve damage to his left wrist after a glass coffee table he was sitting on collapsed and broken glass lacerated his ulnar nerve and three tendons. He underwent five hours of microsurgery to remove glass from his wrist and repair the nerve and tendon damage. Initially expected to miss four to six months, Beezer recovered in time to attend training camp just three months later.

5. B, Carl Hagelin. At least the Ranger rookie sent Alfredsson, a hockey legend back in their native Sweden, a text message apologizing for the hit.

6. A, Tony Amonte. He played his first pro game during the 1991 playoffs but scored his first NHL goal in his first regular season game on October 3, 1991. His 35-goal debut season earned him a spot on the NHL All-Rookie Team, and he was a finalist for the Calder Trophy as top rookie.

7. D, Mike Keenan. "Iron Mike" never played in the NHL.

8. C, Henrik Lundqvist. Andy Bathgate (1956–59) is the only other Ranger to win it at least three years in a row.

9. C, Michal Rozsival. He also led all Rangers defensemen in scoring his first four years with the club.

10. B, Greg Gilbert. A junior member of the Islanders' Stanley Cup championship teams in 1982 and 1983, Gilbert added a third championship to his resume at age 32 with the 1993–94 Rangers.

11. B, Mike Richter and Randy Moller. The photo used on the cover required some alteration. Because the game was licensed only by the NHLPA, the word "RANGERS" had to be airbrushed off Richter's uniform.

12. A, Bill Gadsby. While en route from Southampton, England, to New York in the early days of World War II, Gadsby was one of about 50 survivors who escaped the U-Boat attack aboard a cramped lifeboat.

13. A, Dave Balon. It's not often that a checking line winger leads a team in goals but Balon did it twice, in 1969–70 and 1970–71. That season, he was also named the Rangers' most popular player and appeared in his fourth All-Star Game. Later in his career, Balon began to feel the effects of multiple sclerosis, a degenerative disease that attacks the central nervous system. The diagnosis wasn't made until 1980, nearly seven years after he quit hockey. MS forced Balon into early retirement, then it robbed him of his ability to walk and care for himself. He battled the disease bravely for nearly 30 years until finally succumbing on May 29, 2007. He was 68.

14. B, Henrik and Joel Lundqvist. Joel, Henrik's twin brother, spent three years with the Dallas Stars organization but never played for the Rangers.

15. A, Bob Froese. In 1998, Froese became senior pastor at Faith Fellowship Church in Clarence, New York, a small town northeast of Buffalo.

16. D, Jaromir Jagr. In February 2007, Jagr was roundly criticized after opting out of the tiebreaker during a home loss to the Devils. He participated in future shootouts, but he didn't like it.

17. D, Mike Hartman and Ed Olczyk. The NHL originally left the pair off the Stanley Cup because Olczyk played 37 regular season games and only one game in the Conference Finals while Hartman played 35 regular season games and not at all during the playoffs.

18. B, Esa Tikkanen (1993–94, 1997, 1998–99)

19. A, Eric Lindros.

20. C, Brad Richards. The story goes that Richards purchased the hat straight off the head of a stranger.

21. C, Walt Poddubny. Only two of Poddubny's 11 NHL seasons were spent wearing a Rangers uniform, but they were the two most productive seasons of his career. A skilled center/right winger, Poddubny led the Blueshirts in scoring in 1986–87 and 1987–88. Of his fondness for the Three Stooges, his mother, Nadia, told *Sports Illustrated*: "Walt watches them over and over and never gets tired of them. They calm him down. They lift him up. They're like medicine."

22. A, Theo Fleury, Eric Lindros, and Mike York.

23. D, Brad Park. Park holds the club record with a plus-62 rating, set during the 1971–72 season.

24. D, Dave Kerr. Kerr appeared on the cover of the March 14, 1938, issue of *TIME*.

25. B, Mike Gartner. Appearing in his sixth All-Star Game, and only one as a Ranger, Gartner took home MVP honors by scoring four goals. He also won the Fastest Skater competition for the second time.

33 Big Deal Neil

The architect of the 1993–94 Rangers began his hockey career as a tall, skinny defenseman with decent skills and not much upper body strength. The Islanders drafted Neil Smith out of Western Michigan University in 1974, then tucked him away in the minor leagues for seasoning.

"He was awful," recalled Jacques "Jocko" Cayer, the Rangers' former equipment manager who was working in the IHL while Smith was bouncing around the league on teams like the Kalamazoo Wings and the Muskegon Mohawks. "Just an awful hockey player."

Neil eventually figured that out on his own and after two seasons playing in the Isles' minor league system, he retired in 1980 to become a scout and learn the ropes of hockey management. He studied under one of the best in former Islander head scout Jimmy Devellano, then followed his mentor to the Red Wings in 1982 when Devellano became that club's general manager. Neil oversaw Detroit's scouting and player development and served as general manager of their farm team, the Adirondack Red Wings, which won a pair of Calder Cup titles in 1986 and 1989. At 35, Smith was a rapidly rising star in the management ranks. The Rangers took notice.

On July 17, 1989, the Rangers hired Smith to be their ninth GM in 63 years but their fifth in just the previous 13. Within a month after coming to New York, he revamped the Rangers'

Sabotaged!

Early in the 1999–2000 season, the Rangers brought veteran winger Joe Murphy, an unsigned free agent and career headcase, to New York for a tryout.

The expectation was that Murphy, a fast skater with a good shot, would make the squad. All that needed to happen first was for the Rangers to make room on their roster and for both sides to agree on a contract.

That's where the tale takes a strange turn.

Murphy, it seems, was very eager to sign with the Rangers—so eager that he began to get anxious when the team did not immediately offer him a contract. Neil Smith, who drafted Murphy first overall in 1986 when he worked for the Red Wings, was poised to offer Murphy a deal in the $500,000 range but never got the chance.

Murphy abruptly left the Rangers' practice facility in Rye, arguing with members of the front office and coaching staff on his way out, and accusing Smith of throwing one of his skates into Long Island Sound. His sticks had also been sawed halfway through, probably by Rangers players who weren't thrilled about Murphy joining the team in the first place.

Trouble seemed to follow Murphy, who was eventually suspended and then cut by the Bruins for mouthing off to Coach Pat Burns. And later, while playing for the Capitals, he was smashed in the face with a glass during a bar fight at a lower East Side club.

hockey department and hired Roger Neilson, the veteran coach known as "Captain Video" for his heavy use of videotape to scout and teach.

The first indication that Smith wasn't afraid to make bold moves came in January 1990 when he sent two popular forwards, Tony Granato and Tomas Sandstrom, to Los Angeles for veteran center Bernie Nicholls. A few months later, Smith acquired one of the game's most consistently prolific all-time leading goal scorers— veteran right wing Mike Gartner—from the Minnesota North Stars for Ulf Dahlen.

Nicholls would be traded to Edmonton less than two years later in another blockbuster deal for Mark Messier, the proven winner that so many of Smith's predecessors had searched for in vain. In relatively short order, Smith transformed the Rangers from, as he put it, "a joke, a Broadway show," into a Stanley Cup contender. In 1992, he was named Executive of the Year by *The Hockey News*.

Even as Smith roamed the Garden corridors still wearing the Stanley Cup ring he earned with the Islanders in 1982, he had completely embraced the Rangers and their history. Ending the chants of "1940!" became his obsession, so much so that he was willing to fire Roger Neilson, a coach with whom he'd formed a special bond but who had lost the confidence of team captain Messier, and hire Mike Keenan.

"I've spent every minute of my life the last five years trying to make the Rangers into the old Islanders, the Oilers, the Canadiens," Smith said in 1994. "I wanted the city to kick this '1940' thing. I told all the people I hired, 'Don't do it for me, do it for the logo.'"

And they did. They did it despite a disruptive power struggle between Smith and Keenan that threatened to derail the season before reaching its rapturous conclusion.

Smith's fatal error—and one in which many others share some culpability—was in not blowing up the Ranger roster and starting from scratch when he had the chance. A scout at heart, he'd come to New York with an inclination to build through the draft but in the years after 1994, he continued to chase veterans via trade and free agency: Theo Fleury, Valeri Kamensky, Jari Kurri, Sylvain Lefebvre, Mike Keane, and Brian Skrudland, to name a few. Age was no concern, money no object.

The go-for-broke, win-now strategy that had been so successful in 1994 failed to get the Rangers back to the finals in subsequent years. Just as Smith was coming to terms with the need to make the Rangers younger, new ownership came in and pushed him to trade for Vancouver's Pavel Bure. Smith has always believed that his refusal to make that deal, which would have bankrupted the club of its remaining young players, is what led to his firing on March 28, 2000.

34 "Shoot the Puck, Barry!"

It was with tremendous fanfare that Barry "Bubba" Beck became a New York Ranger, coming over from the Colorado Rockies in exchange for a gaggle of players on November 2, 1979.

"I was shocked when I heard the news," Beck recalled, "since Colorado management had told me that wouldn't happen. There had been rumors that the team was moving to New Jersey. I was renegotiating my contract at the same time that the trade occurred. The Rangers were in town to play us so when the trade came down, I just moved from one dressing room to another."

Six months earlier, the Rangers had unexpectedly crashed the Stanley Cup Finals before losing to the Montreal Canadiens.

"It was sort of common knowledge that Larry Robinson beat us the year before in the finals," said Pat Hickey, one of five players sent to Colorado in the big trade. "We didn't have that one extra element. Barry Beck was the guy that was out there that was like Larry Robinson."

So big things were expected from the big defenseman, and they were expected quickly. He was, perhaps unfairly, cast in the role of a Messiah—the savior that would put the Rangers over the top.

New York City agreed with Beck as he scored 59 points in 61 games, but the club was eliminated in the second round of the 1980 playoffs. The next year he was a key factor in the Blueshirts' march to the semifinals. Beck also served as captain for parts of his seven seasons with the club.

When healthy, Beck was often a dominant presence on the Ranger defense, and his versatility enabled coaches to pair him with a variety of players. If partnered with Reijo Ruotsalainen or Ron Greschner, he could play a simple, stay-at-home style that maximized his strength and toughness. But his willingness to join the rush allowed him to show off his offensive skills. He seemed comfortable in either role.

Rangers broadcaster Bill Chadwick thought that Beck had a tendency to hold onto the puck too long. "Shoot the puck, Barry, shoot the puck!" Bill would shout. Fans picked up on it and "Shoot the puck, Barry!" became a regular refrain at the Garden.

"I took no offence to it," Beck said. "It actually helped me. I had a heavy shot and needed to use it more. I remember one night in Quebec, I had scored a goal and after the game when Bill and I saw each other outside the dressing room, we were both already laughing. He said, 'I told you so!'"

Although Beck believed he played better when he was a little sore, his performance was often hindered by a host of injuries, most notably a left shoulder that never seemed to stay in place. That can be traced to Game 4 of the 1984 quarterfinals when Islanders rookie Pat Flatley hammered Beck into the boards halfway through the third period. Seconds after the hit, with the Ranger captain crumpled in the slot, the Isles took a 2–1 lead and eventually forced a fifth and deciding game. The injury that ended Beck's season doomed the Rangers as well, and they lost the series.

"I was a power player," Beck said. "I loved playing defense. I wanted players and teams I played against to know they couldn't beat me. Once you can establish that, then you can take control of the game. A power player thrives on contact, especially initiating it. You gotta hit to hurt. Unfortunately, that means you're going to get banged up yourself. It comes with the territory, but it's a small

The L.A. Riot

The Rangers and Kings were involved in a notorious bench-clearing brawl in the first round of the 1981 playoffs.

At the end of a fight-filled first period in Game 2, players from both teams squared off as they were leaving the ice. The melee lasted nearly eight minutes and set postseason records for most penalties by one team in a single period (24) and most penalties by two teams in a single period (43). It could have been much worse since Rangers tough guy Nick Fotiu, who wasn't even dressed for the game, got into a fight with a Kings fan near the visitors' bench.

Three players from each team were ejected: Jerry Korab, Jay Wells, and J.P. Kelly of the Kings, and Barry Beck, Ed Hospodar, and Chris Kotsopoulos of the Rangers. That, plus a knee injury to Dave Maloney, forced the Rangers to play the rest of the game with only three defensemen.

The Kings won 5–4 on a late third-period goal by Dean Hopkins. The Rangers eventually won the series 3–1.

price to pay for something you love. Going through those shoulder injuries with the Rangers was devastating. I wanted nothing more than to win the Cup with the Rangers at Madison Square Garden. I got very depressed. For a power player, it is the worst thing that can happen. It was a tough time for me. When I retired, I alienated myself from the game. I felt I had let a lot of people down. I went from captain of the Rangers to a lost soul."

In 1986, dissatisfaction with Coach Ted Sator prompted Beck to announce his retirement at age 29. In the process, he walked away from a $385,000 contract—a lot of money at the time—but decided to come back the following season after Sator was replaced with Michel Bergeron.

During a preseason game in September 1987, Beck re-injured his shoulder and called it quits again. Two years later, he mounted a brief comeback with the Los Angeles Kings but retired for good in March 1990 after deciding he was too slow for the NHL game.

After a long absence from the game, Barry discovered a new career teaching youth hockey—the perfect role for someone who had been so active in children's charities during his playing days.

"I stopped feeling sorry for myself and started living life again," he said. "Then I said to myself, 'I made it to the NHL and was captain of the New York Rangers.' Not too many players can say that. You have to play the hand you're dealt and make the best of it."

35 Flower Power

1988: Hall of Famer Guy Lafleur Makes His Comeback as a New York Ranger

One of the most popular figures in the storied history of the Montreal Canadiens, Guy Lafleur was the first player to score 50 goals with regularity and a member of five Stanley Cup winners in 14 seasons.

But the elegant right winger's final years in Montreal were filled with frustration. When Guy's old linemate, Jacques Lemaire, became coach, he instituted a defense-first system that stifled Lafleur's creativity. Just 19 games into the 1984–85 season, Lafleur retired at age 33 and moved into a rather unfulfilling front office job with the club.

Years passed, and even though Guy had since been elected to the Hockey Hall of Fame, he began to think seriously about making a comeback. Then in 1988, about a week after the Los Angeles Kings acquired Wayne Gretzky, Lafleur asked for an invitation to attend L.A.'s first training camp with No. 99. When the Kings politely declined, Guy reached out to the Rangers.

Rangers tough guy Chris Nilan was a former teammate of Lafleur and offered an enthusiastic endorsement of his friend when GM Phil Esposito came seeking his counsel.

"Espo came to me and asked, 'Listen, do you think Lafleur can still play?' I said, 'Without a doubt.' Guy ran into a lot of nonsense in Montreal. They thought he was near the end. But he just wasn't going to be a player who could fit into Jacques Lemaire's system, and it was sad to see because they had once been linemates. But Jacques had to do what was best for the team at the time. It's hard for superstars in that system. They want to go, they want their cookies. They want their goals. Then Espo asked me if I thought Guy could score 20 goals, and I said of course he could."

Nilan's estimate wasn't far off. Lafleur went on to score 18 goals in 67 games as a Ranger, including two in his memorable return to the Montreal Forum on February 4, 1989. That night, ticket scalpers were asking $400 for a pair of prime seats to witness the homecoming of the man they called The Flower. Before the game, he received a two-minute standing ovation. Chants of "Guy! Guy! Guy!" drowned out the national anthems.

Every time Lafleur's skates touched the ice, the chants would begin anew. The fans went wild in the second period when he picked up a rebound in front of the Montreal net and ripped a shot past Patrick Roy. About six minutes later, they roared with approval again when Lafleur took a pass at center ice, sailed around a defenseman, then rifled a shot between Roy's legs.

Guy was named second star of the game, a 7–5 Canadiens victory.

As much as he appreciated the very warm reception he'd received at the Forum, Lafleur clearly enjoyed being out of the Montreal fishbowl. In New York, he could be just be another face in the crowd.

"It was fun for me to be back with The Flower and to see him outside of Montreal," Nilan said. "To see him *not* get noticed.

He couldn't believe it. To be able to go to a corner store and grab something without everybody being all over him, and then go home and most of his neighbors didn't know him. He had fun with it. Or when he got his first paycheck. He couldn't believe the difference compared to Quebec, where the taxes might've been as high as 50 percent. And all the young players looked up to him."

Lafleur's stint with the Rangers was moderately successful as he helped the team to first place in the Patrick Division before being sidelined with a knee injury. He left New York at the end of the season to follow dismissed Rangers head coach and close friend Michel Bergeron to the Quebec Nordiques for his final seasons.

36 Iron Mike

He coached the Rangers for only one year, but what a year it was.

The team that Mike Keenan inherited when he was hired as coach of the Rangers in April 1993 was largely the same crew that won the Patrick Division in 1991–92 then stumbled to a last-place finish in a season sullied by Mark Messier's revolt to oust Coach Roger Neilson and get him replaced by interim coach Ron Smith. It was a disaster.

Neil Smith figured that what a team this close to winning the Cup needed most of all was a coach who would come in and give it a good, swift kick in the ass. Kicking ass was Iron Mike's forte.

A St. Lawrence University grad who earned his master's degree in education from the University of Toronto, Keenan was an intellectual in a drill sergeant's clothing—at once bright, articulate, thoughtful, and reflective but also not above screaming personal insults at a player he felt wasn't carrying his weight or smashing a stick over a crossbar and banishing the entire team from the ice to conclude a lousy practice.

For those players who responded better to the carrot than the stick, he instituted a financial incentive system to reward players for their performance in five-game segments. There were even motivational quotes posted over the urinals in the practice rink.

Keenan's methods got results, but they also had a way of burning out teams.

After coaching the Flyers to the Stanley Cup Finals twice in four years (1985 and 1987), he was fired in 1988 because players were simply fed up with his tyrannical ways and in near-mutiny. Jeremy Roenick, who was on the Keenan-coached Blackhawks team that made it to the finals in 1992, once said that playing for Keenan "was like camping on the side of an active volcano."

"One of the great things about Mike Keenan, but also what was hard about him, was you worked *every* shift," Mike Richter said. "He didn't want your effort level to ever wane. He would do everything he could do to upset you. Pull a nose hair, get your adrenaline going. He wanted you to bring energy to every shift, and we learned that through the year. We learned that our practices were hard and the expectations were very, very high in that locker room and throughout the organization."

"It was a daily mental challenge with Keenan," Mike Gartner said. "Over the course of the season it created stress, anxiety, and questioning."

For Gartner, some of that stress was alleviated when he was dealt to Toronto at the trade deadline after four-plus exemplary Ranger seasons because he wasn't a "Keenan-type." James Patrick and Darren Turcotte weren't either, and they were shipped off to the Hartford Whalers.

New York City welcomed the spring thaw, but the relationship between Keenan and Smith was getting frostier by the minute. Mike had GM powers when he coached the Blackhawks and wanted more say over personnel decisions with the Rangers. No matter how many trades Smith made to make the Rangers bigger, tougher, and more experienced, Keenan never seemed to be satisfied.

Keenan and Messier, on the other hand, turned out to be an effective team. They both wanted desperately to win, and each man paid the other the respect he craved. And on those occasions when Keenan was in Captain Bligh mode and being irrational, Messier would step in and put the ship back on course.

"Mike would come in and do more damage than he thought he was doing," Craig MacTavish recounted for Rick Carpiniello in *Messier: Hockey's Dragon Slayer.* "He'd be a little more vindictive or berate the team a little more than he himself would have thought. But Mark would quickly put those things in perspective, and if there was any damage control that needed to be done, he did it very quickly. They worked very well together in that respect."

When rumors surfaced that Keenan had held secret discussions with the Detroit Red Wings—during the Stanley Cup

Denis Potvin: New York Ranger?

Yes, Mike Keenan really did ask ex-Islander Denis Potvin, Public Enemy No. 1, to consider coming out of retirement to play for the Rangers. Whether Keenan really believed that Potvin, out of the game for six years and working as a Panthers broadcaster, would take him up on the offer is another story.

The Rangers were in Florida late in the 1993–94 season when Keenan, overstepping his bounds as coach (and the bounds of good taste), mentioned that he thought Denis could help the Rangers' power play.

Potvin was both flattered and shocked by the invitation and did give it serious consideration. But the 40-year-old Hall of Fame defenseman took a quick skate and concluded his body wasn't up for it.

Keenan had to know that word of this would get back to his team. Even if Potvin said no, it would send a message that the coach still wasn't satisfied with the players in the Rangers dressing room and was willing to look outside the organization for help.

Finals!—about becoming their coach and/or general manager the following season, Messier reminded his teammates that they needed to be focused on the next period or the next game, not next year. In so doing, he neutralized a potentially damaging distraction.

The Rangers won the Stanley Cup, and at the post-parade ceremony at City Hall, Keenan and Smith sat side-by-side—the warring couple putting on a brave face for the kids. Fans knew something was up. They'd read the papers. They chanted "Four more years!" to Keenan, letting him know they wanted him to stay and honor his contract.

A month later, Keenan essentially declared himself a free agent on the grounds that the Rangers had breached his contract by being a day late in paying him a $620,000 bonus for winning the Cup. Smith wanted Keenan gone as much as Keenan wanted to be gone—but he wasn't going to just let him pick up and leave. There were lawsuits and countersuits. What should have been a summer of celebration became a summer of strife.

Things really got ugly when Keenan was hired to be the next coach and general manager of the St. Louis Blues.

NHL commissioner Gary Bettman finally stepped in to settle the dispute, allowing Keenan to go to the Blues but suspending him for 60 days and fining him $100,000 for "conduct detrimental to the league." Keenan also had to pay back $400,000 of his bonus to the Rangers. In compensation for Keenan leaving with four years left on his contract, Bettman also approved the Blues' trade of Petr Nedved to New York for Esa Tikkanen and Doug Lidster. In addition, the Blues and Red Wings were both fined for tampering.

Keenan eventually wore out his welcome in St. Louis. And then Vancouver. And Boston. And Florida. And Calgary. In 2013, having seemingly exhausted all of his second chances in the NHL, he went to Russia to coach Metallurg Magnitogorsk of the KHL.

37 Unbreakable Rangers Records

There's an inherent danger in calling any record "unbreakable" because, as the old cliché goes, records are meant to be broken. It was a lesson learned the hard way by one of the authors (we'll identify him only as "A.R.") who once assured the readers of *Hockey Digest* that Terry Sawchuk's record for most career shutouts was "safer than the remote control in your dad's hand on Super Bowl Sunday."

Seven years later, Martin Brodeur held an opposing team scoreless for the 104th time, breaking Sawchuk's mark and making A.R. look a bit foolish.

Here are a few Rangers club records that the authors suspect—but won't promise—will stand the test of time:

Most Career Penalty Minutes: 1,226 (Ron Greschner)
He was, first and foremost, a point-producer. But Gresch was also a big hitter and a willing fighter who spent his entire 16-year career in New York. The closest anyone has gotten to challenging Greschner's career penalty minute total was Jeff Beukeboom, who racked up 1,157 PIMs in 520 games—462 fewer than Greschner.

Most Points in a Season, Defenseman: 102 (Brian Leetch, 1991–92)
Brian Leetch's 23 goals (an NHL record for rookie defensemen) and 71 points earned him the 1989 Calder Trophy as Rookie of the Year. But that was just a warm-up for his next trick—becoming just the fifth defenseman ever to crack the 100-point mark in a single season, recording 22 goals and 80 assists.

More than two decades have passed since Leetch scored in the triple digits, and although there are still plenty of puck-moving blueliners in the game—Mike Green, Kris Letang, Shea Weber, and Keith Yandle, to name just a few—none of them have come close to breaking 100.

Most Career Points: 1,021 (Rod Gilbert)

To score 1,000 points in the NHL requires a rare mix of skill, longevity, and luck. Rarer still is the player who can do it with one team. Rod Gilbert holds many of the Rangers' offensive records but this mark, compiled during 18 seasons and 1,065 games from 1960 to 1978, is the one least likely to be eclipsed.

As the right wing on the Rangers' high-scoring G-A-G Line, Gilbert benefitted from playing with the most skilled players at even strength and on the power play.

Another reason Gilbert broke the 1,000-point mark was that he continued to be a valuable performer well into his mid-thirties, and in fact played some of his best hockey during that time. From 1973–74 to 1975–76, he had three consecutive 36-goal seasons, including a career-high 97 points in 1974–75.

Most Career Hat Tricks: 11 (Bill Cook)

What gives this record an air of unbreakability is the length of time it's stood. Cook played his last game in 1936. If the Rangers haven't found someone with the skills and the staying power to eclipse this mark by now, it's possible they never will.

Most Games: 1,160 (Harry Howell)

This is a record that owed as much to durability—Howell missed only 17 games in his first 16 seasons as a Ranger—as it did to an archaic system that saw players locked in with the same organization for most of their careers.

Frank Boucher's Seven Lady Byng Trophies

Combining gentlemanly play with a high level of skill earned Boucher the Lady Byng Trophy in 1927. He won it again the following year. And the year after that. After winning his seventh Lady Byng in eight seasons, the league gave Boucher the trophy permanently and commissioned a new one. That was quite a gesture since Bobby Orr won the Norris Trophy eight times and not even he got to keep it!

 **1979**

Prior to 2013, when the Boston Bruins faced the Chicago Blackhawks, the last Stanley Cup Final between two Original Six teams was all the way back in 1979, when the Rangers met the Montreal Canadiens.

Coached by Fred Shero, the 1978–79 Rangers won 40 games—ten more than the previous year—and finished third in the Patrick Division with 91 points.

They seemed to have a little bit of everything, this hodgepodge of cagey veterans and wide-eyed youngsters. Phil Esposito, Anders Hedberg, Ulf Nilsson, Ron Duguay, Don Maloney, Don Murdoch, and Pat Hickey led the attack. Walt Tkaczuk and Steve Vickers didn't just kill penalties, they murdered them. And anyone who tried to intimidate the Rangers' skill players would incur the wrath of Nick Fotiu.

Ron Greschner anchored the defense. A punishing hitter, Gresch was also a strong skater who excelled on the power play and handled the puck with ease—so easily that it earned him an occasional shift at center or left wing. Mike McEwen scored a career-high 20 goals and led all Rangers defensemen with 58 points. Carol Vadnais was a stabilizing influence on the ice and in the dressing room. Dave Maloney, recently installed as captain, was at his scrappy best.

The glue that held it all together was goalie John Davidson. J.D. inherited the starter's job four years earlier when the enormously popular Ed Giacomin was placed on waivers. As much as they missed "Fast Eddie," it didn't take long for fans to warm to the new guy. At 6'3" and 200 lbs., Davidson filled a lot of net but he also had great agility. His unorthodox style was not unlike that of six-time Vezina-winner Dominik Hasek.

"When it came to skills," Dave Maloney said, "John was that type of player—he was chaotic. In John you got a big guy in goal who was very, very acrobatic. He was a tremendous athlete."

Cheered on by chants of "JAY-DEE! JAY-DEE!" the tall, mustached goalie looked downright impenetrable as the New Yorkers made quick work of Los Angeles in a best-of-three preliminary round, took four straight from Philadelphia in the quarterfinals after dropping the first game in overtime, and knocking off the Islanders—heavy favorites to win the Stanley Cup—in a six-game semifinal series noteworthy for the stifling defense the Rangers' checkers employed against the Isles' top line of Bryan Trottier, Mike Bossy, and Clark Gillies.

"I won in a few other places," McEwen recalled, "but it was nothing like New York. When we beat the Islanders at the Garden, I guess there were 10,000 people outside and they shut off Eighth Avenue to Seventh Avenue. On 32nd Street or 33rd Street, we had to be escorted out by the cops for about a block because the fans were crazy and everybody was celebrating. I had my family with me from Toronto, and they had four mounted police officers on each side of us. There we were, walking between these four horses through this crowd of crazies who were all happy, yelling and screaming."

The Mafia Line

Phil Esposito had a tough transition period after being traded by Boston to New York, but by 1979 he was living on Manhattan's East Side and finally comfortable in his Ranger silks. Though not as sparkling an offensive force as in his glory days, he looked rejuvenated skating between young guns Don Murdoch and Don Maloney, scoring 42 goals at age 36. That trio, dubbed the Mafia Line because it featured a Godfather and two "Dons," helped power the Rangers to the Stanley Cup Finals.

For the second time in seven years, the Rangers were headed to the finals, a development that nobody on the club could have predicted when the season began. They had accomplished "the impossible" by getting past their rivals from Uniondale. Now all they had to was beat one of the most dominant teams in history.

The Canadiens' roster was loaded with future Hall of Famers: Guy Lafleur, Ken Dryden, Bob Gainey, and Larry Robinson, among others. But the general consensus among many Canadiens fans and critics was that the three-time defending champs weren't as strong as they used to be, and Game 1 seemed to prove the naysayers right. Riding a wave of confidence that seemed to swell with each successive round, the Rangers stunned the Canadiens and the Forum crowd with a 4–1 victory. Vickers, Greschner, Esposito, and Dave Maloney tallied for New York. Afterward, a reporter asked Fred Shero if he was shocked to see Michel "Bunny" Larocque replace Dryden in goal to open the third period.

"I'm not worried about the Canadiens," Shero cracked. "I only watch my team. I haven't worried about the Canadiens since 1957 when they last paid me."

Esposito *was* worried, and not just about the Canadiens. He already owned two Stanley Cup rings but didn't want anyone to jeopardize what was very likely his last shot at a third. Concerned that the Rangers' younger players would want to party after their big win, he urged Shero to get the team out of Montreal before Game 2. But Freddie didn't think it was necessary, so they stayed put.

As the senior-most Ranger, Phil got to room alone at the team's hotel. Around 5:00 the next morning, he was awoken by a ruckus. He went out into the hallway to see some of his teammates wrestling—naked, of course—with a group of lovely locals. Whether that factored in the Rangers blowing a 2–0 lead in the next game and losing 6–2, well, who can say?

"Wait 'til the Canadiens get on our rotten ice at the Garden," Greschner promised. "That'll slow 'em down."

But MSG offered no safe haven for the Rangers—not even with Billy Joel singing the National Anthem—as they lost Game 3 4–1. Serge Savard's overtime goal in Game 4 gave Montreal a 4–3 win and put the Rangers on the brink of elimination.

Davidson, so sharp through the first three rounds, was breaking down. Unbeknownst to anyone outside the club, he'd suffered a knee injury during the semifinals that was becoming more and more painful with every game. Without J.D. at his best, the Rangers stood virtually no chance of getting back into the series.

The finals moved back to Montreal, and Canadiens coach Scotty Bowman was squarely focused on making sure the Rangers never got another home game. Rick Chartraw opened the scoring at 10:36 of the first period and Vadnais tied it 6:00 later. But that was the last puck Ken Dryden would let past him. Jacques Lemaire scored twice in the second period and Bob Gainey would add one more to put Montreal up 4–1. That ended up being the final score of the game and the series as the Canadiens clinched their fourth consecutive Stanley Cup.

And so another Ranger season ended in disappointment. But those six weeks in the spring of 1979, when all of New York City got swept up in the Rangers' cause and it seemed like everyone was a hockey fan, were some of the most exciting and memorable in the team's history. It was a fun ride while it lasted.

39 The Redemption of Jaromir Jagr

Prior to the 2005–06 season, *Sports Illustrated's* resident hockey authority, Kostya Kennedy, predicted that the Rangers would not only finish dead-last in the 30-team league, but that the Blueshirts would likely be dragged into the abyss by their mercurial star, Jaromir Jagr.

"Just as Jagr can take a team to unforeseen heights," Kennedy opined, "no star is better at making a bad situation worse."

Ouch.

Certainly, the perception of Jagr as a moody, coach-killing brat was not unique to the *SI* scribe, who had simply assessed the perpetually dysfunctional state of the Rangers, recalled Jagr's drama-filled final seasons in Pittsburgh, watched his production wane in Washington, and concluded that Jagr and New York would be a match made in Hockey Hell.

The Rangers had pursued Jagr unsuccessfully for years, but it wasn't until January 23, 2004, that they finally got their man. The trade—a future Hall of Famer straight up for Anson Carter—was almost laughably lopsided. To rid themselves of Jagr, the Capitals were even willing to pick up a hefty chunk of his salary.

The Rangers were getting a proven franchise player but, along with him, some uncertainties. Would he be happy in New York? And if not, would he make everyone else miserable?

The Rangers' worst fears never materialized. In fact, as the team returned from another long summer to open training camp in

Jaromir Jagr (right) skates around the right side of the net to shoot against the Pittsburgh Penguins' Marc-Andre Fleury in the second period during Game 3 of an NHL Eastern Conference semifinal playoff game on Tuesday, April 29, 2008, at Madison Square Garden in New York. Jagr scored on the play to tie the score at 3–3. (AP Photo/Julie Jacobson)

September 2005, No. 68 seemed doubly motivated to prove he was still one of the best players in the world. Maybe scathing analyses like the one in *Sports Illustrated* inspired a proud athlete to deliver a prediction of his own—that the bumbling Blueshirts, who had not participated in a postseason contest in seven long years, would finally break that streak.

Czech It Out!

The 2005–06 Rangers had a sizable Czech contingent—part of GM Glen Sather's tacit strategy of surrounding his best player with familiar faces:

Player	Position	Place of Birth
Jaromir Jagr	RW	Kladno, Czech
Marek Malik	D	Ostrava, Czech
Petr Prucha	LW	Chrudim, Czech
Michal Rozsival	D	Vlasim, Czech
Martin Rucinsky	LW	Most, Czech
Martin Straka	C	Plzen, Czech
Petr Sykora	C	Plzen, Czech

Coach Tom Renney called Jagr's declaration "a bold statement by a bold man who can back it up."

He backed it up alright, going on an offensive rampage that saw him pass Jari Kurri as the highest-scoring European in NHL history, set franchise marks for most goals (54) and points (123) in a season, and win his third Lester B. Pearson Award (now the Ted Lindsay Award), a trophy given annually to the league's best player as judged by members of the NHL Players' Association.

With Jagr as a linemate, veteran center Michal Nylander and rookie winger Petr Prucha both enjoyed the most productive season of their careers. But then, that's what superstars do—they make players around them better.

A freak shoulder injury in the first game of the 2006 quarterfinals derailed Jagr's record-breaking season, and without their biggest weapon, the Rangers went on to lose four straight to the Devils. It was a bizarre, abrupt ending to a year that began with so much promise, but the bar had clearly been raised. Thanks in large measure to Jagr, the Rangers were back on the map.

40 The Broadcasters

Some are living, and some are not. They come from eras past and present and have different styles, but they all have one thing in common: they are as much a part of the way fans experience New York Rangers hockey as the games themselves. They are the broadcasters, and they are among the best at what they do.

Here are a dozen play-by-play announcers and color analysts who witnessed the most memorable events in Rangers history and helped shape our memories of those moments with their magic behind the microphone.

Kenny Albert

As a kid, Kenny would tag along to Madison Square Garden as his dad, Marv Albert, prepared to call a Rangers or Knicks game. Once he realized he wanted to follow in his famous father's footsteps, he was determined to do it on his own. And he did. The New York University (NYU) grad worked his way up from a gig calling games for the AHL's Baltimore Skipjacks to succeed Marv as the radio play-by-play voice of the Rangers in 1995 and has held the post ever since.

Marv Albert

A broadcasting legend best known as the TV voice of the NBA—he's actually a member of the Basketball Hall of Fame—Albert also spent three decades calling Rangers games on radio.

Born Marvin Philip Aufrichtig in Brooklyn, Albert was a one-time ball boy for the Knicks. He was still enrolled at NYU when he worked his first radio broadcast for the team as an emergency fill-in for Marty Glickman. His popularity prompted Garden execs to hire him for Rangers games, and he served double duty during the winter, announcing basketball and hockey on radio and TV.

Marv narrated *Rise of the Rangers*, an audio recap of the 1969–70 season produced by Fleetwood Records.

Despite an ever-increasing workload of non-hockey assignments, including football, baseball, boxing and college basketball, Albert continued to lend his distinct voice and style to Rangers broadcasts until 1995.

Bill Chadwick

Chadwick was the first American-born referee in the NHL. He was eventually inducted into the Hockey Hall of Fame and the U.S. Hockey Hall of Fame…an incredible achievement, since he officiated more than 1,000 major league games (a record at the time) with only one good eye.

Nicknamed "The Big Whistle" by team statistician Art Friedman, Chadwick had a passion for hockey—and a soft spot for the Rangers—that was unmistakable. He delighted fans with his trademark calls and phrases (delivered in a thick New York accent), both on radio and television, for 14 seasons from 1967 to 1981. He and partner Jim Gordon became two of the most beloved broadcasters in Rangers history, their popularity only matched in later years by that of Sam Rosen and John Davidson. Like Davidson, Chadwick enjoyed being an ambassador for the club. Unlike J.D., Bill had no filter for his emotions. Whatever he felt, he said.

"Shoot the puck, Barry, shoot the puck!" Chadwick would often exhort Barry Beck. To his credit, Beck took the critique in the spirit in which it was intended.

"Like every other player, I loved Bill Chadwick," Beck said shortly after Chadwick's passing in 2013 at age 94. "He was always willing to give advice to players, good or bad. He cared about the team, as did Jim Gordon. They were both honest, loyal guys who you weren't afraid to have a beer with."

Remembering The Big Whistle

Bill Chadwick was not only the first American referee in the NHL, he was also the first to use hand signals when calling a penalty. The innovation was born of necessity—sometime during the early 1940s, Chadwick was working a Stanley Cup Finals game and it was so loud that he had trouble communicating with the penalty timekeeper.

When he was in his twenties, Chadwick played hockey in the old Metropolitan League. He lost the sight in his right eye in 1935 when he was hit with a puck during a Met League All-Star Game at Madison Square Garden. He continued to play hockey, appearing with the New York Rovers of the Eastern Amateur Hockey League, but two seasons later, he was hit in the left eye by an opponent's stick. That injury was minor, but it persuaded Chadwick to give up competitive hockey.

When Bill decided to pursue a career in officiating, he received a huge boost from none other than Lester Patrick.

"There were some hang-ups about Americans in the NHL in those days," Chadwick told Eric Whitehead in *The Patricks: Hockey's Royal Family*. "But not with Lester. He seemed to have a special appreciation for an American in a Canadian game and always went out of his way to help him. He got me my first officiating job as a linesman for the New York Americans. Whenever he could, he'd watch me and then call me into his office to talk about things I was doing wrong. It was his constructive criticism that got me on my way as an NHL referee."

John Davidson

A fixture on MSG Network telecasts for two decades before he left in 2006 to join the front office ranks, "J.D." was widely recognized as the best color analyst in the business. He was articulate, had an engaging personality, and as a former player had a strong grasp of the inner workings of the game. He and partner Sam Rosen developed an on-air chemistry (and off-air friendship) that is seldom seen in the industry.

"I was lucky enough to work with the best that there ever was in the hockey television business," Rosen said. "So many people stopped me to say, 'You helped teach me the game,' and that was because of John. He had the ability to talk to people on the airwaves without talking down to them and without making the experts feel like he was speaking beneath them. He could relate to all people at all levels. Nobody was like him and that's why when any network did hockey, they hired John Davidson."

Davidson's signature phrase, "Oh baby!" was the title of a video chronicling the 1993–94 season.

Win Elliot

Born Irwin Elliot Shalek, Win worked some of the earliest hockey telecasts in the late 1940s and continued to do play-by-play for the Rangers on TV and radio throughout the 1950s and '60s.

A former goaltender and zoology major at his alma mater, the University of Michigan, Elliot took a communications class in his senior year just to have enough credits to graduate. He did so well that an impressed professor urged Win to consider a career in sportscasting.

Although Elliot took on-air work where he could find it, reporting on boxing and horse racing and even hosting game shows like *Tic-Tac-Dough*, he really made a name for himself announcing for the Rangers. His trademark was a folksy, almost conversational style that conveyed the excitement of hockey without veering into outrageousness.

Jim Gordon

Respected as much for his professionalism as for his ability to capture the drama and excitement of whatever event he happened to be covering, Gordon was hired by Madison Square Garden in 1955 to call Rangers and Knicks games on the radio. For a time, the Queens native was partnered with Monty Hall, the game show host best known for *Let's Make a Deal*.

From 1973 to 1981, Jim worked Rangers telecasts on WOR-TV with Bill Chadwick. The duo complemented each other perfectly—Chadwick the exuberant, sometimes outrageous color man and Gordon the polished pro who knew how to keep the telecast somewhat grounded in reality.

Before he became the voice of the Rangers, Gordon was an accomplished newsman. He reported from the streets during the 1964 Harlem riots and from the subways during the Northeast blackout the following year.

Bert Lee

Bertram Lebhar Jr. was a Cornell grad who attended NYU Law School but gave up a career in law to get into radio advertising sales. He moved up the ranks in New York radio as an executive, eventually becoming vice president of WMCA. Supposedly, he got his first taste of sportscasting filling in for an announcer who was sick. Adopting the on-air name Bert Lee, he went on to work some of the earliest Rangers broadcasts. From 1939 to 1954, Lee was the voice of Rangers hockey on the radio. His partner for much of that time was Ward Wilson.

Dave Maloney

Maloney joined the Rangers' radio broadcast team in 2005. The former Rangers captain has steadily become the most outspoken color commentator associated with the team since the late Bill Chadwick. He's not afraid to be critical of a Rangers player or coach, though his most pointed barbs are usually reserved for the officials. ("Uh oh, here comes the Fun Police.") When he's not playing the yin to Kenny Albert's yang, Maloney can also be seen between periods and during postgame as an analyst on MSG Network.

Sal Messina

He isn't listed as an active player on the Rangers' all-time roster, but Queens native Sal Messina was a veteran amateur goaltender who played for the Long Island Ducks and New York Rovers before becoming the "house goalie" for NHL games at Madison Square Garden in the days when teams carried only one goalie.

Messina was the Rangers' radio analyst from 1973 to 2003, partnered first with Marv Albert (who playfully saddled Sal with the nickname "Red Light") and then Kenny Albert. With his low-key style and personable demeanor, Messina was a natural at the between-periods interview, often chatting with players, executives, and beat writers. In 2005, the Hockey Hall of Fame presented Messina with the Foster Hewitt Award for his outstanding work as an NHL broadcaster.

Howie Rose

Joining MSG Networks in 1985 as a substitute announcer for Rangers radio broadcasts, Rose went full-time in 1989. It was a dream job for the Queens College grad who grew up in Bayside living and dying with the Rangers.

In 1970, at age 16, he bought his first season tickets: Section 429, Row G—the last row of the Garden. It was there that he began his broadcasting career...sort of. Rose would bring a tape recorder to games and do his own play-by-play. And since his seats were right near the Garden's actual broadcast booth, he'd often run into Marv Albert, who would give the kid a copy of that night's press notes to make his "broadcasts" sound more authentic.

Although Rose worked hundreds of Rangers games during his 10 years as a play-by-play announcer on WFAN, he will forever be remembered for his call of Stephane Matteau's double-overtime, series-clinching goal in Game 7 of the 1994 Eastern Conference Finals.

Sam Rosen

The play-by-play voice of the Rangers on MSG Network was honored in 2014 for 30 years on the job.

Rosen's purely platonic love affair with the Rangers began sometime in the late 1950s when he started going to games on Sunday nights at the old Madison Square Garden, located between 49th and 50th Streets. There he finally got to see all the Ranger heroes he'd read about in the newspapers—players like Andy Bathgate, Lou Fontinato, Harry Howell, and Gump Worsley.

In 1973, Rosen went to work for United Press International's Audio Network, and he was assigned to cover hockey at the Garden reporting on not only the Rangers but also all the teams they played against. Five years later, he was asked to fill in for Marv Albert on a Rangers radio broadcast. A major career dream had come true—he was finally calling games for the team he grew up cheering for.

In 1984, Rosen moved from radio to TV, succeeding Jim Gordon. He shared the booth with Phil Esposito for two seasons until Espo moved up to the front office to become general manager. John Davidson stepped in, beginning one of the longest team-specific partnerships in New York sports history.

When the final horn sounded to end Game 7 of the 1994 Stanley Cup Finals, Sam and J.D. were as thrilled as anyone in attendance.

"The waiting is over!" Rosen screamed as fireworks burst in the air overhead. "The New York Rangers are Stanley Cup champions! And this one will last a lifetime!"

Bob Wolff

It's not uncommon these days for the busiest play-by-play announcers to work all four major North American team sports, but Bob Wolff was among the first.

At one point, this native New Yorker was the voice of *eight* teams in *five* different sports: the Rangers; the Knicks and Pistons of the NBA; baseball's Washington Senators/Minnesota Twins; the NFL's Baltimore Colts, Washington Redskins, and Cleveland

Browns; and the Tampa Bay Rowdies of the original North American Soccer League. For many years, Wolff was the play-by-play telecaster for all events originating from Madison Square Garden.

Wolff was a backup play-by-play announcer on the radio from 1970 to 1980 and a color commentator on TV from 1962 until 1974.

41 Practical Jokers

Boys will be boys, as the saying goes, and athletes have been pulling pranks on each other since the first young Athenian chariot racer put shaving cream in his buddy's sandals. And yes, the Greeks had shaving cream.

Hockey players have a long tradition of inflicting petty tortures on one another to lighten the mood of a tense dressing room, kill some time away from the rink, or initiate a naïve rookie.

Depression Era star Ivan "Ching" Johnson was a punishing hitter with a mischievous streak. One of his favorite tricks was to hide a puck in his gloves. Then, during a multi-player scrum along the boards, Ching would drop the concealed puck, causing an immediate whistle and more than a little confusion, not to mention a breather for the smirking defenseman. "I only did it four, maybe five times," Johnson said. "But it was great fun. I even used to do it in practice, but that was tough because Lester [Patrick] used to count the pucks."

Hard-hitting Bill Juzda patrolled the Ranger blueline for five seasons in the 1940s. The target of his mischief was often the senior Bryan Hextall, New York's sharpshooting right winger. If Juzda

170

knew that Hextall's wife, Gert, wanted to hand off parental duties and go shopping when her husband got home from practice, he would say, "Let's stop for a beer—oh, I forgot, Hex, you have to babysit." Hextall would join his mate for a round or two anyway, but Juzda would slip out of the pub first, go to Hextall's house and ask Gert, "Isn't Hex home yet?"

A member of the 1949–50 squad that went to the Stanley Cup Finals, tough defenseman Pat Egan used to wear a bathing cap in the shower because he thought it would prevent him from going bald. His frequent foil, fellow blueliner Wally Stanowksi, would poke holes in the cap.

Former team captain Vic Hadfield was fond of sending teammates off on wild goose chases, but his repertoire also included switching teammates' neckties, fake phone messages (usually from girls), and smearing the inside of shoes with Vaseline or just nailing them to the floor. On the road, he might march up to the hotel's unsuspecting front desk clerk and announce, "I'm Vic Hadfield, captain of the Rangers, and I need a suite for an important team meeting. While you're at it, send up 20 beers." Of course, these "team meetings" rarely had anything to do with business. Or he would lie and tell the clerk that all the players' room assignments had changed, so an incoming phone call for Walt Tkaczuk might be routed to Bill Fairbairn's room.

But the Rangers' undisputed Grand Poobah of Pranks was Nick Fotiu, pride of Staten Island and a Blueshirt for eight seasons. One night in 1976 (possibly '77), Fotiu targeted veteran Bill Goldsworthy. The scene: Toronto's Harbour Castle hotel.

"Me and Ron Greschner were out having a few drinks, feeling good," Fotiu recalled. "The hotel restaurant had a big tank with a lobster in it. Gresch was the lookout while I took the lobster out of the tank. I knew Bill Goldsworthy had had a couple of drinks and he would be in his room, passed out. I let some of the other guys know what was going on. I snuck into Goldy's room and put a quilt over him. Then I put the lobster on the quilt. Meanwhile, all of the guys were watching from the doorway, one standing over the other, like a pyramid. Goldy had the light on, and you could actually see the lobster climbing up his chest. It got near his throat, and all of a sudden, he woke up. You could hear this big scream. So he yells, 'Nicky, you crazy son of a bitch!' That was kind of funny."

Fotiu was also behind a mysterious power outage that only seemed to affect goalies John Davidson and Wayne Thomas.

"We were on the team bus, heading to a hotel in the Boston area," Fotiu said. "I asked J.D. and Wayne Thomas if they wanted to watch a concert on television when we got to the hotel. Thomas says, 'That would be great, we'll get a bottle of wine.' So we're in their room, but I left to go find the hotel's circuit breaker. I turned off the power to their room, and then turned it back on. Then I ran back to the room and watched them call the front desk to complain that the lights were turning off and on. I did that for about half an hour—on and off, on and off. I drove them crazy."

One of Fotiu's favorite gags was putting baby powder in the hairdryers. Another was the booby-trapped donut.

"I used to buy a whole bunch of donuts," he said, "and some were Bavarian cream. The guys would stop by the box of donuts and eat them up like candy. They would go right for it. So what I'd do was stick the nozzle of a shaving cream can in the hole on the side of the donut and fill it until it would puff up, then I'd cover it up with the Bavarian cream. I got lots of guys with that one, but the best was Pierre Larouche when we were playing the Islanders in the playoffs. Larouche had a big mouth—he would never shut up. You could hear him coming down the hall because his mouth was so big. There were like four donuts left, all Bavarian cream. He said 'Oh, Bavarian cream donuts, my favorite.' All of the guys knew these donuts were loaded up with shaving cream. So Larouche takes a bite out of a donut and he's still yapping and yapping. He takes another bite. Then he starts looking around and sees that everybody is laughing. Once he realized what was happening, he ran into the bathroom to spit it out."

42 Wear the Colors

The centerpiece of any hockey uniform is the jersey, or sweater, as it was originally known. That's because the earliest hockey sweaters really were sweaters, crafted from wool. However, since wool is just about the worst material since chainmail to use in an athletic garment, manufacturers eventually turned to lighter, synthetic fabrics like nylon and polyester.

When it comes to hockey apparel, the jersey really is the ultimate expression of fan loyalty. But, as any jersey collector knows, that loyalty comes at a price: an authentic, customized Rangers jersey can run upwards of $350, while replicas—vastly superior in quality to the ones produced 20 years ago—cost about half that much. It pays to be patient and do a little online research before investing in a jersey. The cost-conscious consumer can always find a good deal from a reputable vendor.

Beware Chinese knock-offs found on the internet. Confucius say, "Counterfeit jerseys look good from afar, but are far from good."

Although it's undergone some changes over the years, the jersey of the Rangers is immediately identifiable. Don't agree? Wear one on the streets of Philadelphia and see how long it takes for you to receive some brotherly love.

Here's a brief history of the uniform that inspired the nickname "Broadway Blueshirts":

1926–27: The inaugural Rangers sport a body-hugging light blue sweater with red and white striping on the arms and bottom hem. There are no hockey-stick-wielding cowboys on horseback—the team's original, unofficial crest—just the word "RANGERS" spelled out diagonally across the chest, with the player number on the back. Timeless. Classic. Iconic.

1929–30: Navy blue replaces light blue as the primary jersey color.

1946–47: For one season only, the Ranger jersey features the uniform number on the front with "RANGERS" arched across the upper chest.

1951–52: The Rangers become the last of the Original Six to introduce a road white jersey. All other teams had been wearing

Retired Numbers of the Rangers

One of the very special events a Rangers fan can witness is when the team retires the number of a popular player. It's an occasion to reflect on and celebrate a memorable career. The guest of honor is often joined at center ice by family members and former teammates, showered with gifts, and given an opportunity to address the Garden crowd. The ceremony culminates with the raising of a banner to the rafters.

Here are the eight men who have received the highest honor the club can bestow:

Player	Number	Date Retired
Rod Gilbert	No. 7	October 14, 1979
Ed Giacomin	No. 1	March 15, 1989
Mike Richter	No. 35	February 4, 2004
Mark Messier	No. 11	January 12, 2006
Brian Leetch	No. 2	January 24, 2008
Adam Graves	No. 9	February 3, 2009
Andy Bathgate	No. 9	February 22, 2009
Harry Howell	No. 3	February 22, 2009

white jerseys on the road and dark jerseys at home for years. This season also sees the arrival of the lace-up collar.

1976–77: Blasphemy! GM John Ferguson scraps the classic uniform in favor of a completely new design featuring the Rangers shield on the chest, new name/number font, and new striping. These uniforms are worn for just two seasons, but Fergy takes the basic design with him when he leaves to run the WHA's Winnipeg Jets.

1978–79: The Rangers return to their original uniform design with a few notable differences: player names now appear on home *and* road jerseys, the road blues say "NEW YORK" diagonally across the chest, and the lace-up collar is replaced by a more modern-looking red and white striped collar.

1987–88: "NEW YORK" comes off the road blues and is replaced with "RANGERS."

1996–97: The third jersey craze begins and the Rangers' dark blue "Liberty jersey," with its crest inspired by Mike Richter's mask, is a smash hit. It will remain part of the team's wardrobe until 2007.

1998–99: For one season, the Rangers substitute their dark blue Liberty jersey with a white version. The white Liberty jerseys prove to be much less popular but are far more rare (and valuable) among collectors.

2007–08: The Reebok Edge "uniform system" is introduced for all teams. A radical departure from the standard loose-fitting hockey jerseys that players had been wearing for decades, the new uniforms are more form-fitting but designed with more flexible material. Although some teams use this as an opportunity to roll out completely new uniform designs, the Rangers retain the standard design of their home and road jerseys.

2010–11: In honor of their 85th anniversary, the Rangers introduce a dark blue, retro-style Heritage third jersey. In a nod to some of the great Rangers players of the past, all of the team's retired sweater numbers are stitched onto the inside hem in the back.

2011–12: The Rangers participate in their first Winter Classic outdoor game. To mark the occasion, the team unveils an off-white throwback jersey featuring a large felt crest on the chest, a Winter Classic patch on the right shoulder, and the date of the game—January 2, 2012—printed on the inside collar. The jersey, which draws rave reviews for its simplicity of design, is worn on other select dates throughout the season.

2013–14: The Rangers go with a contemporary design for their Stadium Series jersey. It is white with accents of red, blue, and silver—and it bears more than a passing resemblance to the uniform of their farm team, the Hartford Wolf Pack.

1950

Detroit Red Wings Defeat New York Rangers in Stanley Cup Finals

The Rangers were so bad in the years following World War II that no one gave them a chance to do much of anything when the 1949–50 season began.

Still, their general manager, Frank Boucher, saw some potential that others did not. For starters, he liked their toughness, particularly on defense. He'd brought in Gus Kyle, a hard-hitting ex-Mountie, and the brash veteran Pat Egan, once a rookie star with the rival Americans, to complement regulars Frank Eddolls and Allan Stanley. Up front, Tony Leswick was his usual abrasive self, tying the slick playmaker Edgar Laprade for the team scoring lead with 44 points.

But the biggest reason the Rangers finished fourth in the league and qualified for the last playoff spot was the goaltending of Charlie

Rayner. His worth to the Rangers was confirmed when he was given the 1950 Hart Trophy as league MVP, the first time in more than 20 years a goalie had won the award.

The Rangers needed only five games to eliminate the Montreal Canadiens in the opening round of the playoffs. That set the stage for a final-round matchup with the top-ranked Red Wings, a series Detroit's rising superstar, Gordie Howe, would miss while recovering from a concussion.

Once again, clowns and elephants took over Madison Square Garden, forcing the Rangers to play their "home" games at Maple Leaf Gardens in Toronto. The remaining games would be played at the Olympia in Detroit.

"It was a strange series," Boucher recalled. "We were walloped, as the experts anticipated, in the opener at Detroit by 4–1 but we came back in our first game on Toronto ice 3–1. Then, again playing in Toronto, we dropped the third game 4–0 and it was generally concluded, with all subsequent games slated for the Olympia, that we'd pulled our last surprise."

But then, with the fourth game tied 3–3 after regulation, Don "Bones" Raleigh scored at 8:34 of overtime.

"The silence in the Olympia was deafening," Raleigh remembered. "No one cheered except our guys. I don't think there were ten people in the building rooting for us, but right then we had them on the ropes."

Two nights later, he did it again, breaking a 1–1 deadlock at 1:38 of overtime. Incredibly, the Rangers had taken the lead in a series many assumed the Wings would sweep. With one more win, the Stanley Cup would be Broadway-bound.

The Rangers had a 4–2 lead early in the third period of Game 6, but the Red Wings stormed back with three unanswered goals, edging New York 5–4 to force a Game 7.

Lynn Patrick, in his first and only full season behind the Rangers' bench, did a great job not only of guiding the team to the

Tony Leswick: The Original Sean Avery

What he lacked in stature, Tony Leswick made up for in skill and cunning, and he knew he could give the Rangers a chance to win if he was able to get Gordie Howe, Ted Lindsay, or other stars of the day off their game or, better yet, off the ice.

Tony's favorite target of harassment was Montreal's Maurice "Rocket" Richard, and the long-running, fight-filled feud between the men lasted for years. Leswick knew how to get under Richard's skin and could often draw the short-tempered Habitant into taking dumb penalties. A furious Richard then had to watch a Rangers power play from his seat in the penalty box.

On one such occasion, in January 1950, a packed Montreal Forum watched Leswick and Richard battle throughout the match. Four minor penalties, the last assessed with only 20 seconds of play remaining in a game his Canadiens trailed 3–1, had Richard fuming. When the final horn sounded, Richard erupted into a vicious rage. He hopped out of the box and made a mad dash for Leswick, his fists swinging. Teammates tried in vain to separate the two but the Rocket was so incensed that he even took a wild swing at Rangers coach Lynn Patrick.

seventh game of the Stanley Cup Finals, but in keeping his players' spirits up despite the disappointment of losing the previous match. They never gave an inch, battling the Wings to a 3–3 tie before regulation time expired.

The first 20-minute overtime period hadn't produced a winner. In the second overtime, the exhausted Rangers had two golden opportunities to win the game when both Bones Raleigh and Edgar Laprade beat Detroit goalie Harry Lumley, only to see their shots clang off the post.

"I could've won the game," Laprade said, the regret of that missed opportunity audible in his voice more than 60 years later. "It was around 1:00 AM. I went down the right side, got around the defense, and let my shot go. The puck hit the post, bounced behind Lumley, and went out the other side. If it had just bounced a little differently, it would've gone in the net. That would have been the championship for us. When I came back to our bench and told the rest of the guys, they didn't believe it. But I saw it, and I'll never forget it."

After weathering another Ranger attack, the Red Wings headed back up ice into the New Yorkers' zone. Pete Babando, a reserve forward who'd been benched earlier in the series by Detroit coach Jack Adams, took a pass from linemate George Gee and fired a backhanded shot on goal. The puck slipped past a screened Rayner at 8:31 of the second overtime period, ending the Rangers' season.

"Not a day goes by that I don't think about that goal," Rayner said not long before his death in 2002 at age 82. "What a shame that was. Just one goal, and there never would have been a 54-year drought."

Fred Shero was a spare defenseman on that 1949–50 squad. Shortly after he was hired to manage and coach the Rangers in 1978, he talked about the frustration of missing his one chance to win the Stanley Cup as a player.

"I can honestly say we were robbed," Shero said, "but maybe we could've given it a little more."

44 Domi vs. Probert

The classic first battle between two of the biggest heavyweights of the decade, on February 9, 1992, has been called one of the greatest hockey fights of all time. It's certainly the one that put the Rangers' Tie Domi on the map as a legitimate NHL enforcer.

It was inevitable that Domi, the mouthy, smirking young turk looking to make a name for himself, would eventually collide with the senior Bob Probert, one half of the "Bruise Brothers" with then–Red Wings teammate (and future Ranger) Joey Kocur.

Domi and Probert were lined up for a faceoff after a Detroit goal when the gloves came off. At 6'3", Probert had the size advantage but Tie held his own, going punch for punch with the champ…when he could reach him. He even managed to open up a cut over Probert's eye with a left hook. Most impressive was Domi's ability to absorb a punch. The man's skull had to have been carved from granite.

When it was over, Domi ignored standard hockey protocol by whooping it up, playing to the New York crowd (which was roaring loudly) by strapping on an imaginary heavyweight title belt as he skated triumphantly to the box. It was completely in-character for a player who used to celebrate his goals by riding his stick like a witch's broom.

"It's D-O-M-I, Not D-U-M-M-Y"

On October 14, 1995, ex-Ranger Tie Domi welcomed his former team to Maple Leaf Gardens. Carrying an old grudge against New York's Ulf Samuelsson, Tie chose this night to enact revenge.

Ulfie was a good defenseman but he had a reputation for dirty play—a high stick here, a slew foot there—and a tendency to "turtle" if an opposing player tried to fight him. A year earlier, he'd speared Domi in the groin and escaped punishment.

Late in a game the Rangers would win 2–0, Domi skated up to Samuelsson, who was standing near the Rangers' net, dropped his glove, and sucker-punched Ulf with a solid left hook to the jaw. Samuelsson dropped to the ice in front of Mike Richter, unconscious. He suffered a mild concussion and needed four stitches to patch up the back of his head, which was cut when he hit the ice.

Domi, who claimed Samuelsson egged him on with taunts of, "Come on, dummy, let's fight," was suspended eight games and fined for the punch. But in the eyes of fans who had been waiting years to see the big Swede get his comeuppance, Domi was a hero.

Showing up an opponent is a cardinal sin in hockey, and Domi had just done it on the biggest, brightest stage in sports. Probert was *not* pleased by the outcome or by Domi's showboating, sowing the seeds for a rematch.

The hype leading up to their second fight was unlike anything the NHL had ever seen—a media circus that began with Domi telling a New York paper that he had the next game against Detroit, on December 2, circled on his calendar.

Both fighters threw jabs at each other through the press, and most hockey fans ate it up. Less enthused was league president Gil Stein, who didn't want the NHL to turn into World Wrestling. A week before the game, Stein summoned Domi and Probert to his office in New York to warn them that if they fought, they'd each risk a fine and a lengthy suspension.

The night of the game, Rangers coach Roger Neilson, perhaps wanting to get the "main event" out of the way early, tapped Domi on the shoulder when he saw Probert on the ice for the opening faceoff.

Unlike their last meeting, in which Domi had all but begged for a chance to take on the league's top fighter, this time Probert was the aggressor. He was in full revenge mode and eager to teach his younger opponent a lesson.

The puck dropped and Probert was ready to go, even if Domi—the threat of suspension still fresh on his mind—was not. That moment of hesitation would be his undoing. Probert threw off his gloves and proceeded to pummel Domi, who got in a few shots of his own but was generally overwhelmed.

Despite their on-ice battles—maybe even *because* of those battles—Domi and Probert eventually became friends, though not until after both players hung up their skates.

45 The Shot That Changed the Game

The goalie mask, which evolved from a crude leather contraption worn by the Montreal Maroons' Clint Benedict for a few games in 1930 to the helmet-cage hybrid worn by all of today's pros, did not become standard equipment until the 1960s.

Incredible as it may seem, the mask was once considered a mark of cowardice. That all changed thanks to Canadiens goaltender Jacques Plante, with a little help from Rangers star Andy Bathgate.

It was November 1, 1959, and the Habs were in New York to play the Rangers. Early in the first period, Bathgate skated around the Montreal net and tried to beat Plante on the far side. It's a move he'd used many times before, but this time, Plante was waiting for him. He brought his stick up fast and intentionally clipped Bathgate in the head. Andy suffered cuts to his ear and face and was covered in blood when he returned to the bench.

"He could've broken my neck," Bathgate recalled. "I came off the ice and the trainer said, 'You need a few stitches,' but I told him to just wipe the blood off, it'll be alright. It always looks a lot worse when you're sweating."

Bathgate was fuming. He was determined to exact his pound of flesh on the very next shift. But how? As much as he wanted to, he couldn't just skate up to Plante and throw a punch.

"I was still dazed," he said, "but I knew I had to do something right after the incident. You can't wait a couple of weeks."

Bathgate had already badly injured two other NHL goalies with his famed slap shot, but it was a high backhander fired from close range at Plante's face that would change the game forever.

"That head of his was just sticking out like a chicken in a coop," Bathgate said. "I tried to hit him on the right side, but I hit him on the left side because he turned his head sideways."

Plante dropped to the ice as blood gushed from a gash stretching from his nose to his upper lip. Montreal's team doctor ran onto the ice to help. Gradually, Plante came to his senses, rose to his feet and, propped up by teammates Rocket Richard and Dickie Moore, made his way off the ice to get stitched up.

When Canadiens coach Toe Blake came to the visitors' dressing room to check on his goalie, Plante told him he wouldn't go back into the game without a mask. Blake was adamantly against it, but what choice did he have?

Nearly 25 minutes later, Plante returned to the ice with seven stitches in his lip and wearing a beige, fiberglass mask that he'd previously only used in practice. The Garden crowd was abuzz with a mix of surprise and curiosity.

The Rangers just figured Plante was chicken. Quite the opposite. With his face protected, Plante looked more confident than ever. He backstopped the Canadiens to a 3–1 win that night and remained unbeaten for 17 in a row.

The goalie mask was here to stay.

46 Trading Places

2013: Rangers and Canucks Swap Coaches

What were the chances? What were the odds? How did the stars align just right to make possible a scenario in which the New York Rangers, who won 51 games and finished with the second-best record in the NHL, and the Vancouver Canucks, who also won 51 games and the Presidents' Trophy, would both fire their coaches one year later and then, in the same off-season, hire the man just fired by the other team?

The "trade" of John Tortorella for Alain Vigneault, although not a direct exchange, was believed to be the first of its kind in major league pro sports. The *Vancouver Sun's* Iain MacIntyre cracked that it was the biggest transaction between the Rangers and Canucks since the Mario-Marois-for-Jere-Gillis blockbuster of 1980.

Tortorella played a significant role in transforming the culture of the Rangers organization. The churlish Boston native who treated every reporter's question like a late-night phone call from a telemarketer instilled a work ethic, team-first attitude and religious commitment to blocking shots, all of which resulted in a team that was rather thin on talent earning the best record in the Eastern Conference in 2011–12. His nomination for the Jack Adams Award as Coach of the Year was very much deserved.

But there was no letup with Torts. He was impatient. He was hotheaded. In their exit meetings with Glen Sather following the lockout-shortened 2012–13 season, players made it clear that the dressing room had become a mighty uncomfortable place. They needed to see a new face and hear a new voice.

Despite being the Canucks' all-time leader in coaching wins, guiding the club to six division titles, two Presidents' Trophies, and

---

Top Five Questions the New York Media Never Got the Chance to Ask John Tortorella

1. "Are you still in touch with Sean Avery?"
2. "Exactly what does Mike Sullivan do?"
3. "You often talk about the team needing more jam. What's your favorite flavor?"
4. "Larry Brooks really killed you in today's *Post*. Did you read it?"
5. "Seriously, John, what does Mike Sullivan do?"

an appearance in the 2011 Stanley Cup Finals, Vigneault was cut loose following a pair of early playoff exits.

On June 21, 2013, the Rangers introduced Vigneault as their new coach. Days later, Tortorella sat on a dais in Vancouver talking about how it had been his dream to one day coach in Canada. Under these unique circumstances, it was a given the Rangers and Canucks would be measured against each other all season.

A wave of injuries to key players—and an inability to adapt to changing conditions—doomed Tortorella's first season behind the Canucks bench, and he was fired with four years left on his contract.

The Rangers found patience to be Vigneault's greatest virtue. He gave line combinations a chance to gel and didn't blow them up after one bad shift. He showed a willingness to live with mistakes if players were giving their best effort and trying to create offense. He gave greater responsibility to the likes of Ryan McDonagh, Chris Kreider, and Mats Zuccarello, all of whom responded with career years. Oh, and he guided the team to its first Stanley Cup Finals appearance in 20 seasons. Broadway debuts don't get much better than that.

47 Ranger Firsts

Having been around since 1926, the Rangers have played a role in some landmark events and game-changing innovations:

First U.S.-Based NHL Team to Win the Stanley Cup
On April 14, 1928, the Rangers beat the Montreal Maroons in Game 5 of the Stanley Cup Finals to become the first NHL team

based in the United States to win the trophy. That's an important distinction because, technically speaking, it was the second Stanley Cup victory by a U.S.-based franchise. The Pacific Coast Hockey Association's Seattle Metropolitans won the Cup in 1917, a full nine years before it became the de facto championship trophy of the NHL.

Boardwalk Blueshirts

On December 28, 1929, the Rangers beat the Ottawa Senators 3–1 in the first NHL game ever played in Atlantic City. An announced crowd of about 10,000 filled the old Atlantic City Auditorium, a cavernous convention hall believed to have been the largest in the world at the time. New Jersey Governor Morgan Larson dropped the ceremonial first puck.

The First Televised Game

Although it was not the first hockey game to be seen on television, and the viewing audience was miniscule—just a few hundred people—the Rangers-Canadiens game on February 25, 1940, was the first telecast of an NHL game and the first in the United States.

At the time, televisions were expensive and extremely rare. The entire medium was still considered a fad, but there was enough curiosity about it to warrant a little experiment.

The game was broadcast in the New York area on W2XBS, an experimental TV station used by NBC to test the emerging technology. Broadcasting from a transmitter atop the Empire State Building, the station had already scored a few firsts, including the first televised Broadway drama, the first live telecast of a Presidential speech (Franklin D. Roosevelt opening the 1939 New York World's Fair), and the first live telecast of Major League Baseball.

Screens were small and the resolution was low—probably like watching a hockey game through a fish tank filled with dirty dish water—but viewers would have seen the league's goal-leader, Bryan Hextall, score twice in a 6–2 Rangers win.

Coaching Firsts

In 1939–40, his first season as coach of the Rangers, Frank Boucher came up with a pair of innovations that would not only contribute to a Stanley Cup victory, but would also become standard practice for teams at every level of the sport.

In the old days, it was customary for teams to wait for a stoppage in play to pull their goaltender and replace him with a sixth attacker when trailing by a goal. But Boucher had an idea: why not pull the goalie while play was still in motion? There was no rule prohibiting it and, if executed properly, it could really catch an opponent off-guard. It was so unexpected that the first time the Rangers tried it in a game, they were accidentally whistled for too many men on the ice.

Boucher also agreed to a player's suggestion that instead of backchecking when the Rangers were a man short, they should try going on the attack. This was counter to everything that the finest hockey minds of the day had ever been taught about the game. Teams concentrated on defense when killing penalties: the forwards backchecked the opposing wingers and the defensemen went after the center.

But the concept of offensive penalty killing captured Boucher's imagination, and he had his players practice it carefully before trying it out in a game lest it backfire and they all look like fools. As part of this revolutionary system, Boucher also implemented a box defense in which the four penalty killers would form a loose square in front of goalie Dave Kerr and force attackers off to the sides so any shots on goal would be taken from bad angles. Kerr was good enough to stop most of those.

The system was hugely successful, partly because the Rangers' foes never expected it. Over the course of that season, the Rangers scored more shorthanded goals than power play goals allowed.

First European-Trained Player

In 1965, Ulf Sterner became the first European (and first Swede) to play in an NHL game.

A smooth-skating center with tremendous offensive skills, Sterner was a dominating presence on the international scene before accepting an invitation to try out for the Rangers.

At the time, the idea of a European playing in a league dominated almost exclusively by Canadians was pretty farfetched. Sterner made a strong impression during training camp in 1964, but the Rangers decided he'd be better served by starting the season in the minors.

The only criticism directed at Sterner concerned his reluctance to play physically. This was to be expected since international hockey rules of the day forbade body checking in the offensive zone. The North American pro game featured big hits all over the ice, something Sterner simply wasn't trained for.

The Rangers recalled Sterner from Baltimore of the American Hockey League, and he made his NHL debut on January 27, 1965, against the Boston Bruins. Ulf got pushed around quite a bit that night by the Bruins and showed no interest in pushing back. He went scoreless in four games with the Rangers before being returned to the minors.

It was clear to Sterner that he wasn't going to see Madison Square Garden again…not without a ticket, anyway. At the end of the season, he went back to Sweden for good.

First Game Broadcast in 3D

On March 24, 2010, the Rangers hosted the Islanders at Madison Square Garden for the first network hockey telecast—in fact, the first North American sporting event of any kind—to be produced in 3D.

The tech site Geek.com described the experience as being "like watching sports through a window or in a crystal clear moving diorama. The 3D cameras didn't suddenly send pucks flying at your face, but they did add depth to the game."

Whether you were watching in person at The Garden or at home sporting a pair of funky 3D glasses, it was clear to see that the Rangers were the superior team that night in routing the Islanders 5–0. Marian Gaborik scored twice, and Henrik Lundqvist recorded his 23rd career shutout.

48 Ohh la la Sasson!

Designer jeans took the New York fashion world by storm in the late 1970s. Some of the biggest designers in the industry got in on the phenomenon: Gloria Vanderbilt, Jordache, and Sergio Valente, to name a few. Made for the dance floor and the roller-disco rink, designer jeans were tighter, sexier, and more sophisticated than the loose-fitting Lee jeans your mom bought you at Caldor or Woolworths.

The advertising budgets were huge, so celebrities were often hired to pitch them in commercials (anyone over a certain age is bound to remember a 15-year-old Brooke Shields revealing that nothing comes between her and her Calvin Kleins). That's how Ron Duguay, Phil Esposito, Anders Hedberg, Ron Greschner, Dave Maloney, and Don Maloney got roped into appearing in a pair of TV spots for Sasson jeans.

Ranger Pitchmen

Ad agencies have been using Rangers players to extol the virtues of products for years, though not as memorably as in the Sasson campaign. Can you match each Ranger with the product he endorsed?

1. Frank Boucher	A. Coca-Cola
2. Eddie Johnstone	B. Advil
3. Rod Gilbert	C. Sugar Crisp
4. Don Maloney	D. Camel Cigarettes
5. Brian Leetch	E. Volvo
6. Henrik Lundqvist	F. 7UP
7. Wayne Gretzky	G. Mercury
8. Cal Gardner	H. Rheingold Beer
9. Mike Richter	I. Wendy's
10. John Vanbiesbrouck	J. McDonald's

Answers: 1H, 2A, 3G, 4F, 5J, 6B, 7C, 8D, 9I, 10E

The cringe-inducing commercials featured the players clad in hockey jerseys and blue jeans, skating arm-in-arm and shaking their derrieres while singing the company's French jingle, "Ohh la la Sasson!"

Predictably, the Rangers opened themselves up to plenty of ridicule from players and fans in every arena, including their own. "Ohh la la Sasson!" quickly became "Ohh la la sa-suck!"

"The women loved it, but guys made fun of us," Duguay recalled. "They'd call us sissy, especially in Philadelphia."

"Sure, there were a few players who made comments," said Barry Beck, who appeared in a print ad for Sasson, "but you had to laugh at it. When another player says you have a nice ass, it's hard not to crack a smile…no pun intended."

Mercifully, like disco, the designer jean fad met its demise in the early 1980s. At least one former Ranger is relieved that his face (and rear-end) didn't make it into the Sasson ads. Pat Hickey appeared in an early, un-aired cut of the commercial that had to be scrapped when he was traded to the Colorado Rockies.

"I still got paid," Hickey said, "but I didn't have to take the hit on the embarrassment. It worked out good."

49 The "Forgotten" Cup

Sandwiched as it was between the more celebrated triumphs of 1928 and 1940, the Rangers' Stanley Cup victory in 1933 has been called the "Forgotten Cup."

Murray Murdoch, a left winger who played all of his 508 NHL games with the Rangers, remembered the low-key response to the team's second title. "There was no parade or anything like that," he said. "We took cabs down to City Hall. They shook our hands, and that was that."

The people of New York could be forgiven for having other things on their minds. The stock market crash of 1929 had ushered in a financial crisis unlike any before it, putting millions of Americans out of work. New York City was hit particularly hard. As the Great Depression dragged on, folks had less and less money in their pockets to spend on luxuries like hockey tickets.

Attendance at Rangers games was down. Bill Carey, the president of Madison Square Garden, worried that if fans strapped for cash stopped coming, they might never return. So he slashed ticket prices, twice, for the 1932–33 season. That led to a dispute with the president of the Rangers, John Hammond, who felt that lowering the cost of admission cheapened the value of the product. He resigned a short time later.

Ching Johnson

Ivan "Ching" Johnson was one of the top defensemen in the game and a mainstay on the Blueshirt blueline for the club's first 11 seasons.

Johnson's nickname—fans would shout "Ching, Ching, Chinaman!"—had nothing to do with his ethnicity, since he was of Irish descent. It derived instead from summer camping trips Johnson and his pals would take along the Red River in Alberta. In those days, it was common practice on extended excursions of this sort to hire a man, usually of Chinese descent, to serve as the group's cook. But Johnson usually volunteered for that job, probably to save a few bucks, and one of the least politically correct nicknames was born.

He also went by "Ivan the Terrible," but that tag had nothing to do with his temperament. Johnson was the kind of cheerful, fun-loving guy you'd enjoy meeting anywhere...except in his end of the ice. He was a punishing hitter.

"A big, raw-boned fellow with a bald head, he always wore a grin, even when heaving some poor soul 6' in the air," recalled former teammate Frank Boucher. "He was one of those rare warm people who'd break into a smile just saying hello or telling you the time."

Fans applauded the lower prices and attendance at Rangers games rebounded strongly.

The nucleus of the 1928 Cup team was still largely intact five years later. Murdoch, Frank Boucher, the Cook brothers, and defenseman Ching Johnson had been back to the final round twice since then, in 1929 and 1932, but came away empty-handed.

Led by the NHL's scoring champ, Bill Cook, and buoyed by the solid goaltending of rookie Andy Aitkenhead, the Rangers finished third in their division with a 23–17–8 record.

After series wins over the Montreal Canadiens and Detroit Red Wings, the Rangers met Toronto in a rematch of the previous year's finals. Only the first game of the best-of-five Cup round was played in New York. The Maple Leafs were exhausted from having just played a six-overtime game against Boston the night before, and it showed. The Rangers won easily 5–1 then split the next two games.

Game 4 was scoreless at the end of regulation. About eight minutes into overtime, New York's Butch Keeling hopped over the boards to replace Bun Cook, who had just come off for a line change. Bill Cook and Frank Boucher were heading off, too, when all of a sudden Keeling came up with the puck and fired a rink-wide pass to Bill. The Ranger captain motored into the Toronto zone then ripped a shot that beat ex-Ranger Lorne Chabot stickside for the first Stanley Cup–winning overtime goal in history.

50 Test Your Rangers IQ, Part II

1. Who was the only man to play on both the 1932–33 and 1939–40 Ranger clubs?
    A. Alf Pike
    B. Babe Pratt
    C. Ott Heller
    D. Dutch Hiller

2. In 1993, Ron Duguay married this supermodel.
    A. Carol Alt
    B. Linda Evangelista
    C. Cheryl Tiegs
    D. Kim Alexis

3. This Ranger celebrated scoring a shorthanded goal by holding his stick like a rifle and pretending to shoot Lightning goalie Mathieu Garon, an act of showboating that triggered a melee resulting in 38 minutes in penalties.
    A. Nik Antropov
    B. Ruslan Fedotenko
    C. Nikolai Zherdev
    D. Artem Anisimov

4. He celebrated his first college goal by breaking a stick over his bare head.
    A. Tom Laidlaw
    B. Mike York
    C. Carl Hagelin
    D. James Patrick

5. Six Sutter brothers—Brent, Brian, Darryl, Duane, Rich, and Ron—reached the NHL in the 1970s and '80s. How many of them played for the Rangers?
    A. Three
    B. Two
    C. One
    D. None

6. He scored at 4:07 of overtime in Game 5 of the 1974 quarterfinals to give the Rangers a 3–2 win over the Montreal Canadiens.
    A. Ron Harris
    B. Walt Tkaczuk
    C. Bruce MacGregor
    D. Gene Carr

7. This player was cut by the Rangers on Thanksgiving.
   A. Rich Pilon
   B. Rod Gilbert
   C. Rem Murray
   D. Ed Giacomin

8. All of these Rangers are Boston University alums *except*:
   A. Tony Amonte
   B. Matt Gilroy
   C. Brian Boyle
   D. Dave Silk

9. During the 1992 semifinals against New Jersey, this Ranger set a club record by scoring six goals in one series.
   A. Adam Graves
   B. Mike Gartner
   C. Mark Messier
   D. Tony Amonte

10. Prior to joining the Rangers, this winger lost half of his left thumb in a bizarre farming accident.
   A. Pat Verbeek
   B. Steve Vickers
   C. Wally Hergesheimer
   D. Mike Keane

11. Professional wrestler Chris Jericho is the son of this Ranger left wing from the 1970s.
   A. Vic Hadfield
   B. Dave Balon
   C. Ted Irvine
   D. Greg Polis

12. He holds the club record for most points in a game with seven.
    A. Jean Ratelle
    B. Wayne Gretzky
    C. Ron Duguay
    D. Steve Vickers

13. In 1933, this right winger had eight goals in eight games (plus two assists) to lead all playoff scorers in goals and points.
    A. Butch Keeling
    B. Bun Cook
    C. Frank Boucher
    D. Cecil Dillon

14. In March 2002, Mike Richter suffered a skull fracture when he was struck by a slap shot off the stick of this Atlanta Thrasher (and former Ranger).
    A. Marc Savard
    B. Yannick Tremblay
    C. Chris Tamer
    D. Jiri Slegr

15. He coached only 18 games for the Rangers before being forced to resign due to health issues.
    A. Tom Webster
    B. Ron Smith
    C. Jean-Guy Talbot
    D. Ron Stewart

16. Brian Leetch was briefly the property of—but never played for—this Western Conference team.
    A. Edmonton Oilers
    B. Los Angeles Kings
    C. Vancouver Canucks
    D. Dallas Stars

17. In 2008, the Rangers were involved in a dispute with the National Hockey League over:
    A. The team's uniforms
    B. The team's website
    C. Violation of the league's salary cap
    D. Compromising photos of Colin Campbell

18. When he was a teen, this future Ranger won a Little League World Series Championship.
    A. Mathieu Schneider
    B. Brian Leetch
    C. Darren Turcotte
    D. Chris Drury

19. Who was in net for Montreal the night in 1972 when Vic Hadfield scored his 49th and 50th goals of the season, setting a new club record?
    A. Rogie Vachon
    B. Denis DeJordy
    C. Phil Myre
    D. Ken Dryden

20. In 2010–11, he led the league in blocked shots with 236.
    A. Dan Girardi
    B. Marc Staal
    C. Ryan Callahan
    D. Michael Sauer

21. He was the Rangers' highest Russian-born draft pick.
    A. Alexei Cherepanov
    B. Alexei Kovalev
    C. Fedor Tyutin
    D. Sergei Zubov

22. On January 23, 2002, he scored his first career hat trick and added an assist in an 8–4 win over the Boston Bruins.
    A. Manny Malhotra
    B. Steve McKenna
    C. Jeff Toms
    D. Dave Karpa

23. This left wing drew the plum assignment of skating with Anders Hedberg and Ulf Nilsson on a line dubbed "Swede 16."
    A. Nick Fotiu
    B. Don Maloney
    C. Pat Hickey
    D. Greg Polis

24. He is the only person to have played at least one game for every Original Six team.
    A. Harry Lumley
    B. Vic Lynn
    C. Bronco Horvath
    D. Terry Sawchuk

25. This promising Rangers prospect suffered a severe knee injury in 1999 that would ultimately end his career.
    A. Stefan Cherneski
    B. Tony Tuzzolino
    C. Boyd Kane
    D. Todd Hall

Answers:

1. C, Ott Heller. A steady defenseman, Gerhardt "Ott" Heller played 647 games for the Rangers from 1931 to 1946.

2. D, Kim Alexis. One of the top models of the 1980s, Alexis regularly graced the covers of magazines like *Vogue, Cosmopolitan,*

and *Harper's Bazaar*. She and Duguay were married on January 2, 1993.

3. D, Artem Anisimov. Not one to intentionally show up an opponent, Anisimov quickly apologized for his excessive goal celebration.

4. A, Tom Laidlaw. A rugged defenseman, Laidlaw played on Northern Michigan's first Division I hockey team in 1976–77. New York papers hyped up the stick-breaking story after he was drafted 93rd overall by the Rangers in 1978, in part to show that the Philadelphia Flyers with their Broadstreet Bully image didn't have a monopoly on toughness.

5. D, None. Collectively, the Sutter brothers played nearly 5,000 NHL games for 12 different teams: the Islanders, Blackhawks, Blues, Penguins, Flyers, Canucks, Maple Leafs, Lightning, Nordiques, Bruins, Sharks, and Flames.

6. A, Ron Harris. A defenseman playing right wing in that game, Harris beat Montreal goalie Bunny Larocque with a one-timer off a pass from Pete Stemkowski. The victory gave the Rangers a 3–2 lead in the series, which the Rangers would wrap up at home two nights later.

7. B, Rod Gilbert. Before the start of the 1977–78 season, Gilbert found himself in tense contract negotiations with general manager John Ferguson. Following a 15-day holdout, Gilbert returned to play 19 games before being cut by the club on Thanksgiving Day. It was Ferguson's way of flushing out the last of the Emile Francis–era Rangers, and Gilbert never forgave him for it.

8. C, Brian Boyle. The Hingham, Massachusetts, native attended Boston College.

9. B, Mike Gartner. Despite that performance, Gartner still faced criticism about his postseason play. He might have finally proven his detractors wrong had the Rangers not dealt him to the Maple Leafs for Glenn Anderson in March 1994, one of several big moves the team made in preparation for a run at the Stanley Cup. It was the third time in his Hall of Fame career Gartner had to pack his bags at the trade deadline.

10. A, Pat Verbeek. During the off-season in 1985, Verbeek was working on a corn-planting machine on his 200-acre farm in rural Ontario. He accidentally slipped into the machinery and his left hand went directly into the moving auger, slicing off his thumb between the knuckles. Pat's brother, Brian, rushed him to a hospital but they forgot to bring the severed thumb. Pat's father, Gerry, rushed over to Pat's farm, found the thumb in one of the machine's fertilizer bins, and transported it to the hospital where doctors managed to surgically reattach it. Verbeek's hockey career was saved.

11. C, Ted Irvine. A character player whose robust style was an instant hit with fans, Irvine was also recognized for his work with local charitable organizations, particularly those benefitting children. His son, Christopher Keith Irvine, wrestled under the name Chris Jericho.

12. D, Steve Vickers. On February 18, 1976, future Rangers coach Ron Low was in net for the second-year Washington Capitals when Vickers scored three goals and assisted on four others in an 11–4 Rangers win.

13. D, Cecil Dillon. With three goals and an assist, Dillon was also the leading scorer in the Stanley Cup Finals, which the Rangers won by defeating the Toronto Maple Leafs 3–1.

14. C, Chris Tamer. The incident occurred in the first period of a 5–2 loss to the Thrashers at Madison Square Garden. Richter missed the rest of the regular season.

15. A, Tom Webster. Hired as coach of the Rangers in November 1986 to replace the fired Ted Sator, Webster was plagued by an inner ear disorder that prevented him from flying. He coached only home games for several weeks before announcing his resignation in April 1987.

16. A, Edmonton Oilers. In June 2003, the Rangers traded Leetch to Edmonton for goalie Jussi Markkanen and a fourth-round draft pick. The Oilers made the deal knowing Leetch, an impending free agent, was unlikely to sign with them. A month later, Leetch re-signed with the Rangers and the Oilers received a compensatory draft pick.

17. B, The team's website. The NHL threatened to fine the Rangers $100,000 a day if the team did not hand over control of its website to NHL.com. The club wanted the right to control its own website, and filed an antitrust lawsuit against the NHL. The NHL countersued, threatening to kick Cablevision out of the league. In the end, the Rangers relinquished control of their website and Jim Dolan retained control of his hockey team.

18. D, Chris Drury. A star in baseball and hockey, Drury was a pitcher on the Trumbull, Connecticut, team that defeated Taiwan in the 1989 Little League World Series.

19. B, Denis DeJordy. Playing with a broken thumb, Hadfield scored twice in the final game of the 1971–72 regular season. DeJordy and Hadfield had been teammates in juniors with the St. Catharines Teepees.

20. A, Dan Girardi. Despite the wear and tear on his body, Girardi missed only two games to injury that season and managed to score a career-high 31 points.

21. B, Alexei Kovalev. The Togliatti native was selected 15th overall by the Rangers in 1991. Alexei Cherepanov was chosen 17th overall in 2007, Fedor Tyutin was the 40th overall pick in 2001, and Sergei Zubov went 85th overall in 1990.

22. C, Jeff Toms. On a night in which Eric Lindros (700 points), Theo Fleury (1,000 games played) and Petr Nedved (700 games played) all celebrated career milestones, it was Toms who was named first star of the game. Skating on a line with Lindros and Mike York, the likable journeyman had already notched two goals and an assist late in the game when an errant puck flew off the ice toward the Rangers' bench, striking Toms in the face and breaking his nose. He flew backward, stunned and bloodied, but got back on his feet and into the game. A short time later, he scored his third goal of the match, securing the first hat trick and four-point effort of his career.

23. C, Pat Hickey. "Swede 16" was a play on words—Hickey, one of the fastest skaters in the league at the time, was identified only by his uniform number.

24. B, Vic Lynn. Lynn played one game, his NHL debut, with the Rangers in 1942. Over the next decade, the speedy left winger had stints with the Red Wings, Canadiens, Maple Leafs, Bruins, and Blackhawks.

25. A, Stefan Cherneski. New York's first-round pick (19th overall) in 1997, Cherneski drew comparisons to John LeClair after a successful junior career with the Brandon Wheat Kings. While skating

with the Rangers' farm team in Hartford, the big right winger was checked along the boards and his knee shattered into seven pieces. Cherneski worked hard to come back from the injury, but his knee was never the same. He retired in 2001.

51 The Captains

In other sports, captain is a largely symbolic title given to a member of the team to recognize qualities of leadership. But in hockey, the captain performs a host of duties that are both symbolic *and* functional.

Officially, only the captain is allowed to approach a referee during a game to question a penalty or ask for an interpretation of the rules. Unofficially, a captain's responsibilities often include coordinating off-ice gatherings to build team chemistry, keeping the coaching staff apprised of dressing room morale, or calling that dreaded players-only meeting during a losing streak. How much or how little they say and do largely depends on the personality of the person wearing the "C."

Dave Maloney, captain of the Rangers from 1978 to 1980, notes that the captaincy in hockey has taken on deeper meaning in recent years.

"I don't know if that's just a result of extended media coverage or over-observation," Maloney said. "The role of captain was typically one in which I was kind of in the middle. I never, ever felt that I was in a position to tell the coaching staff, 'You should be doing this or that.' Obviously, with Mark Messier and all the things that happened with him here, the role of captain became more impactful than perhaps it was for the rest of us."

Kelly Kisio, captain from 1987 to 1991, agreed. "I mostly led by example," he said. "I talked a little bit but it wasn't a situation like Messier where I could stand up and give guys shit or anything like that."

The Rangers have had 26 captains, each unique in his own way. Each carried the honor—and burden—of leading one of the oldest and most high-profile clubs in hockey.

Ryan Callahan (2011–14): John Tortorella said that one of the greatest challenges he faced as coach of the Rangers was resisting the temptation to look down the bench and have Callahan hop over the boards on every shift. The Rochester, New York, native earned the trust of coaches at every level with his relentless work ethic and high hockey IQ—that is, the knack for almost always making the right decision in any given situation. Need someone to score a goal? Cally can do that. Throw a big hit? Not a problem. Kill a penalty? Block a shot? Check and check. He never represented the Rangers at an All-Star Game, but No. 24 epitomized what it means to be a Ranger.

Chris Drury (2008–11): A champion at every level in which he competed, Drury came to New York as "Captain Clutch" but left as "Captain Dreary." Age and injuries caught up to the classy veteran, who could never live up to the expectations that accompanied his massive contract. His final NHL goal—and only one of his final season—propelled the Rangers into the postseason in a win over the Devils in the season finale.

Jaromir Jagr (2006–08): Bestowing the captaincy on Jagr was largely a gesture of respect—an acknowledgment of the five-time scoring champ's extensive resume.

Brian Leetch (1997–2000): A quiet and unassuming superstar who never looked fully comfortable wearing the captain's "C" after Mark Messier's acrimonious departure to Vancouver. But Leetch dutifully accepted his role and tried to lead by example during a period marked by disappointing team performances that saw the Rangers miss the playoffs year after year.

Mark Messier (1991–97, 2000–04): The captain against which all others are measured. Messier was an outspoken leader who dared teammates to dream big and had the talent to back up his words. He was absolutely fearless and completely focused on winning. His first act as captain was to rearrange the locker room at MSG. A table that held skates and Gatorade was dividing the room, so Messier had it removed. He noticed the defensemen had their lockers behind a pillar, so he moved them, too. The reason? He wanted to be able to look into every teammate's eyes. He demanded accountability from the men he played with—more than a few felt his wrath for giving less than 100 percent—but he also went to great lengths to make everyone feel welcome and part of the team. When the Rangers called up a rookie enforcer named Darren Langdon from the minors for his first NHL game, he found a brand-new Hugo Boss suit hanging in his dressing room stall—a gift from No. 11.

Kelly Kisio (1987–91): What he lacked in star power, Kisio made up for with moxie. His heart was barely big enough to fit in his 5'9", 170-lb. body. Kisio was a team leader, playmaker, checker, penalty killer, and power-play specialist.

Ron Greschner (1986–87): As one of the oldest and longest-tenured Rangers, Greschner was the logical choice to replace Barry Beck when his former defense partner left the team in 1986.

Barry Beck (1981–86): Giving Bubba the captaincy was the organization's way of letting the world know that he was going to lead the Rangers to the Promised Land. He didn't, but he gave it his best shot.

Walt Tkaczuk (1980–81): The big checking center was named captain in his 14th and final NHL campaign…but only for a third of the season. Management felt at the time that it would be better for the team to have a rotating captain.

Dave Maloney (1978–80): A playmaking defenseman whose skating and hockey sense made him an important member of both the power play and penalty-killing units, Maloney was also a scrappy leader in the defensive zone. That scrappiness earned him the captaincy when he was only 19 years old. He's still the youngest captain in the club's history.

Phil Esposito (1975–78): A reluctant captain, Espo was given the "C" before he ever played a game for the Rangers. Years later, he asked the team's former coach and GM, Emile Francis, why the captaincy hadn't gone to a career Ranger like Rod Gilbert. "I wouldn't have made Rod Gilbert captain," Francis supposedly replied, "if he was the only player on the team."

Brad Park (1974–75): The star defenseman figured that because he was the Rangers' captain and Most Valuable Player, he wouldn't get traded. He figured wrong.

Vic Hadfield (1971–74): Size and toughness gave Vic a competitive advantage, but a mischievous sense of humor gave the G-A-G Line left winger locker room credibility, which in turn made him a more effective leader.

Bob Nevin (1965–71): A natural leader, he ably captained the team during its return to respectability in the late 1960s. But Nevin, a solid defensive forward, came to New York in a massive trade for Andy Bathgate and spent much of his Rangers career trying to win over the Garden's balcony brigade. His subtle contributions to the team too often went unnoticed, but not by those closer to the action.

Camille Henry (1964–65): At 31, "Camille the Eel" was one of the senior-most Rangers on the team when Andy Bathgate was traded to Toronto. Generously listed at 5'8" and 150 lbs., Henry was probably about 20 lbs. lighter.

Andy Bathgate (1961–64): For future Ranger stars like Rod Gilbert, Vic Hadfield, and Jean Ratelle, there really was no better role model than Bathgate. Unfortunately, he ran afoul of general manager Muzz Patrick one day by suggesting that Ratelle, a slick young center, not be included in a rumored trade. A short time later, Bathgate was enjoying a pre-game meal at the Royal York Hotel in Toronto when he was summoned to Patrick's room. He arrived to learn that he'd just been traded to the Maple Leafs.

George Sullivan (1957–61): True to the color of his hair, George "Red" Sullivan was a fiery competitor, a sparkplug center who supplied guts and character for Ranger teams that were mostly unremarkable.

Harry Howell (1955–57): The Rangers were so impressed by Howell's poise as a young defenseman that they named him captain when he was just 22. He gave up the captaincy two years later to

Defenseman Harry Howell poses with his son, five-year-old Danny, at New York's Madison Square Garden, where Howell was working out on January 4, 1965. (AP Photo/John Lent)

focus on improving his play. He did, and it earned him a spot in the Hockey Hall of Fame.

Don Raleigh (1953–55): Back when uniform numbers really meant something, the Rangers assigned Raleigh No. 7—a high honor, since only Frank Boucher and Phil Watson had worn it previously for 22 consecutive seasons. They wanted a guy headed for stardom, and they wanted a center. Raleigh was both.

Allan Stanley (1951–53): A defensive defenseman painted by the Rangers front office as a potential savior, Stanley was given the captaincy in part to turn the tide of fans' displeasure over his efficient but not overly physical style. But that didn't silence the boo birds, who were on Stanley every time he touched the puck, then every time he got on the ice, and then when he was just sitting on the bench. The booing got so bad that Rangers coaches would sometimes play him only on the road. Only a trade to the Maple Leafs brought him relief.

Frank Eddolls (1950–51): A shutdown defenseman, Eddolls starred for the Blueshirts on their run to the 1950 Stanley Cup Finals. He was held in high regard as a leader—so much so that while he was still playing, he was named temporary head coach of the Rangers' farm team in Saskatoon when Bill Cook was promoted to coach the Rangers.

Buddy O'Connor (1949–50): The Rangers have had dozens of clean, gentlemanly players but the cleanest of them all, hands down, had to be Herbert William "Buddy" O'Connor, a diminutive center who stood 5'7" and weighed just more than 140 lbs. The statistics alone tell the story: 238 games as a Ranger, 12 penalty minutes. In fact, Buddy played two full seasons with the Rangers without drawing a single penalty.

Neil Colville (1945–48): A superb stickhandler and a deft playmaker, Colville began his NHL career as a center on the "Bread Line" between brother Mac Colville and Alex Shibicky. But after missing two full seasons in the Canadian military during World

War II, he returned to the Rangers as a defenseman in 1945 and was quickly named the club's fourth captain.

Ott Heller (1942–45): A rash of injuries to the Rangers defense corps led to Heller's call-up from the minors in January 1932, and he was a fixture on Broadway for the next 14 seasons. As durable as he was tough, Ott—his real name was Ehrhardt—played an amazing 26 professional seasons all over the hockey map.

Art Coulter (1937–42): A punishing hitter and willing shot-blocker, Coulter lent strength to the Rangers' smaller players. If an opponent tried to physically intimidate one of his teammates, Coulter was sure to intervene. "He was a great team man, a great captain," Frank Boucher said. "The team always came first with him."

Bill Cook (1926–37): The Rangers couldn't have picked a better man to be their first captain. Cook's toughness undoubtedly traced to his service, starting at the age of 17, with the Canadian armed forces in World War I. He survived battles at Ypres, Vimy Ridge, the Somme, and Flanders. A fellow soldier once described Cook as one of the bravest men he'd ever seen.

52 The Fog

Savant (noun): a person of profound or extensive learning; a scholar.

When it came to studying the science and art of hockey, Fred Shero was certainly that. He was an innovator, often credited with being among the first Western coaches to study Soviet hockey and review game film.

But, like many exceptionally bright people, Shero could also be aloof. Although well-read and well-versed on a variety of subjects outside of hockey, he sometimes had difficulty connecting with his players one-on-one, preferring to let his assistant, Mike Nykoluk, do much of the talking. "The Fog" was a nickname that fit Freddy to a T.

Pat Hickey noticed that during games, Shero always seemed to be scribbling something onto a little piece of paper.

"So I went over and talked to Freddy on the bench," Hickey recalled. "I looked down at the paper and you know what was on there? Nothing. I asked him about it and he said, 'It's just my act. I like to keep people guessing.'"

The 1978–79 season saw Shero return to the city where he had gotten his start in pro hockey. The onetime Ranger defenseman (1947–50) also enjoyed a lengthy stint as a minor league development coach (1959–71), winning championships in four different leagues while sending many young players on to NHL careers.

Despite his success at that level, Shero hadn't been given a shot to coach the Rangers, so he left the organization in 1971 to work for the Philadelphia Flyers. In three short seasons, he turned them into Stanley Cup champs.

Although Freddy still had a year left on his contract at the end of his seventh season behind the Flyers' bench, he had begun to feel that his players were tuning him out. He was ready for a change and jumped at the chance to go back to New York to run his former team as coach and general manager. The Rangers were eventually forced to give up a first-round draft pick in 1978 to the Flyers in exchange for releasing Shero from the last year of his contract.

Telling reporters that his heart had always been in New York, Shero officially took over the Rangers' hockey operations on June 2, 1978. Among the first accomplishments of his stewardship—after announcing that the club would throw out the garish uniforms introduced by John Ferguson and return to wearing its traditional threads—was the signing of a pair of high-priced free agent Swedish scoring stars: Anders Hedberg and Ulf Nilsson.

Under Shero, the Rangers improved by ten wins and eighteen points from the previous season and then defeated Los Angeles, Philadelphia and the New York Islanders with a cumulative 10–3 playoff record to reach the 1979 Stanley Cup Finals. By the time the championship series opened at the Montreal Forum on May 13, Shero was being billed as a miracle worker. His reputation soared after the Rangers took the opening game with relative ease 4–1. But then the Canadiens roared back with four straight wins, sending Freddy and the Rangers home empty-handed.

The sudden downfall of Shero and the Rangers was chronicled in Larry "Ratso" Sloman's *Thin Ice,* a warts-and-all look at the team as it emerged from the decadent, hedonistic '70s with a major hangover. Embedded with the team like a war correspondent, Ratso had unprecedented access to the players and management. He wrote what he saw, and what he saw was a dysfunctional mess.

Although he was technically GM, Shero didn't have a head for the administrative functions of the job, leaving many of those duties to his assistant, Mickey Keating. The players didn't respect Keating, and neither did the press.

Then there was the time Shero traded Don Murdoch for winger Cam Connor when he thought he was getting defenseman Colin Campbell (yes, *that* Colin Campbell). Garden boss Sonny Werblin was especially ticked about the trade of Murdoch, since Donnie was one of his favorites and he hadn't been told of the deal in advance.

And then there was the matter of Shero's drinking. That he enjoyed warm beer was strange, but not a firable offense. The fact that he seemed to be drinking at all hours, including during morning practices, led some to believe that perhaps Freddy's fog wasn't a fog at all but an alcohol-induced haze that clouded his judgment. He finally admitted to the *New York Post* that yes, he did have a drinking problem, yes he had it under control, and no, it never affected his job.

Besieged by injuries, the Rangers won just four of their first 20 games to open the 1980–81 season, but Shero took all the blame. Two days after losing at home to the Flyers 5–1 on November 19, Shero was dismissed and replaced in both of his jobs by 34-year-old Craig Patrick.

Shero died in November 1990 after a long battle with cancer. He was 65.

In 2013, after several failed attempts by his backers to get Shero inducted into the Hockey Hall of Fame, the Fog finally got his due.

53 Maskless Marvels

There's no doubt about it: New York is a goalie town. Always has been, always will be. Fans of the New York Rangers have always had a thing for goaltenders. Perhaps that's because there have been so many good ones over the years, dating back to the days when facial protection consisted of a five o'clock shadow and not much else.

Here's a look at some of the best and brightest from the team's first era:

Lorne Chabot (1926–28)

When the Rangers first joined the NHL, someone in the front office, probably PR man Johnny Bruno, decided that the team needed a more ethnic flavor to attract the city's rapidly growing immigrant population. So Lorne Chabot, a French-Canadian from Montreal, became the deliberately Semitic-sounding "Lorne Chabotsky" in press releases and box scores. He was not pleased.

Although Chabot and the team put that botched publicity stunt behind them, the nickname stuck with him for years.

At 6'1" and 185 lbs., Chabot was an exceptionally large player by the standards of the era, but he had terrific mobility and focus. He was honest, too. Reportedly, he turned down a sizable bribe to throw a game and immediately reported the incident to his manager and coach, Lester Patrick.

In 1927–28, Chabot played all 44 regular season games and blanked the opposition 11 times while helping New York reach the Stanley Cup Finals. But in Game 2 of that series, he was knocked unconscious by a shot and replaced by Coach Patrick. Chabot eventually made a full recovery but he lost the confidence of Patrick, who seemed to fear that the injury might leave the net-minder a bit "puck shy." So in October 1928, the Rangers traded Chabot to the Toronto Maple Leafs with $10,000 for goalie John Ross Roach.

John Ross Roach (1928–32)

At 5'5" and tipping the scales at only 130 lbs., Roach was certainly the smallest goalie ever to guard the Blueshirt cage. Appearing anxious and fidgety, he was known to be in almost constant motion in front of his net. Off the ice, at least one former team-mate described Roach as moody—hardly a novel observation when applied to goalies.

Although saddled with the redundant nickname "Little Napoleon," Roach covered enough of the net to record 13 shutouts and a 1.41 goals against average in his first Ranger season—marks that have yet to be eclipsed. He was equally stellar in the postseason, earning three more shutouts and posting a miniscule 0.77 goals against average as the Blueshirts advanced to the 1929 Stanley Cup Finals. But Roach was outplayed by Boston's stellar rookie goalie Cecil "Tiny" Thompson, earning the Bruins their first championship.

Roach started every game for the Rangers during the next three seasons, and after stonewalling the Canadiens in the 1932 semi-finals, he and the Blueshirts were back in the Cup round facing Toronto. After falling tantalizingly short of the silver chalice in his last finals appearance, Little Napoleon had a shot at redemption. What followed was one of the most lopsided finals ever played. The press dubbed it "The Tennis Series" after the Maple Leafs scored six goals in every game of their three-game sweep. That embarrassment was more than Lester Patrick could stomach, and after the season he sold Roach to Detroit.

Andy Aitkenhead (1932–34)

Lester Patrick was so eager to get John Ross Roach out of town that he was willing to rest the team's hopes on a relative unknown: rookie Andy Aitkenhead.

Nicknamed "The Glasgow Gobbler" because he was born in Glasgow, Scotland, and presumably because he gobbled up pucks like a hungry octopus, Aitkenhead arrived in New York a year earlier to take a job stopping rubber for the Can-Am League's Bronx Tigers. Accustomed to playing before sparse crowds at the old Bronx Coliseum near Webster Avenue, Aitkenhead was soon the darling of 15,000 fans at Madison Square Garden. He posted a 23–17–8 record and was equally marvelous in eight playoff appearances, winning six and recording two shutouts en route to a four-game victory over Toronto in the 1933 Stanley Cup Finals.

At just 29 and already a playoff hero, Aitkenhead looked set to be the team's goalie for the foreseeable future. But then, following a 3–2 loss to the Bruins on March 15, 1934, it was reported that Aitkenhead suffered a nervous breakdown severe enough to prompt Patrick to ask permission to borrow Ottawa goalie Alec Connell for the playoffs if his own netminder was unable to perform. Aitkenhead recovered in time to close out the regular season and prepare for another run at the Stanley Cup. His play was sharp but

Eggs a la Gump

In Gump Worsley's day, it wasn't uncommon for rowdy fans to hurl objects at opposing players. Gump was reminded of this when he returned to Madison Square Garden on March 12, 1967, as a member of the visiting Montreal Canadiens.

Worsley was in net that night for the Habs, and he surrendered the first goal of the game to Jean Ratelle at 2:45 of the first period. Moments later, a fan hurled an egg at Worsley from about 100' away, splattering the right side of his face with yolk. Dazed, Gump left the game and was replaced by his 21-year-old backup, Rogie Vachon.

The 25-year-old assailant, who had a bag of eggs with him when he was nabbed by Garden cops, got off easy when Gump refused to press charges.

the Rangers were upset by the Maroons in a best-of-three quarterfinal series.

Patrick's confidence in Aitkenhead didn't waver again until the goalie dropped seven of his first ten starts the following season. A shakeup was required, and as swiftly as his Ranger career began, the Gobbler lost his job to veteran Dave Kerr.

Dave Kerr (1934–41)

Purchased for $10,000 from the Montreal Maroons in December 1934, Dave Kerr would bring stability to a position that had been largely unsettled for the first eight years of the Rangers' existence. He became the bellwether of Ranger squads for the next seven seasons.

An amazingly durable player, Kerr would miss only one game during the entire course of his Ranger career—an incredible stretch for anyone, especially a goaltender. The pinnacle of Kerr's career was 1939–40 when the Rangers won their third Stanley Cup. He had an NHL-leading eight shutouts, a miserly 1.54 goals-against average, and eight wins in the playoffs. He also won the Vezina Trophy, the first Ranger to do so.

"Davey was tremendously important to the 1940 team," recalled his coach, Frank Boucher. "He was always in fantastic shape and was really an inspiration for the other fellows. Plus, the fans really liked him." Off the ice, Kerr was a pretty well-rounded guy. He attended McGill University, was a stockbroker in Toronto during the summer, and to keep his conditioning up and reflexes sharp, he played lots of tennis and handball.

He was also pretty protective of his eyesight. He'd wear sunglasses if it was snowing (to reduce the glare) and avoided movie theaters on game days to "save" his eyes.

And to relax, he would occasionally have a glass of wine with his pre-game meal in the afternoon. This was done in the privacy of his own home, of course, since no coach—past or present—would tolerate a player drinking alcohol before a game.

Chuck Rayner (1945–53)

Claude Earl "Chuck" Rayner had a relatively short career, but he hung around long enough to become one of the most popular Rangers of his time.

"Bonnie Prince Charlie" was voted the team's Most Valuable Player three times and won the Hart Trophy as league MVP in 1950, only the second goalie to do it. That was the season he backstopped a Cinderella Rangers squad to the Stanley Cup Finals and very nearly won it. Big for a goalie at 5'11", 190 lbs., Rayner was remarkably agile and a powerful skater who often left his net to carry the puck, an unheard-of practice at the time.

He is believed to have been the first goalie in history to score a goal in an official game. It happened in 1944 while he was playing for the Royal Canadian Armed Forces team in Halifax, Nova Scotia. He skated the length of the ice and scored. Knee problems forced Rayner into premature retirement following the 1952–53 season. In that last year, he shared duties with a hot rookie named Lorne "Gump" Worsley.

Gump Worsley (1952–63)

The late Canadian sportswriter Jim Coleman remembered the first time he saw a Gump in net at Madison Square Garden.

"He looked like a kid who had just sneaked over the fence and got into the game," Coleman said. "He had a head of closely cropped hair, the Ranger uniform flopped all over him, and he flopped all over the ice. It was just incredible what he was doing, but he still gave you the impression that he shouldn't be there… that he just sneaked in."

When Worsley won the Calder Trophy as Rookie of the Year, playing for a weak team, it proved he did belong.

In addition to New York's hockey fans, the press also loved Worsley, grateful as they were to be covering a guy as colorful and quotable as the team has ever had. Gump—the nickname came from the popular comic strip character Andy Gump—usually saved his best wisecracks for Phil Watson, his bombastic coach for three-plus seasons in the Big Apple. Short and stocky, Gump hardly had an athlete's physique. That made him a target of Watson's verbal barrages. Typically, these played out in the press.

Despite a career-long battle with his weight, Worsley was surprisingly nimble. He had to be—he routinely faced more shots than any goalie in the league. "Remember," Harry Howell noted, "we weren't exactly a first-place team at the time." Indeed, when asked once which team gave him the most trouble, Gump replied, "The Rangers."

54 Party Like an All-Star

There will always be jaded fans who'll complain that the NHL All-Star Game is a meaningless exhibition. But, as meaningless exhibitions go, it still beats the Pro Bowl.

The league held its first All-Star Game in 1934 as a benefit for injured Maple Leafs player Ace Bailey and his family, but it didn't become an annual event until the 1947–48 season. The format has changed several times over the years. Initially, the defending Stanley Cup champions would play against a team comprised of First and Second Team All-Stars from the other five clubs, plus a few extra players to make sure all teams were represented. Since 1968, the league has experimented with other formats, including East vs. West, North America vs. the World, and Team This Guy vs. Team That Guy, but the result is usually the same: lots of goals, not many hits.

It is, ultimately, a league marketing tool—a showcase of stars and their stunning skills that usually can't be displayed in meaningful competition. It's evolved from a mere game to a weekend-long party…and a big-time money-maker.

Madison Square Garden has hosted the event twice:

26th All-Star Game, January 30, 1973: East 5, West 4

By 1973, the idea that players chosen for the two All-Star teams should be the best at the time of the game, rather than the best of the players from the prior season, had quickly gained popularity. Thus, Brad Park, Jean Ratelle, Ed Giacomin, and Gilles Villemure were chosen to represent New York on the East Division squad.

Since the Bruins' defeat of the Rangers in the 1972 Stanley Cup Finals was still painfully fresh in fans' memories, Boston

Ranger All-Star MVPs

Player	Year	Host City	Notes
Don Maloney	1984	East Rutherford, New Jersey	Goal, three assists
Mike Gartner	1993	Montreal, Quebec, Canada	Four goals, assist
Mike Richter	1994	New York, New York	19 saves, two goals allowed
Wayne Gretzky	1999	Tampa, Florida	Goal, two assists
Marian Gaborik	2012	Ottawa, Ontario, Canada	Three goals, assist

players were roundly booed when they were introduced as members of the "home" team.

Bobby Orr was expecting that kind of reception, and decided to take a well-choreographed fall at center ice during pregame player introductions. The crowd got a good laugh out of it.

45th All-Star Game, January 22, 1994: East 9, West 8

Like the league itself, the 1994 All-Star Game had a very different look from games of years past. New conference names, new uniforms, and new incentive to play with intensity: a $5,000 bonus for every player on the winning team.

Led by the Rangers' "Core Four" of Mark Messier, Brian Leetch, Adam Graves, and Mike Richter, the Eastern Conference set an All-Star record with 56 shots on goal. With 19 saves on 21 shots (including four breakaway attempts by Pavel Bure) during the second period, Richter was named the game's Most Valuable Player and won a Dodge pickup truck.

If You Go...

All-Star tickets can be hard to come by. The game sells out quickly because priority is given to corporate sponsors and season ticketholders.

Since All-Star Weekend is held in a different location every year, you'll want to do a little advance scouting on the host city before planning to attend, especially if you're hoping to sample the local nightlife. Don't be duped into believing that Newark and Winnipeg will be as much fun as New York, Miami, or Los Angeles.

No matter where it's held, the event will include a fan festival for people of all ages featuring interactive games and attractions, memorabilia shows, autograph sessions with stars of the past and present, displays of NHL trophies, live TV and radio broadcasts, music, food, and lots of other things to see, do, and buy.

The night before the big game, there's always a star-studded party somewhere in town with a Grade-A catered buffet—imagine shrimp the size of your fist—live music, and plenty of VIP guests. A select few have been able to crash the party by purchasing tickets through scalpers...but you didn't hear that from us.

55 Desperate Measures

There were times during that lengthy wait between championships when the Rangers were willing to try just about anything to change their losing ways.

It was during the 1950–51 season that Herb Goren, the team's publicist, heard about a New York psychologist and hypnotist named Dr. David Tracy who had been watching the Rangers and wanted an opportunity to work with the players.

"It can't do any harm," Goren told the Rangers' general manager, Frank Boucher. Goren had a point—the team had gone winless for 12 in a row. And with causes for celebration few and far between, the occasional publicity stunt was necessary to stay on the public's radar.

Boucher reluctantly gave his blessing, hoping that at the very least, a session with the good doctor might relax his players and persuade them to grip their sticks a little less tightly.

About an hour before the next home game, Dr. Tracy came into the Rangers' dressing room and spoke in a calming, reassuring voice to each of the players...all of them except Nick Mickoski, who ran out of the room because he was afraid he was going to be hypnotized.

The Rangers played a good game that night against the Bruins, but with the score tied 3–3 in the closing minute, Boston scored the go-ahead goal and extended New York's winless streak to 13 games.

"Tracy," Boucher concluded, "couldn't put the puck in the net or keep it out any better than I could."

Then came Leone's Magic Elixir. A secret concoction of Gene Leone, owner of Leone's restaurant and a huge Ranger fan, the non-alcoholic potion was guaranteed to restore the confidence and vitality of any slumping Ranger who consumed it.

The Rangers got their first taste of the stuff one night before a home game against Detroit. A large black bottle arrived at their dressing room with a note from Gene Leone that read, "Drink it and win."

So the players sipped the brew from paper cups, then beat the Red Wings 3–2. Two nights later, they beat the Bruins 4–2. After each win, Boucher—trying desperately to keep a straight face— would explain to reporters that the magic potion provided by the restaurateur had a transformative effect on his team.

Soon, the story of Leone's Magic Elixir was all over the papers...and not just in New York. Even the Toronto press wrote about it after the Rangers earned their first road win over the Maple Leafs in three years. The team won 10-of-12 games and climbed as high as third place in the standings.

Eventually, of course, whatever psychological boost the Rangers had received from the drink, later revealed to be a simple mixture of ginger ale, orange juice, and honey, wore off and the Rangers slid back into last place.

56 Beat the Crapitals

Before we get into the Washington Capitals' successes against the Rangers, some of which are painfully fresh in our collective memory, here are a few things you absolutely must know about New York's southern-most rivals:

1. Traffic in Washington, D.C., is already among the worst in the nation. A Stanley Cup parade would bring the city to a standstill. Luckily, in 40 years of Capitals hockey, this has never been a problem.

2. The Capitals have, for much of their history, employed a logo that features the team name spelled out in all lower case letters—a lower case logo for a lower case franchise playing in a lower case sports market.

3. Capitals fans are the biggest bandwagoners in the National Hockey League. You can be sure that five minutes after their franchise player, Alex Ovechkin, abandons the Beltway for a fat, tax-free KHL paycheck and endless rivers of vodka in his native Russia, the sea of red No. 8 jerseys at Verizon Center will be washed away by a sea of empty seats…empty, save for that one pathetic soul who shows up every night to blow his stupid plastic horn. He has no place else to go.

John Pence, a lifelong Capitals fan and a season ticket holder since 2006, offers an opposing view.

Rangers All-Time Record vs. Capitals (1974–2014)

GP	W	L	T	OL
201	89	88	18	6

"I never really understood the characterization of D.C. as a bandwagon hockey town," Pence said. "People come here from all over for work, for school, and for a better quality of life. So I contend that D.C. is *not* a bandwagon sports town but rather a transient-rich sports melting pot. Much of the misdiagnosis of fair-weather fandom can be attributed to simple arithmetic. If the Rangers didn't have the luxury of a 48-year, multi-generational head start in terms of establishing history, lasting traditions, and therefore a larger fanbase than the Capitals, the perception would be different. The Capitals may not enjoy as large a following or as long a history as the Rangers, but that doesn't mean Capitals fans are any less passionate or dedicated to their team."

Although Pence freely admits that Jeff Beukeboom, Esa Tikkanen, Theo Fleury, Matt Barnaby, and Sean Avery top the list of Rangers he's wanted to see pulverized by a fleet of Waste Management trucks, he is surprisingly complimentary toward Rangers fans.

"I've found that the majority of our respective fanbases are intelligent and well-rounded in their understanding of hockey," he said. "There's nothing like sitting down with a knowledgeable student of the game to discuss the sport I play and love, and there are many Rangers fans I'm proud to call friends and teammates. I've found that, unlike fans of other teams in our division who come here, Rangers fans wear their passion on their sleeve but are usually able to keep it in check."

The Rangers-Capitals rivalry dates back to 1979 when Washington moved into the rough and tumble Patrick Division. Split up from 1998 to 2013, the teams were reunited in the absurdly named Metropolitan Division.

New York and Washington have played their share of chippy regular season games—the likes of Dale Hunter, Craig Berube, and Kevin Kaminski enthusiastically embraced the villain's role at Madison Square Garden—but the biggest fireworks in this rivalry are traditionally reserved for the postseason.

It's always a thrill when the capitol of the United States meets the capitol of the Known Universe in the Stanley Cup playoffs:

1986 Patrick Division Finals: The Rangers, who finished 29 points behind Washington during the regular season, stun their opponents, the press and themselves by winning the series in six games. Two of New York's victories come in overtime.

1990 Patrick Division Finals: Fresh off winning their first division title since 1942, the Rangers are defeated by the Capitals in five games.

1991 Quarterfinals: The Rangers take a 2–1 series lead over Washington before losing three straight. "FIFTY-ONE YEARS OF FUTILITY AND COUNTING," reads the *New York Times'* post-mortem. "CAPITALS ELIMINATE RANGERS FOR SECOND STRAIGHT YEAR."

1994 Semifinals: Neil Smith had to admit that beating the Capitals in the playoffs was something he wanted very badly. "They're a monkey I'd like to get off our backs," he said. Smith got his wish in 1994, though Washington put up a much tougher fight than the 4–1 series result would indicate. Series highlight: Midway through the second period of the Rangers' 3–0 win in Game 3, Caps tough guy Keith Jones tries to goad Esa Tikkanen into taking a penalty. A smirking Tikkanen responds by planting a kiss right on the bridge of Jones' nose.

2009 Quarterfinals: The worst postseason collapse in Rangers history. The Capitals complete their comeback from a 3–1 series deficit, beating the Rangers 2–1 in Game 7. Series highlight: John Tortorella throwing a water bottle then brandishing a stick at a drunken Caps fan who may or may not have poured beer on him.

2011 Quarterfinals: After the top-seeded Capitals lose Game 3 in New York, their coach, Bruce Boudreau, rips Madison Square Garden on a D.C. radio station. "The reputation of being in Madison Square Garden is what makes it famous," he says. "Also, our building's a lot louder." With the Rangers leading 3–0 in Game 4, Rangers fans start chanting "Can you hear us?" at Boudreau. Their smugness is quickly negated when the Caps storm back to win 4–3 in double-overtime. Washington goes on to win the series, four games to one.

2012 Semifinals: Marian Gaborik scores in triple-overtime to win Game 3. The Rangers come back to tie Game 5 on a goal by Brad Richards with only 6.6 seconds left in regulation before Marc Staal wins it in overtime. Washington receives strong goaltending from Braden Holtby throughout the series but is outdueled by Henrik Lundqvist. The Rangers win Game 7, 2–1.

2013 Quarterfinals: Different year, same result. Washington's top line of Alex Ovechkin, Nicklas Backstrom, and Marcus Johansson is held to just three goals in the series, and Lundqvist posts back-to-back shutouts in Games 6 and 7. Derick Brassard, acquired at the trade deadline from Columbus for Marian Gaborik, leads the Rangers with a series-high nine points (two goals, seven assists), all compiled during the final five games.

57 Trader Phil

Phil Esposito had a tough decision to make: stay in broadcasting and potentially have a job forever, regardless of whether the Rangers won or lost, or accept Garden management's offer to replace Craig Patrick as general manager of the Rangers and await his turn to get fired.

He chose the latter.

On July 14, 1986, one of the greatest (and most outspoken) players in NHL history gave up the security of a gig as TV color commentator to satisfy a competitive streak that served him well during an 18-year Hall of Fame career as a player with Chicago, Boston, and New York. Phil was also going to double his salary, no small incentive in taking the post.

Although he lacked managerial and coaching experience, Esposito was extremely aggressive in trying to transform the Rangers into a winner. He was also a natural-born salesman and used that ability to the fullest throughout his tenure during which he pulled off so many trades and other roster moves that he soon became known in the hockey world as "Trader Phil."

He'd only been on the job for a couple of weeks when he traded goalie Glen Hanlon and two draft picks to Detroit for Kelly Kisio, Lane Lambert, and Jim Levins, and a draft pick; acquired Walt Poddubny from Toronto for Mike Allison; signed a pair of former Rangers in Lucien DeBlois and Doug Soeteart; and inked college free agents Mike Donnelly and Norm MacIver.

But what Esposito felt the Rangers needed, more than anything else, was a player like Gary Carter of the New York Mets—a franchise cornerstone. An established star to build around. A proven winner. As early as 1986, he identified Edmonton's Mark Messier as such a player. Capitalizing on the Oilers' well-documented financial problems, he negotiated a trade for Messier that would have cost the Rangers Kisio, John Vanbiesbrouck, Tomas Sandstrom, a second-round draft pick, and $5 million in cash. Espo's excitement turned to disappointment when Garden management refused to let him include that much cash in the deal. A couple of years later, he tried to make a similar deal for Wayne Gretzky, only this time the Oilers asked for $15 million. Again, Espo's bosses balked.

Trader Phil vs. Trader Neil

When it came to dialing up their fellow GMs to talk trades, who had the itchier finger: Phil Esposito or his successor, Neil Smith? According to nhltradetracker.com, Esposito completed 43 trades in three seasons for an average of 14 per season. Smith made 102 trades in 11 seasons as GM for an average of nine per year.

Esposito started taking some heat from fans and the press for his seemingly incessant roster reshuffling. As much as he was fond of saying that he didn't care what anyone thought about him, Phil didn't always handle criticism well.

"My first year with the team," recalled the Rangers' former equipment manager, Jocko Cayer, "Phil traded Tommy Laidlaw to Los Angeles for Marcel Dionne. One morning, I'm in early making coffee, and Phil comes in. He says, 'Lemme ask you a question— what do you think of the trade?' And I said to Phil, 'Do you think that this trade will benefit the hockey club?' He said yes. And I said, 'Then end of story.' He knew a lot of people were pissed about the deal, but I reminded him that people were going to get pissed any time he did anything. That's the way it is. There are a jillion people out there who think they know more about hockey than you do. And as it turned out, the Rangers got the better of that deal."

One of Esposito's most high-profile moves was the hiring of Michel Bergeron, "Le Petit Tigre," as coach in June 1987. As Bergeron was still under contract with the Quebec Nordiques, Esposito had to negotiate some form of compensation with the Nords' team president Marcel Aubut. They settled on $100,000. Later, Espo learned that in separate discussions, his bosses had also agreed to send Quebec a first-round draft pick. He was livid.

"The next day," he said, "in the papers all I read was that I had given Quebec too much for Michel Bergeron."

Their relationship began smoothly enough, with Esposito suggesting to his new coach that he might try coaxing Guy Lafleur out of retirement to play for the Rangers. Bergeron thought it was a good idea. Phil was pleased that they seemed to be on the same page.

It was all downhill from there.

"Esposito and Bergeron were very much alike," said hockey historian Bruce "Scoop" Cooper. "Temperamental, sometimes intemperate, demonstrative, passionate, impetuous, ardent, ambitious, egocentric, self-indulgent, affable, and sentimental. Not surprisingly, neither man was very good at taking a backseat to the other—nor to anybody else—and over the next two years, that would lead to plenty of fireworks. The media circus in New York loved it, of course."

"I wouldn't say Phil had a thin skin," Cayer said, "but he's Italian and he'll hold a grudge. He and Bergy butted heads all the time because Bergy knew who he was going to play and he stuck with his guys. Phil was bringing guys in when they were at the end of their careers and they couldn't f---ing play anymore, like Brad Maxwell. We had enough guys like that on the team already."

What really set Esposito off, more than anything, was when Bergeron went over his head to complain to Rangers team president Jack Diller. Espo tried to fire him, but Diller wouldn't let him. The team was winning.

When he found it had happened again, late in the 1988–89 season, Esposito hopped on a plane to meet up with the team in Pittsburgh to fire Bergeron personally. The Rangers were on a 43–10–0 slide at the time, so Diller didn't stand in the way. But he did insist that Phil take over as coach.

Esposito was behind the bench for the last two games of the regular season (both losses) and the opening round of the playoffs against Pittsburgh. Although he had veteran goalies Vanbiesbrouck and Bob Froese at his disposal, Esposito summoned rookie Mike Richter to New York and decreed that he wouldn't hesitate to start the kid against the Penguins. Three consecutive Ranger losses prompted Esposito to make good on his threat and on April 9,

1989, Richter became the first goalie in club history to make his NHL debut in a Stanley Cup playoff game. Espo's decision to start a rookie in an elimination game drew harsh criticism, even more so after Pittsburgh swept the series.

In the three years since Esposito had replaced Craig Patrick, the Rangers had gone through three full-time and three interim coaches, had a sub-.500 record, and won just two playoff games.

On May 24, 1989, the ending that Esposito had expected from Day 1 on the job arrived in the form of a visit to his office from Jack Diller, accompanied by a pair of Garden security guards.

"Phil," Jack said, "we're making a change."

58 The 2012 Winter Classic

If there were any hockey fans who dismissed as gimmicky the concept of an outdoor regular season NHL game, they have surely been won over by now by the Winter Classic, an event envisioned by Gary Bettman to challenge college football for bragging rights as America's favorite New Year's Day sporting event. Amazingly, it has done just that.

The Winter Classics played so far have been among the most-watched hockey games ever. The first, in 2008, featured the Buffalo Sabres versus the Pittsburgh Penguins at Ralph Wilson Stadium.

After a few years—and a second appearance by Sidney Crosby's Penguins—Rangers fans started getting restless. When was the team from the world's No. 1 sports market going to get a turn?

In September 2011, the league formally announced that the Flyers would host the Rangers at Citizens Bank Park in Philadelphia at the 2012 Winter Classic. The even better news was that the lead-up to the game would be chronicled on the HBO series *24/7*.

Playing on a rink that stretched from first base to third base, the Rangers made the league's fifth Classic event a memorable one, beating the Flyers 3–2 to hold their place atop the Eastern Conference standings.

Like any great spectacle, this one was full of secondary story-lines and subplots, including:

Milbury's Flub

During a live pregame interview with Bob Costas that aired nationally on NBC, analyst Mike Milbury tried to explain how the Rangers had shed their once-soft reputation to become one of the toughest, hardest-working teams in the league. "These aren't the Blueshirts from Broadway anymore," Milbury said in as earnest and respectful a tone as he could muster, "they're the Blueshits from the brickyard."

Come again?

The knee-jerk reaction of some viewers who caught Milbury's slip of the tongue was that it was no slip but an intentional dig at the Rangers. That, of course, is utter nonsense.

Would he have preferred not to use profanity on national television and risk a reprimand from NBC? Absolutely. But did the man who once climbed into the stands of Madison Square Garden to brawl with Rangers fans lose any sleep over his gaffe? Probably not.

Marc Staal's Return

At an impromptu pregame press conference, Coach John Tortorella announced that Marc Staal, who missed the first 36 games of the season due to lingering effects from a concussion he suffered on a hit by his own brother, Carolina's Eric Staal, nearly 11 months earlier, would make his season debut in the outdoor game.

View of the stadium during the singing of the Canadian National Anthem prior to the 2012 NHL Winter Classic between the New York Rangers and the Philadelphia Flyers at Citizens Bank Park in Philadelphia, Pennsylvania, on January 2, 2012. (Cal Sport Media via AP Images)

The 24-year-old defenseman, who had actually written off the possibility of playing in the Winter Classic, was pleasantly surprised to be cleared by his doctor to participate in full-contact drills about a week before the game.

Tortorella wisely brought Staal along slowly, limiting his ice time to just more than 12:00—about half of what he usually played.

"My first shift," Staal said afterward, "I felt lost. I was a bit of a wreck there, but as the game wore on, I felt more and more comfortable."

Rupp to the Rescue

Signed in July 2011 to add some size, toughness, and experience to the forward ranks, Mike Rupp had been having a frustrating first year in New York. The former Devil suffered a knee injury in training camp that hampered him all season.

The Rangers were trailing 2–0 late in the second period when Rupp rifled a shot past Flyers goalie Sergi Bobrovsky then celebrated the goal by mimicking ex-Ranger Jaromir Jagr with a salute to the crowd. Early in the third period, Rupp tied the game for New York with a soft snap shot taken from a bad angle. Brad Richards scored what turned into the game-winner with 14:39 still left to play.

Half of all the goals Rupp ever scored as a Ranger were scored in that game. He was traded the following season to the Minnesota Wild.

Conspiracy Theories

Tortorella questioned several calls that were made—and not made—by referees Ian Walsh (a Philadelphia native) and Dennis LaRue late in the game, including a penalty shot that was awarded to Philadelphia with 19.6 seconds left in regulation.

Ryan McDonagh dove into the crease to corral a loose puck behind Henrik Lundqvist, but he was called for covering the puck in the crease. Lundqvist stopped Danny Briere on the penalty shot attempt, and the Rangers hung on for the win.

After the game, an enraged Tortorella called the officiating "disgusting" and suggested that NBC and the NHL might have been in cahoots to get the contest tied and drag out the drama.

Although he'd later apologize and dismiss his comments as ill-timed sarcasm, Tortorella was slapped with a $30,000 fine by the league…or roughly 12 times what the average player could expect to pay for elbowing an opponent in the head. Seems fair.

59 Moscow on the Hudson

Much credit has been given to all the former Edmonton Oilers and Chicago Blackhawks on the 1993–94 Rangers. Receiving less fanfare was another, smaller subgroup that, in hindsight, had greater historical significance: Sergei Nemchinov, Alexei Kovalev, Sergei Zubov, and Alexander Karpovtsev, were the first Russians to have their names engraved on the Stanley Cup.

Although he ranked among the Soviet Elite League's scoring leaders, Nemchinov wasn't cut from the same mold as flashier stars like Alex Mogilny and Pavel Bure. The big centerman was considered a defensive player whose leadership skills and sense of loyalty suggested he was also a person of character.

Neil Smith, general manager of the Rangers, took Nemchinov in the 12th round of the 1990 draft on the off chance he would be able to get Sergei released from his commitments back home. Smith initially tried waving some green in front of Red officials, but they showed little interest in negotiating for Nemchinov's services. Pressed on whether he might encourage the player to defect, the Ranger boss coyly replied, "I can't have any influence in that. And if I did, I wouldn't admit it."

Making his NHL debut in 1991, Nemchinov proved to be a far better scorer and stickhandler than anyone expected. He was an ideal trailblazer because he made everyone in the organization believe that Russians could be good teammates. It was something that Canadians and Americans who grew up during the Cold War were only going to learn from experience.

Kovalev couldn't have been more different from Nemchinov in terms of playing style and personality. Unlike the disciplined and grim-faced Soviets who dominated international hockey throughout the Cold War, Kovalev was a free-spirited, spotlight-adoring kid who had, as Smith once termed it, "the curse of great talent."

The first Russian drafted in the first round (15th overall in 1991) might have gone a few picks earlier had he not still been bound to his club team, Moscow Dynamo. But when the Soviet Union crumbled, Kovalev made his way to America to play for the Rangers, the team he'd followed since childhood.

The 6'2", 220-lb. forward was so strong on his skates that it was almost impossible to knock him over…unless, of course, he felt like taking a tumble to draw a penalty. He had a deft passing touch, a hard and accurate shot, and no shortage of confidence.

The "curse," in Alexei's case, was having all the physical tools to be a megastar but not understanding that games are won on goals, not style points. That was a lesson Smith and the Ranger coaches tried to hammer home during Kovalev's rookie season in 1992–93 when his poor defensive play and habit of overhandling the puck—like a game of keep-away with everyone on the ice— finally earned the likable but stubborn youngster a demotion to the minors.

Irina Cytowicz Tesoriero, who served as the Russians' interpreter, remembers Kovalev as the troublemaker of the group.

"Whenever he did an interview," she said, "he would purposely wait until I had a mouth full of food and then wait on me to answer. He was waiting for the food to come flying out of my mouth."

Irina can laugh about that time in 1991 when she helped Kovalev buy a car. She wasn't laughing then.

"Alex wanted a black convertible," she recalled. "He was so tall he was having trouble fitting into cars, and we finally found a car in Smithtown, Long Island: an Oldsmobile Cutlass Supreme convertible. It was black, black, black. He fell in love with it. I drove him back out to the dealership to pick it up and he was so excited. And I said, 'Okay, but you have to follow me home.' On the drive home he kept fooling around and pulling ahead of me. I rolled down the window to tell him not to do that because it gets congested near the Throgs Neck Bridge. Lo and behold, he makes a wrong turn at the split and misses the turn to go over the bridge."

Irina panicked. Kovalev didn't know the area and barely spoke English.

"I was thinking, *Oh my god! I just lost Neil Smith's star rookie in New York*. I pulled up to the toll booth and asked if they'd seen him and they said, 'Do you know how many cars go through here each day?'"

She called the Ramada up in Armonk where he was staying. Then she called Mike Gartner.

"I had to tell him that I lost Alex," she said. "And he said, 'What do you mean? He doesn't speak English and has no idea where's he going. How do I tell Roger Neilsen about this?' Other players were calling all over the place."

By now, it had been more than three hours since Alex ditched Irina on the thruway.

"I was hysterical," she said. "I called the police. Then I finally got through to his room at the Ramada and this maid kept saying, 'He no here.' I tried to leave my phone number but she kept repeating the same phrase, 'He no here, he no here.' Now it's going on four hours."

Using the Empire State Building as his navigational tool, Alex drove past LaGuardia, over the George Washington Bridge, through the Lincoln Tunnel, and back to Madison Square Garden. From there, he was able to get back to his hotel.

"He finally calls and says, 'I wanted to be alone in my car.' I said, 'Couldn't you have told me?'"

For one season at least, Kovalev found an unlikely fan in Coach Mike Keenan, a man not generally known for his patience. Iron Mike loved Alexei's enthusiasm for the game. He liked to tell the story about how he once left Kovalev on the ice for multiple shifts to teach him a lesson, but it backfired because Alexei thought he was being rewarded with more ice time.

It's hard to imagine Russian hockey icon Vladislav Tretiak being as animated after any of his world championships as Kovalev was after winning the Stanley Cup. With lucky troll doll in hand and drenched in champagne, Alexei bounced through the victors' locker room wearing a grin so big it seemed to envelope his entire face.

Like a great point guard in basketball or a strong midfielder in soccer, Zubov was able to control the tempo of a hockey game. Although his Ranger career was brief—a scant three seasons—he made the most of his time in New York.

Among the best stickhandling defensemen in the history of the NHL, Zubov was a superb passer who excelled at working the puck out of his own zone before spearheading a counterattack. His arsenal included an accurate and powerful slap shot, but he was just as comfortable threading a gorgeous pass through traffic to the open man as he was letting one rip from the point.

Before arriving in North America, Zubov spent four years on the Central Red Army club, a team he was groomed to join from childhood. There he played with some of the biggest names in Russian hockey, including Sergei Makarov, Igor Larionov, Slava Fetisov, and Vladimir Konstantinov.

"That Red Army club was great," he said. "I'd say we could easily outmatch any team on the planet—not just in the Russian league. It was just amazing to play with guys like Larionov and Fetisov. Even the guys of my generation like Sergei Fedorov, Pavel Bure, and Alex Mogilny—they were all unbelievable individuals. It was hard not to learn from them. I'd just watch, listen, and try to do the same thing."

But at the end of the 1991–92 season, the club failed to pay its players, triggering a mass exodus to the NHL. By then, Zubov had already been drafted by the Rangers and informed his parents that if an opportunity to play in New York presented itself, he would go.

Using buddy Nemchinov as an interpreter, Zubov met with Neil Smith in a Moscow hotel room and signed his first NHL contract. He and Kovalev were on a plane to New York a few days later.

The Russian rearguard arrived to find that the Rangers didn't have room for him, so he ended up with their AHL affiliate in Binghamton. Since players of Zubov's caliber tend not to stay in the minors very long, he soon joined the varsity on Broadway.

His all-around play (and conditioning) improved markedly under the watchful eye of Mike Keenan, who delivered this ultimatum to the young defenseman early in the 1993–94 campaign: shape up or go back to Binghamton. Zubie responded to Keenan's threat by leading the Rangers with 77 assists and 89 points, many of those scored during the man-advantage. With Zubov at one point and Brian Leetch at the other, the Rangers' power play was lethal.

Karpovtsev was a reliable, defense-first blueliner with great strength and the willingness to play tough against the toughest players. In his six Ranger seasons, "Potsy" was a second/third pairing defender whose subtle contributions were often overlooked. It wasn't until the 1997 playoffs that his presence—or lack thereof—was fully felt.

The Rangers were battling injuries that spring but had managed to split the first two games of the Eastern Conference Finals against Philadelphia. Coach Colin Campbell sent Karpovtsev and defense partner Ulf Samuelsson over the boards every time the Flyers' big captain, Eric Lindros, was on the ice.

But when Karpovtsev left the team to return to Russia to attend the funeral of his mother, the Rangers had to regroup. No matter who Campbell sent out against Lindros, No. 88 was pretty much able to do whatever he wanted. His hat trick in Game 3 powered the Flyers to a 6–3 victory and swung momentum in the series in Philadelphia's favor. The depleted Rangers had no chance.

Tragically, Karpovtsev was killed in the September 2011 air disaster in which a plane carrying players and staff of the KHL's Lokomotiv hockey team crashed near the Russian city of Yaroslavl. Karpovtsev was one of the team's assistant coaches. Former Ranger defenseman Karel Rachunek and onetime Ranger draft pick Jan Marek also died in the crash that claimed the lives of 43 of the 45 people on board.

60 The Barstool GM

The Rangers are on a two-week Western road trip to open the season because the Garden is being "transformed"…again. You decide to hit the streets in search of a venue where you can watch the game in the company of your fellow Rangers fans. Here are some of Gotham's finest:

Blarney Rock Pub
137 West 33rd Street, New York, New York
(212) 947–0825
www.blarneyrockpub.com
"Everybody is going to family restaurants these days," lamented *The Simpsons'* cantankerous bartender Moe Szyslak. "Seems nobody wants to hang out in a dank pit no more." Like the fictional Moe's Tavern, the Blarney Rock Pub just wouldn't be the same without "the dank." Established in 1969, this local landmark is an authentic neighborhood bar, not some glistening Times Square tourist trap.

Framed Ranger jerseys adorn the walls, and there are plenty of TVs scattered throughout so you won't miss any of the action. In the old days, the Rock was a favorite hangout of NHL referees like Bruce Hood. Must-have menu item: Owner Tom Dwyer—a Ranger fan since 1948—recommends the Full Irish Breakfast (eggs, sausage, Irish bacon, black and white pudding, grilled tomatoes, baked beans, and potato).

Blondies Sports
212 West 79th Street (between Broadway and Amsterdam), New York, New York
(212) 362–4360
www.blondiessports.com
Blondies is a classic, Upper West Side sports bar with great staff and no shortage of TVs. You get the best of both worlds here: an electric atmosphere when the big game is on, and a mellow, laid-back vibe the rest of the time. Owner Ken Hartmann wants Rangers fans to know they're always welcome. "The beauty of Rangers fans is that it's mostly a blue-collar fan base. I love the Rangers. As long you hate anything Boston, I can be your buddy." Must-have menu item: The wings are outstanding but you will not find a better boneless Buffalo chicken tender anywhere in the city. Pair up some with a basket of waffle fries.

Café 31
220 West 31st Street, New York, New York
(212) 695–5966
www.cafe31nyc.com
A Nicky Fotiu favorite! Directly across from the World's Most Famous Arena, Café 31 is packed with fans having pregame meals on nights when the Rangers or Knicks are at home but quite a bit less busy when they're on the road. The best reason to watch a

game here is the layout and an abundance of TVs. Most sports bars in the city can get a bit cramped but Café 31, being more restaurant than bar, has to be bigger to accommodate all the tables. The staff is among the friendliest around. Must-have menu item: Keep it simple and stick with drinks and nachos.

The Flying Puck

364 Seventh Avenue (between West 30th and 31st Streets),
New York, New York
(212) 736–5353
www.theflyingpuck.com

Is this a Ranger bar? Well, they have a stained glass Ranger logo on the ceiling, so you be the judge. Located just a half-block from Madison Square Garden, the Flying Puck opened in 2009 with a clear objective—to give the city's hockey fans a watering hole they could call their own. If you go, go early, because the Puck can get a little tight on game nights. Must-have menu item: A robust selection of draught beers and kickin' Buffalo wings are an unbeatable combination.

Hudson Station Bar & Grill

440 Ninth Avenue, New York, New York
(212) 244–4406
www.hudsonstation.com

Located on the edge of Hell's Kitchen, Hudson Station features 25 HDTVs and two projectors spread out over three floors. Hudson Station has hosted viewing parties and player autograph signings in cooperation with webleedblue.com. Must-have menu item: Hudson Station is a gastropub, so the menu trends toward high-end interpretations of familiar pub fare. Try the pulled pork sandwich with Chef Matt's famous Carolina-style BBQ sauce. Save room for their Cookie Smash (baked cookie dough topped with ice cream).

Manny's On Second

1770 Second Avenue (between 92nd and 93rd Streets),
New York, New York
(212) 410–3300
www.mannysonsecond.com
At last count, Manny's had more than 40 HDTVs, so it's virtually impossible for you to be here on a game night and not be able to watch the Rangers. Must-have menu item: Buffalo wings are Manny's signature dish.

The Molly Wee

402 Eighth Avenue at 30th Street, New York, New York
(212) 967–2627
www.themollywee.com
Just one block south of Madison Square Garden, this prototypical Irish Pub is a favorite hangout of Dancin' Larry. Must-have menu item: Imagine our disappointment when we ordered the Leprechaun Soup and learned it was not made from real Leprechauns. Next time, we're ordering the Chicken Delight (grilled chicken breast, crispy bacon, melted mozzarella, and BBQ sauce on a hero).

Slattery's Midtown Pub

8 East 36th Street, New York, New York
(212)683–6444
www.slatterysmidtownpub.com
A two-for-one drink special during weekend Ranger games (as long as you're wearing Rangers gear or carrying a ticket to the game) lets you know this revered sports bar is serious about catering to Rangers fans. In 2013, the pub hosted a live viewing party with Ron Greschner. Must-have menu item: Try the Maryland crab cake appetizer and the Dublin-style fish and chips.

Stout

133 West 33rd Street, New York, New York

(212) 629–6191

www.stoutnyc.com

Stout is a massive place but has enough semi-private nooks and crannies to provide a more cozy sports-bar vibe. Screens are large and plentiful. The beer selection is outstanding. Must-have menu item: Of all the standard pub fare, you'll want to try one of Stout's many gourmet burgers. There's a burger for every palate, even vegetarian.

Warren 77

77 Warren Street (between Greenwich and West Broadway), New York, New York

(212) 227–8994

www.warren77nyc.com

Rangers fans come in all shapes and sizes, and Warren 77 should appeal to the fan who wants to watch a game in a more laid-back, lounge-like environment. Co-owned by Sean Avery, this unassuming Tribeca meeting place opened in 2009 as a "sports bar with a sense of style." Imagine a cookie-cutter chain like ESPN Zone, and now imagine the exact opposite. With a decor inspired by old New York, Warren 77 is a sports bar that purposefully defies classification and attracts an eclectic clientele. The three-dimensional wooden mural chronicling New York's rich sports history might be one of the coolest works of art in the city. Flat-screen TVs are cleverly hidden behind sliding panels when not in use. Must-have menu item: The meatball sliders are almost good enough to make you forget the Rangers haven't had a legitimate power play point man since Brian Leetch.

61 John Amirante

It's part of the ritual, the tradition, of attending a Rangers game, and it begins with an announcement over Madison Square Garden's public address system.

We ask that you please rise and remove your caps for the singing of our National Anthem. And now, please welcome John Amirante.

He's been at it for more than three decades, this soft-spoken Bronx native who, as a kid, daydreamed of performing at the Garden...but not as the anthem singer.

"I always envisioned myself here as a player," Amirante said. "We played roller hockey in the streets and made our own rinks. I had a close friend who was also into hockey. We used to go to games at the old MSG and get a student discount. I remember watching Edgar Laprade. I used to emulate him when I played in the street. I wore No. 10, just like him. My buddy, who was a goaltender, would say he was Chuck Rayner."

By the 1970s, John was working in the North Tower of the World Trade Center at the naval architecture firm owned by John McMullen. In 1979, McMullen purchased the Houston Astros.

Amirante's coworkers knew he moonlighted as a singer—he sang at Ron Gilbert's wedding—and they encouraged him to try out to sing the National Anthem at Shea Stadium when the Astros came to town to play the Mets. Weeks later, on August 2, 1980, Amirante was belting out the anthem behind home plate at Shea in front of 50,000 people.

"After that, I contacted MSG and sent in a tape," he said. "They called me back and rattled off the dates for three Ranger games and two Knickerbocker games. I was thrilled. I'd only asked to do one game."

New York Rangers favorite John Amirante sings the National Anthem with the NYPD before the game between the New York Rangers and the Boston Bruins at Madison Square Garden in Manhattan, New York, on November 19, 2013. The Bruins defeated the Rangers 2–1. (Cal Sport Media via AP Images)

His first game at the Garden was on November 2, 1980, Kings at Rangers.

"When I stepped out onto the ice, I said to myself, 'Oh my God, a dream has come true,'" he recalled. "When I finished, I got a tremendous round of applause. I came off the ice and the production coordinator at the time, Paulette La Melle, came over to me and said, 'You were great!' That was really nice to hear."

The Los Angeles Kings won that night 6–3, but John was in Heaven just the same.

In 1982, McMullen bought the Denver-based Colorado Rockies, moved the team to New Jersey, and renamed it the Devils.

Amirante sang the first-ever anthem at a Devils game, but when a contract offer to be the team's permanent anthem singer followed, Amirante politely declined. His heart belonged to the team on the other side of the Hudson.

He's been with them ever since, and on a verbal contract. There's nothing in writing.

"The feeling I get is tremendous," he said. "The fans are great. I love doing it, and I know they love me doing it. I feel I've been blessed."

62 Derek Being Derek

On the ice and off, Derek Sanderson couldn't resist being the center of attention and getting into trouble. The titles of his two autobiographies—*I've Got To Be Me* and *Crossing the Line*—convey the devil-may-care essence of the man.

Emile Francis knew what he was after when he acquired Sanderson from the Boston Bruins in exchange for center Walt McKechnie on June 12, 1974: grit and character. He got both, and then some.

"I knew that our team at the time needed some new blood," Francis recalled, "so I went after Derek. Hey, he had won two Stanley Cups with the Bruins, and he always played great in the playoffs and always played great against us. At the time, I thought it was a terrific fit."

Years earlier, in Boston, Derek was called "Little Joe," a reference to Joe Namath, the flamboyant leader of the New York Jets with whom Sanderson would later open a nightclub on the Upper East Side.

> ## Noise Pollution
> "Air horns were very common at the Garden in the 1970s. So many fans complained that they were finally banned. The teenager who sat in front of me used one every game. His name was Mike Mesaros and he later became one of the original members of the rock group The Smithereens."
>
> Stu Dolgan, East Windsor, New Jersey
> Rangers fan since 1962

Like they did with Namath, New York fans developed a great fondness for Derek, if only for a short period of time. They loved his bold, abrasive style of play but also his *chutzpah*, which anyone who drives a Rolls Royce, wears a full-length fur coat, and parties with Playboy Playmates must have in spades.

While many Rangers lived out in Long Beach near the team's practice rink, Derek made his home in Manhattan. He reveled in the New York nightlife where one didn't need a reason to celebrate. When you were out on the town with Derek, every night was New Year's Eve…and he was happy to pick up the tab.

Judging by his extravagant lifestyle—the WHA's Philadelphia Blazers once made him the highest paid athlete in the world—it was clear that money wasn't of great importance to Sanderson. Anyone who didn't believe that before witnessed it with their own eyes one night in 1975 at Il Vagabando, the players' favorite Italian restaurant on East 62nd Street. Derek was dining out with a group of teammates and instead of agreeing to split the check, as was customary, he pulled out some cash to pay for everyone. Rod Gilbert objected. The next thing everyone knew, Sanderson had a lighter out and he was burning a $100 bill…a foreshadowing of dark days to come.

Sanderson played 75-of-80 games in his first season as a Ranger, and he contributed solidly, if not spectacularly, with 25 goals and 25 assists. The next season, he played only eight games before Francis shipped him off to the St. Louis Blues in exchange for a first-round draft choice that turned out to be Lucien DeBlois.

By then, Sanderson was losing a battle with drug addiction and alcoholism, a battle that nearly killed him after his hockey career ended. He flushed away his fortune and wound up penniless and in poor health. But with the help of former teammates, chief among them Bobby Orr, Derek beat his addictions and found work first as a sportscaster and then—irony of ironies—as a financial advisor for pro athletes.

63 L'Affaire de Lindros

They didn't know it at the time, but when the Rangers lost the battle for the rights to Eric Lindros in 1992, it might have been a blessing in disguise.

Labeled "The Next One," Lindros was the most hyped prospect to come out of junior hockey in a decade. The 6'4", 229-lb. center was blessed with the size and vision of Mario Lemieux and the fearlessness and physicality of Mark Messier.

But any team that drafted Eric would also be drafting Carl and Bonnie Lindros, the ultimate hockey hover parents whose meddlesome ways had been driving coaches and other parents nuts from the time Eric was an adolescent. If they didn't think Eric's wingers were quite up to par, or if Eric wasn't getting enough power play time, they wouldn't hesitate to pick up the phone and give some poor soul an earful.

The Quebec Nordiques were expected to use the first overall pick at the 1991 NHL Entry Draft to select Lindros. But Eric made it abundantly clear to the Nordiques that he would never play in Quebec due to a laundry list of concerns: the city, the language, the culture, the organization, etc. "I want to go where Eric Lindros will be happy," he would say, referring to himself in the third person.

The Nordiques drafted him anyway. And, true to his word, Eric refused to sign with them and returned to his junior team, the Oshawa Generals. His agent and his parents asked the Nords to trade his rights, but they weren't going to be coerced by an 18-year-old kid and his handlers. As far as the Nordiques were concerned, Lindros could rot in Oshawa.

The stalemate lasted until January 1992 when the Nordiques, who had to sign or trade Lindros by June 1993 or risk having him go back into the draft, decided to start fielding serious offers for the stubborn superstar. The Rangers' Neil Smith reportedly put in an initial bid that was deemed inadequate, but six months later Smith sweetened it as only a general manager desperate to end his team's 52-year Stanley Cup drought could. In exchange for the rights to Lindros, the Rangers offered Tony Amonte, Alexei Kovalev, John Vanbiesbrouck, Doug Weight, two first round draft picks, *and* $12 million in cash. Although marathon talks hadn't resulted in a deal, both Smith and Quebec GM Pierre Page came away sensing they were very close.

Unbeknownst to Smith, the Nordiques had already reached a tentative deal with the Flyers—but they continued negotiating with the Rangers.

Toronto arbitrator Larry Bertuzzi (a relative of Todd Bertuzzi) was called in to resolve the matter, ultimately ruling in Philadelphia's favor.

Had Bertuzzi ruled in favor of New York, would the Rangers still have won the Stanley Cup in 1994? Perhaps, perhaps not. With Lindros in the lineup, the Rangers might not have missed the playoffs in 1993, in which case there would not have been any reason to pursue Mike Keenan to coach.

"A player like Lindros comes along only once a decade," Smith told an interviewer several years later. "When you have an opportunity, you owe it to your fans to try. If another opportunity were to present itself for a player like that, I'd do it again."

Still, it was also Smith who once said, "There's no such thing in hockey as one player so dominant that he's worth all the problems he might bring." Especially if those problems are named Carl and Bonnie.

Nine years and at least four concussions later, Lindros became a Ranger—acquired from Philadelphia on August 20, 2001, for Jan Hlavac, Kim Johnsson, Pavel Brendl, and a third-round draft pick.

64 Herb Brooks

In a touch of irony, the man Craig Patrick hired on June 4, 1981, to take over the Rangers' bench was the same man who had hired him a little more than two years earlier to be his top assistant with the gold medal–winning U.S. Olympic Hockey Team: Herb Brooks. By leading that group of underdog collegians to their "Miracle on Ice" at Lake Placid, Brooks had become probably the best known and most highly praised coach in any sport in the nation.

When Herb returned to the United States in 1981 after a brief coaching stint in Europe to work in New York, the world's biggest and most important professional sports market, it naturally created quite a buzz. It also quickly returned the Rangers to being one of the highest profile clubs in pro sports. Unfortunately for both the new coach and his team, however, at the same time three of the Rangers' Patrick Division rivals—the Islanders, Flyers, and Capitals—were also then among the top teams in the NHL.

No Broadway Encore for Brooks

After the Rangers missed the playoffs in 2001–02, GM Glen Sather fired Coach Ron Low and began the search for a replacement. One of the people he interviewed was Herb Brooks, who had been out of coaching for a few years but expressed interest in returning to the NHL as long as it was with the Rangers. He was briefly the frontrunner for the job but eventually withdrew his name from consideration, possibly because he had second thoughts about being away from his family back in his native Minnesota. Sather eventually hired Bryan Trottier. The following August, Brooks died in a motor vehicle accident north of the Twin Cities. He was 66.

Herb implemented a hybrid system that incorporated a crisscrossing, European-style of playmaking and good old North American–style checking. The Rangers needed something new because the Patrick Division of the early 1980s might have been the most competitive in hockey. In their first season under Brooks, the Blueshirts improved by 18 points to 92 and earned second place in the division only to fall to the Islanders in the Division Finals.

Realizing he couldn't treat professional players like college kids, Brooks adjusted his approach to focus more on each man as an individual. In the early going, most responded well.

"When Herb Brooks came in my second year," Tom Laidlaw recalled, "he pulled everybody to center ice one day after practice at Playland. He was giving one of his preseason speeches, telling each player what his role was. When he came to me, right in front of the whole team, he said, 'Laidlaw, if you get the puck, give it to somebody else. You're not supposed to have it.' The guys got a chuckle out of that. It was kind of harsh, but he was sending a message in a funny way that I didn't have a whole lot of offensive skill. At the same time, Herbie also gave me a heck of a lot of confidence because he treated me very well and gave me a big role on that team."

Brooks and Ron Duguay, on the other hand, was hardly a marriage made in heaven. The two inevitably clashed, Brooks the disciplinarian and Duguay the freewheeling kid who had become a celebrity and teen heartthrob on Broadway.

Doogie's habit of coming late to practice, a $50 fine for each offense, was particularly galling to Brooks. Late in the 1982–83 season, Duguay was late again. He paid his fine and promptly asked a trainer how many practices were left for the season. "Four," he was told. Doogie brashly wrote a check for $200. That summer, he was traded to the Red Wings.

The Rangers had their best regular season under Brooks in 1983–84 when they won 42 games and amassed 93 points but still finished in fourth place behind the Islanders, Caps, and Flyers. After two seasons of advancing to the Patrick Division Finals, this time the Rangers didn't make it past the semis, knocked out by the Islanders for the fourth consecutive year.

The next season, Brooks' Rangers went into a tailspin after the team was hit with a tidal wave of injuries. Tensions ran high as he tried to keep the team afloat and in the playoff hunt. Then, in early January 1985, Brooks was quoted in a *New York Times* story in which he called team captain Barry Beck a "coward" and criticized the big defenseman for not playing up to his full potential. The two men moved quickly to patch up their differences, but it damaged Herb's credibility in the dressing room and was an unnecessary distraction.

Behind the scenes, too, Brooks was embroiled in a power struggle with Craig Patrick. Herb felt he needed more say over player personnel decisions and clearly did not like being subordinate in those matters to a general manager who had once been his assistant coach. It was a significant role reversal that altered the dynamic of their relationship. It also bothered Herb that Patrick didn't place more of the blame for the team's problems on injuries.

By mid-January, the Rangers were stuck in fifth place with a record of 15–22–8 after an ugly 7–1 loss in Washington on January 19, 1985.

Brooks, who came to New York to engineer another miracle but went out of his way to never get anyone's hopes up, was fired two days later.

In a rare interview with Brooks' biographer, John Gilbert, Mark Pavelich looked back at his five Ranger seasons and thought about how things might have been different. He also disputed criticism that Brooks' time in New York had been a failure.

"It was really unfair," Pav said, "because we were a really good team under Herbie, up in the 90-point range, and the only problem we had was that the Islanders were always there."

65 The Czechmates

In the blackest night, a pinpoint of light can shine as brightly as the sun. Maybe that's why, during the darkest of dark ages for the Rangers, the Czechmates seemed so luminous.

Or maybe they were just that good.

In January 2000, in an effort to ignite the slumping Petr Nedved, Coach John Muckler had a brilliant (but in hindsight, obvious) idea: why not slide his struggling center between fellow Czechs Radek Dvorak and Jan Hlavac? The trio clicked immediately. In his first game with new wingers, a 3–2 win over the Maple Leafs, Nedved scored his first goal in 13 games and won 12-of-19 draws.

That might not sound like a big deal, but at the time the Rangers and their fans had to be satisfied with small victories.

Despite often having the highest payroll in hockey, the team missed the playoffs every year from 1998 to 2004. Coaches came and went and aging veterans dragged their dispirited bodies from one end of the ice to the other while the splendor of 1994 got smaller and smaller in the rearview mirror.

But with their instant chemistry and creativity, the Czechmates became one of the hottest lines in hockey. They brought excitement and an ounce of hope back to the Garden at a time when there was precious little of either.

Nedved, the playmaker, was the engine that made the line go. He'd played for the team once before, during the lockout-shortened 1994–95 season, and simply ran out of time to alter people's perception of him as a skilled but soft player who wouldn't battle through checks and put in the dirty work that is part of winning. He was eventually traded with Sergei Zubov to the Penguins for Luc Robitaille and Ulf Samuelsson.

There was something unmistakably different about Nedved now, and the Rangers noticed it immediately. The tall, lanky kid they had discarded three years earlier was gone, and in his place was an older, tougher competitor who no longer shied away from the physical aspects of the game but actually thrived on going head-to-head with the league's top forwards.

Dvorak was one of the four or five fastest skaters in the game and a natural scorer who didn't score often enough for Florida Panthers coach Terry Murray, prompting his trade to New York. But in 2000–01, the right winger's first full season as a Ranger, "Devo" broke out with a career-high 31 goals and 67 points.

Hlavac was the finisher—a good skater with great hands and an accurate shot. His 28 goals and 64 points in 2000–01 were also career-highs.

Together, the Czechmates—or "Czech Posse" as they liked to call themselves—carried the Rangers offensively for the better part of two seasons. They were also surprisingly effective defensively, often matched against the opposition's top line because they could cycle the puck in the offensive zone and thus prevent the other team from scoring against the Rangers.

Off the ice, the three were thick as thieves, dining on sushi or taking in Knicks games when the Rangers had the night off. Both of the younger Czechs viewed Nedved as something of an older brother—someone who could help them get acclimated to the big city and let them crash in his apartment until they found more permanent lodging.

Since one-line hockey teams are rarely successful, a roster shakeup was inevitable. In August 2001, the Czechmates were broken up when Hlavac was included in a multiplayer trade with the Philadelphia Flyers for Eric Lindros.

66 Howe He Got Away

Oh, how different the Rangers' fortunes might have been had the legendary Gordie Howe chosen to begin his pro hockey career in New York instead of Detroit. It almost happened.

In 1934, the Rangers moved their training camp to Winnipeg, Manitoba. This coincided with the establishment of the Lester Patrick Hockey School in that city, which would become the proving ground for an entire generation of Rangers players. Teenagers would come to the Patrick School and essentially try out for spots in the organization. If Patrick and the Ranger scouts liked them, they would be signed and often end up playing with the New York Rovers, an amateur team that also played at the Garden. This helps explain why so many great players from the city of Winnipeg, most notably Andy Bathgate, ended up playing for the Blueshirts.

Gordie was only 15 (but 6' tall and 200 lbs.) when he and a group of friends from Saskatoon, Saskatchewan, drove more than 400 miles to Winnipeg to attend camp at the Patrick School in 1943.

Up until then, Howe had never been out of Saskatoon except to play one game in Regina…and it showed. Alf Pike, a Rangers veteran nicknamed "The Embalmer" because he'd once been a licensed mortician, took the kid under his wing.

"[Pike] would get me into the food line at the hotel so I could be sure to get something to eat," Howe recalled. "I was so backward then, I'd just sit in the background and watch everyone else."

Yes, Gordie was lonely and feeling a bit overwhelmed in his first NHL camp, but that's not why he left. Nor is it true that the Rangers cut him. In fact, management saw great potential in Howe and sat him down to discuss their plans for him. First, they wanted to get his signature on a form that would've given the Rangers exclusive rights to negotiate a contract with him down the line. Then they wanted him to go to the Notre Dame School, a parochial school in Saskatchewan, to work on his hockey skills. Their thinking was that, from there, he could transition into their farm system and eventually make the varsity in New York.

"The first thought I had was, *I'm not Catholic*," Howe explained. "And the second thought was, *I'd be going to a regimental school awfully far from home.* Heck, I decided I'd rather go home, and that's what I did."

The following year, Howe was invited to the Detroit Red Wings' camp. When told he'd get to play with friends from Saskatoon on the Wings' junior team in Ontario, Howe committed himself to the Detroit organization. He'd make his NHL debut in 1946 and spend the next 25 seasons in a Red Wings uniform.

Would Gordie have gone on to become the cornerstone of a Stanley Cup dynasty in New York, or ended up a "Lone Ranger" like Bathgate—a superstar who'd spend most of his career shackled to mediocre teams? We'll never know.

67 The Comeback

Trailing the favored Penguins 3–1 in the 2014 semifinals, the Rangers were on the ropes and pretty much written off by all but their most fanatical followers. The Blueshirts, who'd won the first game in overtime before dropping three straight, had never come back from a 3–1 deficit to win a playoff series in their 87 seasons. Nor had they won a series against the Penguins in any of their four previous meetings.

When the Rangers arrived in Pittsburgh the day before Game 5, they learned that France St. Louis, mother of Martin St. Louis, had died unexpectedly from a heart attack at the age of 63. Marty immediately left the team to be with his family in Montreal. But believing that France would not have wanted her son to miss such an important game, the St. Louis family encouraged Marty to rejoin his teammates. The next day, he returned to Pittsburgh and was in the lineup for Game 5.

"You want to play hard for a guy like that who's coming from such a tragedy," Marc Staal said. "You want to rally around it."

And rally the Rangers did, outplaying and outworking the Penguins in a 5–1 win.

St. Louis' father and sister were in attendance for Game 6—on Mother's Day—at Madison Square Garden. In the first period, they watched as Matt Niskanen's clearing attempt bounced off

St. Louis' leg and past Penguins goalie Marc-Andre Fleury. No highlight goal, to be sure, but an emotional one for Marty. And it sparked the Rangers to a 3–1 win.

Yes, the passing of France St. Louis was a catalyst in the Rangers' resurgence, but there were others of equal significance. Start with the man between the pipes for New York, Henrik Lundqvist, who made 35 saves in Game 7—some of them otherworldly—in fending off the panicking Pens. He was brilliant in protecting New York's tenuous 2–1 lead late in the third, stopping Evgeni Malkin and James Neal at point-blank range.

And in limiting the regular season scoring champ, Sidney Crosby, to just one goal and two assists in the series, the Rangers effectively neutralized Pittsburgh's most dangerous offensive weapon.

If you know anything about the Rangers-Penguins rivalry, then you can appreciate why knocking the NHL's golden boys off their perch was so satisfying for the Rangers and their fans.

A Protected Species

The Penguins joined the NHL in 1967 but didn't share a division with the Rangers until 1981–82. Before tanking the 1983–84 season so they could finish last and draft Mario Lemieux, the Penguins were the definition of an irrelevant hockey club and a distant, distant third in local fan support behind the Steelers and Pirates. Flightless waterfowl suited them well as a mascot.

Lemieux's rapid ascension to superstardom saved pro hockey in Pittsburgh but also created rivalries where none existed before. The Rangers and other Patrick Division foes employed any and all tactics to contain Mario, and the Penguins did what they needed to do to protect their franchise player. Opponents who dared target No. 66 did so at their own peril, risking retribution from his teammates or the heavy hammer of discipline from the league.

On October 30, 1988, at Madison Square Garden, Rangers defenseman David Shaw chopped at Lemieux with his stick in retaliation for an earlier crosscheck. Lemieux dropped to the ice for several minutes while fights broke out all over the ice. He eventually left the game with a bruised sternum and did not return. Everyone else spent the closing minutes slashing each other and fighting. The third period took an hour to complete as referee Andy Van Hellemond assessed 18 major penalties, including a match penalty to Shaw. Nine players were ejected. After the game, which the Rangers won in a 9-2 rout, Garden security actually ordered taxis into the building and up the ramp so the Penguins could exit the arena in safety. Shaw was eventually suspended 12 games for the hit on Lemieux, the third-longest ban in league history up to that point.

The following April, the Penguins had all the motivation they needed to sweep the Rangers out of the 1989 semifinals.

By 1992, Mario and the Penguins were defending Stanley Cup champs. Their biggest obstacle to repeating would come from Mark Messier and the Presidents' Trophy–winning Rangers. In Game 3 of the 1992 Patrick Division Finals, Adam Graves slashed Lemieux across his left glove. It was a routine play for the time, but Lemieux crumpled to the ice in agony.

"[Adam] took a good swing at him, there's no question," Brian Leetch recalled, "but I knew he hit him in the glove. So my initial reaction was that Mario was overreacting and trying to draw a bigger penalty." It wasn't until later that X-rays confirmed Lemieux had a broken hand.

Graves received a two-minute minor penalty for the slash that some conspiracy theorists, Lemieux chief among them, believed had been ordered by Rangers coach Roger Neilson. The league suspended Graves four games—an excessive ban. He wasn't surprised to receive supplemental discipline but was stunned by accusations that he'd intentionally injured another player.

With Lemieux out, the Rangers won Game 3 and appeared to be headed to a commanding 3–1 series lead in Game 4 with

Rangers All-Time Record vs. Penguins (1967–2014)

GP	W	L	T	OL
258	120	105	23	10

a two-goal lead when the unthinkable happened: Ron Francis fired a harmless shot on goal from the neutral zone that went on edge and squeaked through Mike Richter's pads. Just a minute and a half later, Troy Loney tied the game for Pittsburgh 4–4. Neilson changed goalies, but John Vanbiesbrouck surrendered the game-winner to Francis at 2:47 of overtime. Building off the momentum of that come-from-behind victory, the Penguins won the series in six games and, in fact, never lost again that postseason.

When it came to torturing the Rangers, it seemed that nothing could slow down Super Mario...not even cancer. In January 1993, he left the Penguins to undergo treatment for Hodgkin's lymphoma. He returned four months later and on April 9 scored five goals in a 10–4 blowout over the Rangers at Madison Square Garden. One of New York's most hated rivals received a rare standing ovation for that performance.

Three years later, in the 1996 semifinals, the Rangers were completely overmatched by Mario and Jaromir Jagr, who combined for 15 goals in a five-game rout.

Le Hypocrite

As owner of the Penguins, Lemieux has spoken passionately and publicly about enforcing rules on obstruction and harsher punishments for players who attempt to injure opponents. Those comments would sound reasonable if they hadn't come from the employer of Matt Cooke, one of the dirtiest NHL players in recent memory. Cooke was suspended in March 2011 for concussing Ryan McDonagh with an elbow to the head.

A Parent's Nightmare

"In February 1999, my wife, who is also a Rangers fan, gave birth to our first child. We named her Destiny and made sure that she was baptized in a Rangers jersey. At her baptism, my wife, myself, and my stepdaughter all wore our Rangers jerseys. Years later, as Destiny learned about hockey, she came to me and said, 'Daddy, I like the Penguins. They're cool!' I immediately called my lawyer friend, wanting to sue the doctor who delivered her. God does have a sense of humor."

James Valenzano, Maricopa, Arizona
Rangers fan since 1970

John Tortorella, furious over Brooks Orpik's dangerous knee-on-knee hit on Derek Stepan just one year later, said what so many in and around the hockey world were thinking when he called the Penguins "one of the most arrogant organizations in the league." Then he singled out Pittsburgh's two "whining stars," Crosby and Malkin.

"They whine about this stuff all the time," Tortorella fumed, "and look what happens. It's ridiculous, but they'll whine about something else over there, won't they? Starting with their two f---ing stars." Tortorella was fined $20,000 for that outburst.

"I don't doubt that [Crosby] gets the benefit of some calls," one longtime Penguins insider said. "Virtually every superstar does. He did a lot of yapping at officials early in his career, and I think that's where the reputation is rooted. I don't happen to believe it's accurate because I see what kind of beating he absorbs on a nightly basis. But when you're a high-profile guy who isn't shy about expressing yourself to the officials, that reputation is likely to develop. Funny, though, that a guy like Ron Francis, who yapped about every single infraction for which he was ever called, never got a reputation like the one Crosby has. Not sure why that is, frankly."

68 Down and Out in Broadway Blue

The trappings of fame—being young, rich, feeling invincible—can drive athletes to make some pretty bad choices. Pile on the pressures that accompany a high-profile occupation and whatever demons they might be lugging around from their past, and it's almost a miracle that every one of them isn't in rehab.

Most find healthy ways to cope with those stresses. Some bend. A few break. A tiny fraction break so badly that their troubles get aired out in public, bringing embarrassment to themselves, their families and their teams.

Don Murdoch was on the fast track to stardom, but in an era of excess, a career that began with so much promise was derailed by substance abuse.

Injuries limited the Ranger rookie to 32 goals in a season that saw him finish runner-up to Atlanta's Willi Plett for the 1977 Calder Trophy. The future looked bright for the hotshot that teammates nicknamed "Murder."

But as he embraced all the perks and pleasures that came with being a star for the Rangers, Murdoch's frequent partying began to affect his job. He was suspended by Coach Fred Shero for missing a team flight to Detroit after he'd been out all night doing God-knows-what. There were times when his own teammates were afraid to be on the ice with him because he was still half in the bag.

"One time, [John Ferguson] took Murdoch in the back room and smacked him," Phil Esposito recalled. "I also did that once. I told him, 'Straighten up, you son of a bitch,' and I slapped him across the face. He was numb. When he was clear-headed, he was a heck of a hockey player. He pissed away what could have been a great, great career."

In August 1977, Murdoch was caught at the Toronto airport with almost five grams of cocaine, becoming the first NHL player to be charged with drug possession. Years later, he admitted that the strain of his newfound fame had turned a drinking habit into a drug addiction. After pleading guilty to the charge, Murdoch was suspended for the entire 1978–79 season by NHL president John Ziegler. The sentence was later cut in half for good behavior.

Murdoch returned to take part in the 1979 playoff run and had some success playing on the "Godfather Line" with Esposito and Don Maloney, but he had done irreparable damage to his image in the eyes of the Rangers' brass. When the partying got out of control again, it was clear that his days in New York were numbered. The next season, Murdoch was traded to Edmonton where he played on a line with Dave Semenko and a young Mark Messier. He had a last shot with the Detroit Red Wings before ending his career in the minors.

"Donnie was a great talent, an unbelievable goal scorer, and just an absolutely great guy in the room," said Mike McEwen, who teamed with Murdoch for three seasons in New York. "He was one of the funniest guys around, telling stories. If he had taken better care of himself, he would have had a great career. He just burned the candle at both ends."

Like Murdoch, **Kevin Stevens** had no enemies. His warmth, generosity, and sense of humor were as renowned as his deft scoring touch around the net, which allowed him to amass 329 career goals over the course of 15 seasons. Wayne Gretzky and Mario Lemieux were among Stevens' closest friends in the game.

There were reports that the Rangers knew Stevens had a drinking problem when they acquired him in 1997 from the Kings in exchange for Luc Robitaille, but they were willing to take a chance on him anyway because he'd spent some time at an L.A. rehab facility.

Even if Stevens was clean when the 1999–2000 season began, his career was headed south in a hurry, and he knew it. He was among the team's highest earners but wasn't producing. Depressed, he started drinking again. Then he hit rock-bottom. Following a 4–1 win over the Blues in January 2000, Stevens was arrested at a seedy motel in Collinsville, Illinois, with a prostitute, her pimp, and the remnants of somebody's crack cocaine binge. At the time, Stevens was married with two children, with a third one on the way.

That episode was the humiliating wakeup call Stevens needed to put his life back on track. He got clean, played briefly for the Flyers and Penguins, and retired in 2002. He stayed in the game as a broadcaster and scout.

Theo Fleury signed with New York as a free agent in 1999. At 5'6", the former Calgary Flame was at one time the smallest player in the league, but his intensity, fearlessness, and high level of skill made him a star. Fleury was leading the Rangers with 30 goals and 74 points in February 2001 when he unexpectedly left the team to enter the league's substance abuse program.

Drugs, alcohol, gambling, strippers...you name the vice, and Theo blew money on it, as much as $50 million, by his own estimates.

Back in uniform for the Rangers in 2001–02, he notched his 1,000[th] career point with a pair of assists against Dallas on October 29 and scored 20 goals through the first three months of the season playing on the "FLY Line" with Eric Lindros and Mike York. Unfortunately, the inner demons the feisty forward had battled for so long resurfaced, and it showed in his erratic behavior. He walked out on the team during the third period of a game in Pittsburgh and then, moments after being ejected from a game in San Jose, punched out team mascot Sharkie.

It wasn't until after he retired as a player that Fleury began to open up about some of the likely causes of his addictions, including his abuse as a teenager at the hands of junior coach Graham James. Fleury has found a new career as a motivational speaker, sharing his story of recovery.

69 "Darth" Sator

After parting ways with Herb Brooks in 1985, the Rangers turned to another American to fill their coaching vacancy: Ted Sator.

Like Brooks, Sator was a product of U.S. college hockey, having both played and coached at Bowling Green State University. But unlike Brooks, Sator—rumored to have beaten out more than 20 other candidates for the job—promised to be the kind of coach his players could talk to. He had a reputation for stressing the fundamentals and had recently worked as an assistant under Mike Keenan in Philadelphia. Plus, he spoke Swedish fluently! At first blush, there was a lot to like about the tall, ruggedly handsome 35-year-old from Utica.

Sator's brief turn as coach of the Rangers is notable for the speed with which he got results—the team advanced to the 1986 Conference Finals but was defeated by the eventual champion Montreal Canadiens—and the haste with which players under his command were banished to the minors, fled the country, or chose retirement rather than spend another second playing for him.

Sator introduced a new dump-and-chase brand of hockey that some of the skill players found stifling. And despite all his talk about being the kind of guy players could relate to, Sator proved to be anything but. He seemed to have two settings: cold and distant, or mean enough to make a grown man cry.

Ye of Little Faith

"My first game at The Garden without my parents was a win for the Rangers and for me. I had some money left over, so I bought an entry into the section pool. To get in on the pool, you paid a few bucks to pick a piece of paper out of a bag. Each piece of paper had a uniform number written on it, and if that player was the first one to score, you won the pool. I pulled No. 29, Reijo Ruotsalainen. I thought, 'Well, there goes a couple of bucks.' But then Sexy Rexi put one in from the point. I was so excited the Rangers scored, I almost forgot I won the pool."

Ed Stein, Gallatin, Tennessee
Rangers fan since 1973

"Ted was such a perfectionist," Don Maloney said, "you worried too much about making a mistake."

"He had trouble with older players," Ron Greschner said. "We were almost the same age, making more money. It was tough for him to handle. He reacted to it by benching players and humiliating them."

Reijo Ruotsalainen got so fed up he went back to Finland. Mark Pavelich and Barry Beck quit the team. Nick Fotiu, Glen Hanlon, Pierre Larouche, Brian MacLellan, Stephen Patrick, Peter Sundstrom, and Mike Rogers were among the other veterans who showed themselves to the door or were forced out.

"Ted Sator took the team to the Conference Finals," Beck said, "so he must have been a good coach. But players are professionals and should be treated as such. Everyone needs a kick in the ass once in a while at every level of hockey, even the NHL. But you do it with respect. That's the one word you will hear more than any other during the season: respect. Some players thought Ted didn't do that, so they left. I was one of them. Players don't mind criticism, but you've got to do it right."

When Phil Esposito replaced Craig Patrick as general manager of the Rangers, he initially opted to keep Sator as his coach. But

Espo held Sator responsible for the mass exodus of veterans like Beck and Pavelich and was annoyed that other players he'd gone to the trouble of acquiring couldn't crack Sator's lineup. That, and the stark differences in the two men's personalities and approach to the game suggested that this was a relationship that probably wouldn't last. And, of course, it didn't.

Sometimes when a coach gets fired, pro athletes express disappointment or a sense of guilt over having let him down. A reporter making the rounds to get players' reactions to Sator's firing in November 1986 discovered this was not one of those times.

Said Willie Huber, "There's no guilt here."

70 Build Your Own Rangers Fan Cave

You're a rabid Rangers fan in need of a room to watch games in comfort and privacy—your own little Miniature Square Garden.

One could easily sink $50,000 into a project like this, and some high-rollers surely have, complete with NHL-licensed leather home theater seating, a state-of-the-art sound system, and an Aaron Voros lookalike to serve drinks (or, for a few bucks more, the real Aaron Voros).

But you shouldn't have to choose between creating a Rangers-themed refuge from the ravages of the work day and putting a kid through college. Here are some tips on how to build a respectable Rangers fan cave on a modest budget:

Plan it Out

First, choose the room that's about to be redecorated (or, in Gardenspeak, "transformed"). Have an extra bedroom? A finished

Mudge's Square Garden

Perhaps the most famous Rangers fan cave anywhere belongs to Bill Mudge of Commack, New York. In 1998, Bill completed Mudge's Square Garden, a basement hockey shrine billed as "Home of the Boys in Blue." It features stadium seating from the old Commack Arena (former home of the Long Island Ducks), a turnstile from Playland, a full bar, and countless pieces of Rangers memorabilia.

"During the playoffs, we'd have all kinds of hockey stuff hanging up around the house," Bill recalled. "My wife suggested that we move it all to the basement. It was getting to be a disaster, so I agreed. We did all the work ourselves, from putting in the seats to hand-painting the floor to look like the ice at MSG. I've got sticks signed by Mike Richter and Adam Graves, a glove signed by Mark Messier and some of the other guys from '94, a Wayne Gretzky jersey, a Henrik Lundqvist jersey...lots of other stuff. It's basically full now."

Bill had season tickets for 23 years but had to give them up due to rising costs. He'll never have that problem at Mudge's Square Garden which, he's proud to say, has hosted the Stanley Cup on more than one occasion.

"When Craig Campbell and Phil Coffey from the Hockey Hall of Fame came in and saw the basement, they said it was the best hockey place they've ever seen," Mudge said. "And they've been in millionaires' houses, too."

basement? In the long run, square footage will be less important than finding a space that can be sufficiently compartmentalized and sealed off from the rest of humanity.

Make some rough sketches of what you want your fan cave to look like. You're not Leonardo da Vinci, so don't worry if your crude doodle isn't a work of art. It's just to help you build a visual of the room before you start populating it with stuff.

Take some measurements, too. As much as you would love to hang that framed Zdeno Ciger jersey your brother (who doesn't watch sports) gave you for your birthday, sadly there might not be room for it.

Think about colors, too. A blue, red, and white motif screams Rangers, but your memorabilia is more likely to stand out in a neutral color scheme. Don't underestimate the power of taupe!

Everyone Loves a Bargain

One fan's junk is another fan's treasure. Websites like eBay and Craigslist can be useful in finding affordable Rangers bric-a-bracs to decorate your fan cave. Here you will find jerseys, photos, pennants, pucks, posters, old equipment, and a million other novelty items you never knew existed. A Rangers Stanley Cup PEZ dispenser? Sure, why not.

If you decide to go the eBay route, try shopping during major holidays and obscure hours such as the middle of the night when people are less likely to be trawling the internet for Mark Messier bobblehead dolls. Fewer bidders equals lower prices. And of course, be wary of dishonest sellers. If someone auctions off a jersey that looks like it has been dragged behind the Seventh Avenue Local but is described as "new without tags," keep shopping.

It's not the best site to browse for sports collectibles, but Craigslist might be a good option if your fan cave needs furniture. There are always sweet deals to be had on couches, chairs, coffee tables, entertainment centers, etc. Sometimes, people are so eager to rid themselves of these items, either because they're moving or upgrading, that you can get them for free. That's right, free.

Be Creative

How about a hockey stick hat rack to show off all your Rangers caps? All you need is a drill, an old stick (preferably wood), hardware to mount it on the wall, and a few hooks or pegs to hang the caps. Don't pay $45-$75 for a premade rack when you can make one just as good at a fraction of the cost.

There are plenty of other great ideas for do-it-yourself projects on websites like Pinterest, where we discovered a hockey stick Adirondack chair.

Don't Rush It

Madison Square Garden wasn't built in a day. Neither will your fan cave. Take your time and grow your collection gradually, if need be, to get the biggest bang for your buck.

71 Leapin' Lou Meets His Match

It wasn't a fight so much as a dismantling of one player's face by another.

Leapin' Lou Fontinato—he got his nickname from hopping all over the ice when he thought he'd been unfairly penalized—was among the most feared enforcers of his time and the first NHL player to rack up 200 penalty minutes in a season. That made Gordie Howe's pummeling of the rambunctious Rangers defenseman at Madison Square Garden all the more surprising.

Howe was involved in a scuffle near the Rangers' net with Fontinato's teammate, left wing Eddie Shack, when Louie barreled halfway across the rink to take on the Red Wings star.

"I saw Louie coming at me," Howe recalled years later, "thinking he was swinging at a dead target. He didn't know I saw him out of the corner of me eye. I slipped my hands out of my gloves, just holding onto them with my fingertips, and waited 'til he threw his right hand at my head. Then I moved and he missed, thank God."

Fontinato's first punch didn't hit its mark, but he managed to get in a few hard shots before Gordie, holding off the Ranger with his left hand, returned fire with his right in a series of devastating uppercuts that broke Fontinato's nose and dislocated his jaw. Howe hit Fontinato so hard that Howe dislocated a finger.

Concerned for his own safety, referee Art Skov stood back and let the fight take its course. "Howe," Skov recounted, "cleaned Fontinato like you've never seen."

One media report from the day described Fontinato's face by saying, "It looked like he ran the 100-yard dash in a 90-yard gym." Indeed, his nose appeared to have been smeared halfway across his face.

Both men played the rest of the game, but when it was all over and the teams boarded a train for a rematch in Detroit, Fontinato stayed behind in a New York hospital so a surgeon could repair his mangled nose and badly bruised face. There he was photographed by *Life* magazine, and the picture of him peering out through bandages that almost completely covered his face, like a mummy, ran in the magazine two weeks later.

"Howe needn't think he's Jack Dempsey just because he put me here," *Life* quoted a defiant Fontinato.

The fight further solidified Howe's reputation as a great player who did not need anyone to stand up for him, though after bloodying Fontinato, he rarely had to drop his gloves again.

Louie, whose colorful career ended when he suffered a broken neck while playing for the Canadiens in 1963, was as defiant as ever when *The Hockey News* reached him at his beef farm in Campbellville, Ontario, 40 years later to talk about the famous fight. He still refused to concede defeat.

"It was no worse than a draw," Louie said. "No way. I'm sure I must've thrown a few punches to go that far."

72 Draft Day Hits and Misses

More than one NHL general manager has described the annual Entry Draft as a crapshoot—sometimes you hit, sometimes you miss. When choosing from among the hundreds of eligible young prospects, the best that any team can hope to do is make an educated guess.

Different teams employ different strategies. Some use the draft to fill an immediate, specific need, though most adhere to the philosophy that it's wiser to take the best player available because a team's positional needs can change rapidly and a young player chosen today might not be ready to step in for another three or four years.

The Rangers' director of player personnel, Gordie Clark, orchestrates the team's draft efforts. Gordie won't discuss specific players—club policy—but he did shed some light on the challenge of developing players in an environment where they can be crushed beneath the expectations of others.

"There's a hype that the media can build up about a player," Clark said, "and sometimes it's their parents or their agents that say the kid can play in the NHL. All of a sudden, they put that pressure on them. And then the reality kicks in that it's tough to play in the NHL. Some guys get traded away because of it. How many never play for the team that drafted them? It's always been in our game that we get so high on them and then down on them. You have to be patient, especially with these young guys in the minor leagues. That's the name of the game. You have to develop these guys to get them ready. We can't just buy them."

It's Gordie's job to be patient, to not rush to judgment on young players who might be late bloomers. Fortunately, the authors are under no such obligations.

Miss: Dylan McIlrath (10th overall, 2010)

Expending a pick this high on a blueliner known more for his fighting ability than his skating, defensive zone coverage, or offensive skill, will rank as one of the Rangers' great draft day blunders… especially after the Anaheim Ducks chose offensive defenseman Cam Fowler two picks later. In 2014, on the same day the Hartford WolfPack were giving away McIlrath "bobblefist" dolls, Fowler scored a goal for Team USA at the Winter Games in Sochi.

Hit: Ryan Callahan (127th overall, 2004)

Callahan posted impressive numbers as a junior player with the Guelph Storm and was projected to be a top-nine NHL forward. But his intangibles—work ethic, intelligence, versatility—were off the charts. Callahan would have been selected two or three rounds earlier had teams known what he would bring to an NHL locker room.

Miss: Hugh Jessiman (12th overall, 2003)

The 2003 draft was stocked like the MGM Grand buffet. It was virtually impossible not to come away satisfied. But the Rangers shocked the crowd by choosing Jessiman, a 6'6", 220-lb. forward out of Dartmouth College. Until he finally laced up his skates for the Florida Panthers in February 2011, "Huge Specimen" had the dubious honor of being the only player selected in the first round of that draft who hadn't played a single game in the NHL.

Hit: Henrik Lundqvist (205th overall, 2000)

It's not every day you discover a future Hall of Fame goaltender in the seventh round. This could be the pick of the decade, the century, and the millennium.

Miss: Pavel Brendl (fourth overall, 1999)

Neil Smith traded up to draft Brendl, a goal-scoring right wing from the Czech Republic who played junior hockey in Calgary.

Envisioned as a potential franchise forward, Brendl came to training camp the following year out of shape. He never played for the Rangers and in 2001 was traded to the Flyers as part of a package for Eric Lindros. Factor in the selection of center Jamie Lundmark ninth overall and a bevy of other prospects who never played in the NHL, and the 1999 draft might be the Rangers' worst ever.

Hit: Sergei Zubov (85ᵗʰ overall, 1990)

Zubov was often criticized by Coach Colin Campbell for his poor positional play and for taking too many risks. Then again, Zubov was a fifth-round pick who led his team in scoring four years after he was drafted. The Rangers gave up on him too soon.

Miss: Michael Stewart (13ᵗʰ overall, 1990)

Michigan State defenseman spent several years in the minor leagues before continuing his career in Europe. He never played in the NHL. Players drafted after Stewart in 1990 include Keith Tkachuk (19ᵗʰ overall to Winnipeg) and Martin Brodeur (20ᵗʰ overall to New Jersey).

Hit: Reijo Ruotsalainen (119ᵗʰ overall, 1980)

Dynamic though undersized offensive defenseman was a threat to score every time he stepped on the ice. Occasionally used at left wing, Rexy was one of the fastest skaters in the league.

Miss: Al Blanchard (10ᵗʰ overall, 1972)

Blanchard's stock was high going into this draft because he'd scored a lot of points playing on a line in Kitchener with future Flyers star Bill Barber. He spent a few years toiling in the minor leagues before retiring as the only first-round pick from the 1972 draft never to have played in an NHL game.

73 9/11

On the morning of September 11, 2001, the Rangers were scheduled to take their physicals at Madison Square Garden in preparation for the start of their first training camp ever held in New York City when word broke of the horrific terrorist attacks on the World Trade Center and the Pentagon.

Players were originally slated to stay at a Marriott right at the foot of the twin towers beginning on September 10. For logistical reasons, arrangements were changed a week earlier. Much of the hotel was destroyed when the South Tower collapsed.

The city, the entire nation, was shaken to its core by the events of that day. Players were like anyone else who lived or worked in New York in that they either lost friends in the attacks or knew others who had.

In the weeks that followed, Mark Messier showed once again why he was such an inspirational leader. The Rangers captain stressed to teammates the need not only to mourn the victims, but also to get back to the routine of hockey because that would be the best therapy for them and for their grief-stricken fans.

On September 28, Mike Richter, Eric Lindros, and a small group of front office staff joined Messier for a surprise visit to Ground Zero to honor the victims and to salute the workers laboring at the site. They brought hats, T-shirts, souvenirs, anything that wasn't nailed down, and distributed them to the workers.

"They were still trying to recover bodies," Messier recalled. "We were there when the firemen and policemen would come back and tell the families, who were in a waiting room, whether they had found anybody. It was an incredible experience to see the pain of those people."

The Rangers didn't want any press coverage on this particular public relations outing—it was meant to be a private affair—but they got some anyway when Canadian media recognized Messier.

"Mess isn't that easy to hide," Richter said.

Nine days later, the Rangers played their regular season home opener at the Garden against the Buffalo Sabres. During a pre-game tribute to the victims, the first responders and all those still working around the clock at Ground Zero, Mark was handed the helmet of Ray Downey, a fallen fire chief. A visibly touched Messier donned the helmet then flashed his famous smile as the Garden erupted in cheers.

The Rangers and Sabres both wore special jerseys with "New York" written diagonally across the chest that were later auctioned off to raise money for the 9/11 victims fund.

For a few hours at least, the 18,000 fans in attendance could focus on something other than the feelings of pain and helplessness that had consumed them for nearly a month.

Messier, who had pledged that the Rangers would dedicate their 2001–02 season to the first responders, set up the game's first goal, which happened to be Lindros' first as a Ranger. Taking their cue from their charismatic leader, the Blueshirts went on to beat the Sabres 5–4 on an overtime goal by Brian Leetch.

The victory capped off an emotional evening but it was just the beginning of the Rangers' involvement in the city's post–9/11 healing. They continued to honor victims and heroes throughout the season and beyond. Following the last home game on the schedule, Messier gave the jersey off his back to Rosalie Downey, Ray Downey's widow.

74 Superfans

Every team in every sport has that one fan who everybody knows by name—someone whose enthusiasm for and devotion to the home team has earned them a degree of local celebrity. The Rangers have had many such fans over the years.

Bob "The Chief" Comas was an eccentric character from Brooklyn who took his job as unofficial team mascot *very* seriously. For more than 20 years, Bob wandered around Madison Square Garden wearing his trademark feathered headdress, shaking hands, whooping, and doing a war dance when the Rangers scored a goal. Between periods, he'd come down from his seat in the blues to entertain fans in the lower bowl by contorting his body to spell out R-A-N-G-E-R-S. Chief had his share of hecklers, some of whom would try to pluck out the feathers from his headdress, but most fans saw him for what he was—a harmless obsessive who just desperately loved the team. Chief took off his headdress for the last time in 1995, one year after the Rangers won the Stanley Cup. He passed away in 2009 at age 62.

Another lifelong fan, **Steven McDonald**, was a New York City police officer shot in the line of duty when he was 25 years old. He was left paralyzed as a result. During McDonald's recovery in the hospital, he passed the time by watching videotapes of Rangers games. Players who visited him to lift his spirits came away inspired by his strength and courage. In 1987–88, the Rangers created the Steven McDonald Extra Effort Award "for the player that goes above and beyond the call of duty." McDonald is there every spring to congratulate the winner, as voted by the fans.

Ceil Saidel was hardly a character—more of a fixture, really—and the team's No. 1 fan for more than 50 years. Ceil was an original member of the Rangers Fan Club and did everything the fan club ever needed. She went out of her way never to bother the players, from Andy Bathgate, Lou Fontinato, and Rod Gilbert to Eddie Giacomin, Mark Messier, and Brian Leetch.

In May 1994, just a month before her beloved Rangers would win the Stanley Cup, Ceil was brutally murdered in her own apartment building on Sedgwick Avenue in the Bronx. She was 67. Rangers fans young and old and the Rangers themselves were shocked and saddened. Ceil hadn't missed a Rangers game in 22 years. Her seat (Section 230, Row A, Seat 12) remained empty through the balance of the playoffs, adorned only by flowers and dozens of remembrance messages.

To honor Ceil's memory, the Rangers Fan Club established the Ceil Saidel Memorial Award "for dedication to the organization on and off the ice." Fittingly, Adam Graves won it the first seven years it was presented.

Larry Goodman, or **Dancin' Larry** as he's known to the latest generation of fans, has been doing his hip-hop dance routine up in Section 407 since late 1996. Immediately recognizable because of his shaved head, Larry moves out into the aisle to dance to "Strike It Up" by Black Box, his every move captured on the Garden's main scoreboard screen. When he's done, he walks down to the railing at the foot of his section and urges everyone in the arena to stand up in their seats.

Like The Chief before him, Larry has had to contend with the taunts of fans who don't appreciate his Jumbotron gyrations. Relentlessly positive, he takes it in stride.

"He gets threatened all the time not to do the dance because some idiots feel it's a jinx and the other team always scores," said Eddie "The Mouth" Gieck, co-host of Blueshirt Underground Radio. "But I like Dancin' Larry. He makes other humans smile."

75 Score One for Slats

His critics have called him a dinosaur—a cigar-chomping relic from an earlier age who rode into the Hockey Hall of Fame on the coattails of Wayne Gretzky and Mark Messier. They say he's completely out of touch with today's game and cite as proof the disastrous free-agent signings of Wade Redden, Bobby Holik, Darius Kasparaitis, and others. They accuse him of hiding from the press in his executive suite like the Great and Powerful Oz, pulling levers and pushing buttons behind a curtain of secrecy. They lament his unprecedented job security and wonder how many more coaches he'll send to the guillotine before his own neck is on the line.

They say all of those things and a whole lot more about Glen Sather. But for all the flak he's taken since being hired as general manager of the Rangers in 2000, Sather also deserves much of the credit for a trade that ranks among the club's best ever: the one for Ryan McDonagh.

Rewind to July 1, 2007. On the first day of free agency, the Rangers make a huge splash by signing not one but both of the most coveted players to hit the market: centers Chris Drury and Scott Gomez. The price was steep—their two contracts combined were worth more than $86 million.

Money aside, these were no-brainer hockey moves. Gomez and Drury were proven winners—each a former Rookie of the Year, each a Stanley Cup champion, each admired for his clutch play in big games, and each young enough to contribute meaningfully to the Rangers for years to come.

"BROADWAY BLITZ," screamed the cover of *The Hockey News*, which featured Gomez and Drury decked out in their new

Ranger threads and smiling like two guys who'd just won the lottery (which in a sense, they had). "IN A NEW YORK MINUTE RANGERS BECOME A CUP FAVORITE."

But excitement quickly turned to disappointment as both players struggled to replicate the success they'd enjoyed on other teams, Gomez more than Drury. A second line center earning megastar dinero, Scotty underachieved first for coach Tom Renney and then for John Tortorella. Gomez's game—one built on playmaking and skating—simply vanished before our eyes. The former Devils star was not yet 30 years old and already looked washed-up.

Sather shopped Gomez around for months to clear cap space, but who would take on the five years and $33.5 million left on his contract? What team would gamble that Gomez just needed a change of scenery to resuscitate his career?

The Montreal Canadiens, having failed in their highly publicized bids to land Vincent Lecavalier and Mats Sundin, were still in the market for a veteran center. Sather had found his mark.

On June 30, 2009, the Rangers traded Gomez and minor leaguers Tom Pyatt and Michael Busto to Montreal for McDonagh, Chris Higgins, and Pavel Valentenko.

In one transaction, Sather not only extricated Gomez from the Rangers' payroll, but also added a proven goal scorer in Higgins *and* a blue-chip defense prospect in McDonagh. Then he used his newfound cap space to sign free agent Marian Gaborik.

For once, the Rangers were involved in a lopsided deal and emerged as the clear victors.

In Gomez's three seasons as a Canadien, his point production dropped from 59 to 38 to 11. The team finally decided to cut its losses by sending him home and buying out the remainder of his contract.

Although Higgins didn't pan out in New York and Valentenko returned to Russia after two seasons in Hartford, McDonagh steadily entrenched himself as a cornerstone of the Rangers defense corps—a top-two blueliner with smarts, speed, skill, toughness, and incredibly, the potential to get even better. In 2013–14, he received the Players' Player Award and became the first Ranger in eight years *not* named Henrik Lundqvist to be named team MVP.

"I think every time we go to Montreal, they cringe looking at what Ryan McDonagh has become," Sam Rosen said. "They virtually gave him away. When you look back through history, that trade will be known as one of the great steals. From the moment he got here, you could see the great natural ability he has and it starts with his skating. A couple of strides and he's at full speed. And his offensive game has evolved by leaps and bounds under Alain Vigneault. He has a good shot and sees the ice very well. He's the full package, and everything on the chart is still going up."

Bravo, Slats. Bravo.

76 Loose Lips, Funny Quips, and Famous Last Words

"As a coach, he was a good waiter."
—*Gump Worsley, on his low opinion of Coach Phil Watson*

"You're not really a hockey player 'til you've lost a few teeth."
—*Bill Gadsby, on why hockey players keep dentists so busy*

"We always took the train. There were a few bridge players among us. We used to get into it but we didn't have the whole car to ourselves, so we'd go into the ladies' dressing room and keep playing cards in there for hours until we got back to New York."
—*Edgar Laprade, on how the Rangers passed the time on road trips*

"I'm glad I won the award now because I expect it's going to belong to Bobby Orr from now on."

—*Harry Howell, after winning the Norris Trophy as the NHL's best defenseman in Orr's rookie season. Howell was right—Orr went on to win the next eight Norris Trophies presented*

"Brad Park and I were coming back from Minnesota aboard a charter flight one night around 2:30 AM. We were tired. We got off the plane at Kennedy and hopped into Brad's car. He had a new 1969 Dodge Charger. So we're driving and we end up behind a big DeSoto—a '53 or a '54. The DeSoto stalls and Brad hits the guy's rear bumper. It was so big it cracked the Charger's whole front end, but the other car's bumper had no marks. We both get out of the car to give the guy shit, and six guys pop out of the DeSoto. I put my hands up in the air and said, 'Sorry guys, it's all our fault.' They took off and Park looked at me and said, 'That was good thinking.'"

—*Walt Tkaczuk, a 14-year NHL veteran who knew when to drop the gloves and when to skate away*

"I kept punching and all I could reach was his throat."

—*Brad Park, on how he was able to hold his own in a fight with Vancouver's Pat Quinn, at the time one of the biggest players in the league.*

"I've seen Emile change lines *while* he's fighting."

—*Rod Gilbert, on how Emile Francis may have lost his temper, but he never lost control as coach*

"The reputation was 'Rod Gilbert: Playboy' all throughout my career. If the definition of being a playboy is enjoying good food, enjoying traveling, enjoying the company of beautiful ladies, going out and enjoying life and dancing, then I'm a playboy."

—*Rod Gilbert, redefining what it means to be a playboy*

"I couldn't believe how stupid they were. Rod Gilbert should have been the team captain, or Walt Tkaczuk, not me. Years later I asked Emile Francis why and he said, 'I wouldn't have made Rod Gilbert captain if he was the only player on the team.'"

—Phil Esposito, on his surprise at being named captain of the Rangers immediately after being traded to New York

"The nights in Philadelphia when Stemmer and Moose Dupont stood nose-to-nose arguing, everybody thought, 'Oh, there's going to be a brawl right here,' they were actually talking about *All My Children*."

—Ted Irvine on how Pete "Stemmer" Stemkowski used a daytime soap to teach former Rangers teammate Andre "Moose" Dupont how to speak English

"The Hall of Fame is a joke. It's a complete joke. I have never seen anything like it in my whole life. I'm not saying who doesn't belong. Bobby Orr belongs in there. Marcel Dionne belongs in there. Gretzky and Messier, too. But there's lots of people who don't belong. Oldtimers *and* newtimers. I just don't understand. In baseball, that s--t don't happen."

—Ron Greschner, on the Hockey Hall of Fame's induction standards

"I'm just glad it wasn't machete night."

—Bob Froese, after Rangers fans threw mugs on the ice during mug night

"I've always liked the Rangers, I just don't like Ranger fans. I've never seen people so vulgar, like a bunch of animals, in my entire life. To call other human beings what they do. Maybe I'm naive, but that gets me pumped up."

—Islander Bob Bourne, on his motivation to beat the Rangers

"Back when Tomas was new to the team and his English wasn't that good, he said something that came out in a way that our goalie, Glen Hanlon, didn't like. Glen was still steaming about it during practice. So Tomas came skating down in warm-ups and fired a hard shot that went close to Glen's head. Glen came rushing out of the net to chase Tomas down. Half of us were dying laughing because we could see this whole thing had developed because Glen just didn't understand what Tomas had said. And the rest of us were like, 'Oh my God, here's our goalie chasing Tomas Sandstrom all over the rink.' So we settled everything down and got Glen back in the net. Well, Tomas was such a fiery competitor, and by now he's mad too. So the warm-ups continued and as he came down to take another shot, he fired another high, hard one right at Glen's head. Again, Glen came out of the net and chased Tomas all over the ice. We later came to realize that Sandstrom was a great team guy and that whole episode had just been a big misunderstanding."

—*Tom Laidlaw, on teammate Tomas
Sandstrom's uncompromising style*

"Lord, I feel for those fans. If I had the bottle, the genie, the one wish, it would be to see the Stanley Cup carried around Madison Square Garden, and carried by Rangers. My life would be just about complete."

—*Hall of Fame goalie Eddie Giacomin, speaking in 1989
on the eve of his No. 1 jersey being retired by the club.
Five years later, Giacomin's wish would come true.*

"If you take out fighting, what comes next? Do we eliminate checking? Pretty soon, we will all be out there in dresses and skirts."

—*Tie Domi, writing in* USA Today *about
the sanctity of fighting in hockey*

"The playoffs separate the men from the boys, and we found out we have a lot of boys in our dressing room."

—*Neil Smith, after the Rangers lost to the Washington Capitals in the 1991 playoffs*

"If we were picking first, we were picking Brendl. We had him No. 1. He should be a franchise player in the NHL."

—*Neil Smith, on why he traded up to select Pavel Brendl fourth overall in the 1999 Entry Draft. One of the great draft-day busts, Brendl arrived at his first training camp out of shape. He never played a game for the Rangers and was eventually traded to Philadelphia.*

"In our opinion, he's the best first passer in the game."

—*Glen Sather, on why he inked Wade Redden to a six-year, $39 million contract, widely considered to be the worst free-agent signing in the history of hockey*

"I'm excited about this. I've never had a coach who was a center-man before."

—*Eric Lindros, on the hiring of Bryan Trottier as coach of the Rangers*

"I don't enjoy hockey-obsessed Canadians, the [currency] exchange is not very good right now, and it's going to cost me a lot of money in tickets for people I don't even like."

—*Sean Avery, Canadian, on why he wasn't looking forward to a game in Toronto*

"He specifically told me I got it because [Kovalchuk] is a superstar, and I can't go after a superstar. I told him I make $4 million. I'm a superstar, too."

—*Sean Avery, recalling what he told referee Paul Devorksi after receiving a 10-minute misconduct for exchanging words with Devils star Ilya Kovalchuk*

"P.A. skated by the bench and basically mocked us. It was the wrong move for a guy like that. He's never going to get himself into a club in the city after I send out e-mails."

—*Sean Avery, on the steep price Islander P.A. Parenteau would pay for talking smack against the Rangers*

"Even a milder version of Sean Avery is still not that mild."

—*Sean Avery, on being on his best behavior after returning from a lengthy league-imposed suspension*

"There's winning and misery, and there was a lot of misery in my last few years. I think things would have been different for myself if we were winning 50 games a year and having a good time doing it. It would have made my decision to retire harder."

—*Mark Messier, on why he didn't return for a 26th NHL season*

"Watching a shootout is like admitting you watch *Survivor* or search the Internet for porn."

—*Brendan Shanahan, comparing the tie-breaker to other guilty pleasures*

"Because he stinks on the power play. He stinks. I don't know why. I wish I could put him on the power play, but every time I put him on, he stinks."

—*John Tortorella, on why he stopped using Carl Hagelin on the power play*

77 Sad End for Sawchuk

The final act of the tragedy that was Terry Sawchuk's life played out in New York City as the legendary goaltender spent his 21st and final NHL season as a Ranger.

Once the backbone of a Stanley Cup dynasty in Detroit, the 11-time All-Star and four-time Vezina Trophy winner was now a journeyman in the twilight of his career, his body broken down from injuries too numerous to list. But Emile Francis sensed that "Ukey," a nickname tracing to Terry's Ukranian heritage, had just enough hockey left in him to provide an occasional breather for starter Ed Giacomin.

Sawchuk appeared in eight games for the Rangers that season, starting seven of them. His 103rd and final career shutout was a 6–0 trouncing of the Pittsburgh Penguins on February 1, 1970.

Fundamentally, Sawchuk was still sound. He practiced hard and had no illusions about supplanting Giacomin as the team's No. 1 goalie. But off the ice, a change of scenery hadn't improved the Winnipeg native's surly disposition. He battled alcoholism and depression throughout his career, and teammates, opponents, fans, and family members were subjected to his trademark mood swings. Those troubles cost him his marriage.

Weeks after the end of the season, Sawchuk and teammate Ron Stewart got into an argument at a bar in Long Beach, not far from the house they were renting together.

"It was over a phone bill," Francis said. "Christ, it was about an $8 phone bill. The season had been over for a month. Terry had gone back to Detroit, hoping to have a reconciliation with his ex-wife, but it didn't work out. So he came back to New York and shared a place with Stewie. They were out at a bar one day, having

Do They Have Phones in Italy?

"The game in which Terry Sawchuk shut out the Penguins was the first sporting event I ever went to. Years later, Rod Gilbert told me that he'd been on vacation in Rome when one of the hotel managers there told him that his goalie had passed away. For two days, Rod was going crazy looking for an *International Herald Tribune* to find out what happened to Ed Giacomin."

Phil Czochanski, Old Bridge, New Jersey
Former statistician for Rangers broadcast team
Rangers fan since 1970

a few drinks, when Stewie brought up how much Terry owed him for the phone bill. If he was drinking, Terry could get a little mean. Well, he told Stewart he wasn't going to pay him, and all a sudden, he threw a punch. A friend who was there jumped in and broke it up, and Stewart was smart enough to take off."

Sawchuk followed him home.

"Back at their place, they started arguing again," Francis said. "Stewart tried to walk away again. He was walking down the steps when Terry came up behind him and took another swing. They both rolled down the steps and ended up outside on the lawn. Sawchuk fell into a barbecue pit, and Stewart rolled on top of him. Right away, Terry knew he was hurt bad. He said to Stewie, 'Call an ambulance.'"

Sawchuk was rushed to the hospital. His internal injuries were so severe that his gallbladder had to be removed. Despite Terry's insistence that the entire episode remain a secret, a doctor tracked down Francis at a junior hockey tournament in Quebec and urged him to get back to New York as soon as possible.

"They weren't sure he would make it through the night," Francis said.

When Francis got to the hospital the next morning, Terry told him the whole story.

"Don't blame Ron Stewart," Sawchuk said, "because this is my fault."

Sawchuk was transferred to a hospital in Manhattan where doctors planned to perform another operation—this one to remove blood from a lacerated liver. Before being wheeled off to the operating room, he asked for a priest to administer last rites.

"I was there with him," Francis recalled, "and I told him not to worry and that I'd be there when he got out. And he took off a ring—his Detroit Red Wings ring—and he said, 'In case I don't make it, can you please give this to my son?' Then he asked me if I could get his kid, who was also a goalie, a tryout with Kitchener. I told him not to worry, that he was going to come out of this okay. They took him in for surgery a little after 6:00 PM and didn't finish until around midnight. At that point, the doctors came out and said there was no sense in waiting around. There was nothing more that anyone could do. Now we had to wait. They sent me home and told me they'd call if they needed me."

Sawchuk never recovered, and he died on the morning of May 31, 1970. He was 40.

With Terry's ex-wife in Michigan and brother in Canada, it fell on Francis to identify Sawchuk's body at the morgue on Second Avenue.

"Terry was in a bag," Francis remembered, "like a hockey stick bag, with a tag around his neck. Believe me, that's not something I'd ever want to do again. The people there didn't know who Terry Sawchuk was. To me, there was no better goalkeeper than Terry Sawchuk. And to see him lying on that floor, just 40 years old, Christ, it made me sick. I didn't sleep for at least three nights."

Although cleared of any wrongdoing in Sawchuk's death, Ron Stewart spent the rest of his life racked with guilt. As compassionate toward his players as he was demanding, Francis kept Stewart in the organization for as long as he could. Eventually, he chose Stewart to succeed him as Rangers coach.

Francis also got Terry's son, Jerry, that tryout with Kitchener, and he made the team.

In 1971, Sawchuk was elected posthumously to the Hockey Hall of Fame—one of the few NHL greats who had the three-year waiting period waived for their induction.

78 So Long, Cally

Rangers Trade Ryan Callahan to Tampa Bay for Martin St. Louis

From time to time, Ranger Nation wakes up to the harsh reality that NHL hockey is more than just a sport played at its highest level. It's also a multibillion-dollar business. As much as we want it to be about the Cup and nothing but the Cup, it's also about collective bargaining agreements, salary caps, and no-trade clauses.

That's why, in March 2014, the Rangers traded fan-favorite Ryan Callahan just two seasons after naming him captain. But rationalizations like "It's part of the business" and "If Gretzky can be traded, anybody can be traded" provided little or no consolation to those who had watched No. 24 play every shift as if it was his last for seven-plus seasons.

Lacking the All-Star pedigree of a Mark Messier or a Jaromir Jagr, Callahan represented a departure from the marquee-name-as-captain. But it was a much-deserved honor for a heart-and-soul right winger who led by example on and off the ice. He called to mind self-made stars of the past like Ted Irvine, Eddie Johnstone, Don Maloney, Kelly Kisio, and Adam Graves—never the biggest, fastest, or most skilled Rangers, but completely fearless, focused, and team-oriented.

*Ryan Callahan (24) in action during the game between the Chicago
Blackhawks and the New York Rangers at the United Center in Chicago,
Illinois, on March 9, 2012.* (Cal Sport Media via AP Images)

Thank You, Cally

"Every single shift, Ryan Callahan went out there and showed why he was the heart and soul of the New York Rangers. I loved him as a player, and always will, because of the emotion he showed on the ice. The trade hurt my heart a lot."

Jessica LaPorte, Nutley, New Jersey
Rangers fan since 1985

"He'll battle in any way possible to win the game," play-by-play man Sam Rosen said. "If this guy were 6'2" and 210 lbs., he'd be a First Team or Second Team All-Star every year of his career. That sometimes went unnoticed about him. There's no team that couldn't use Ryan Callahan."

The 2011–12 season was a special one for the Rangers and for Callahan. In his first year as captain, he scored a career-high 29 goals and 54 points as the Blueshirts won their first division title since 1994 and finished with the best record in the Eastern Conference.

The secret of New York's success was no secret. The Rangers won because they had the best goalie in the world in his Vezina Trophy–winning season and a coach in John Tortorella who demanded 100 percent effort 100 percent of the time. But it was Callahan—throwing hits, blocking shots, killing penalties, forcing turnovers—who set the tone.

There was the night at Scotiabank Place in Ottawa when the Rangers were trailing the Senators three games to two in a tough quarterfinals series. Callahan took a blistering slap shot to his left hand off the blade of Chris Phillips and was in so much pain that he couldn't even hold his stick. Yet he stayed on the ice and almost blocked two more shots. He went off, got checked out, and at the next whistle, hopped back over the boards for a Rangers power play. Classic Cally.

The Rangers came back to beat the Senators in seven games then went the distance with Washington in the semis before falling to New Jersey in the Conference Finals.

New York wasn't quite ready to say goodbye to Callahan—not the majority of fans and certainly not his teammates. Nor did he give any indication that he wanted to play anyplace else. But in talks with the Rangers on a new contract, it was clear that the impending free agent and the club had placed very different valuations on his worth. To borrow a baseball analogy, Ryan was a singles hitter who wanted to be paid like a home-run hitter.

As the trade deadline approached, the Rangers and Callahan inched closer on a six-year extension. The two sides were no longer that far apart on dollars, but Callahan's insistence on a no-trade clause ultimately forced Glen Sather's hand. The general manager was reluctant to give that kind of job security to an injury-prone player who, because of his all-out style of play, would always be one blocked shot away from another extended absence from the lineup.

Meanwhile, down in Tampa Bay, Lightning captain Martin St. Louis was putting his general manager, Steve Yzerman, in an awkward spot by requesting a trade to the Rangers and *only* the Rangers.

And so, unable to reach an agreement with Callahan, and unwilling to risk losing him for nothing in the off-season, Sather swapped him and a pair of high draft picks for St. Louis, a 38-year-old reigning Hart Trophy winner.

It was part of the business.

If Gretzky can be traded, anybody can be traded.

We had to accept it. We didn't have to like it.

79 Inkreidable!

They say living well is the best revenge. Even if Chris Kreider didn't have revenge on his mind, many of the 18,000 spectators who watched him score a hat trick against his former coach surely did.

Rangers fans and the New York media had November 30, 2013, circled on their calendars—the day John Tortorella was coming back to Madison Square Garden as coach of the Canucks. Anyone expecting Tortorella to break character and suddenly become sentimental or nostalgic about his four-plus seasons as Rangers coach would be disappointed. To him, this was just another game on the schedule.

"I am going to coach this game," he told reporters during a brief but cordial pregame interview, "hopefully kick their ass, and get out of here."

Kreider, the big left winger relegated to the minors by Tortorella for half of the previous season, had other plans. He scored twice in the first period—on a wrist shot off assists from new linemates Rick Nash and Derek Stepan, and then off a deflection of Ryan McDonagh's power play pass—then completed the hat trick 9:38 into the third period by tipping Anton Stralman's point shot past backup goalie Eddie Lack.

Final score: Rangers 5, Canucks 2.

Afterward, Kreider refused to admit to having any extra motivation to show up Tortorella. Instead, he took the high road, insisting there were no hard feelings and that he learned a lot from his former coach. No one familiar with Chris as a player or as a person found that surprising.

From his days at Andover Academy, the Boxford, Massachusetts, native exuded poise, humility, and the smarts to know that, despite being blessed with god-given talent, he didn't have all the answers. His coaches there, and later at Boston College, adored that about him.

The Rangers made Kreider the 19th overall pick of the 2009 draft. The team hoped he would leave school to turn pro after his sophomore season but Kreider, committed to getting his degree and hungry to win a national championship, declined the Rangers' repeated overtures and returned to BC for his junior year.

He took accelerated courses that brought him within four classes of earning his degree, won a national championship, then hooked up with the Rangers in time for the Eastern Conference Quarterfinals against Ottawa. Making his NHL debut in Game 3 of that series, Kreider brought an infusion of speed and energy to a club that won 51 games during the regular season but was starting to run out of gas. There were nights during that whirlwind spring when Kreider was the Rangers' best forward.

His banishment to Hartford the following season was not a banishment at all, but a necessary part of the learning process for a young player who struggled with consistency. In 2013–14, he didn't look at all out of place skating on the Rangers' top line with Stepan and Nash, and he was an early favorite to win the Calder Trophy as Rookie of the Year. He missed the end of the regular season and the start of the playoffs with a fractured left hand but returned in time to help the Rangers reach the Stanley Cup Finals.

"I've seen growth in him as a professional and as an NHLer," said one Rangers insider. "When he first started out, he was a little bit hesitant and maybe too deferential to his linemates. Now he's much more assertive, and players look for him. They realize he has great speed and skating ability and will look to hit him with a lead pass. He'll skate to the puck at full speed to take a shot or drive hard to the net. I think he surprises some defensemen with how big and strong he is. When he's playing physical, he battles for the puck and usually wins. The more he does that, the better he gets."

Chris Kreider celebrates after scoring during the third period of a game against the Vancouver Canucks on Saturday, November 30, 2013, at Madison Square Garden in New York. It was Kreider's third goal for a hat trick, leading the Rangers to a 5–2 win. (AP Photo/Bill Kostroun)

80 The Furious Finish

The great *New York Times* sportswriter Gerald Eskanazi called it one of the most important and decisive victories in the Rangers' loss-strewn, 44-year existence. The team's 9–5 win over the Red Wings earned them a playoff berth on April 5, 1970, the last day of the regular season.

After a strong start to the 1969–70 campaign, the Rangers made life very difficult for themselves. Five weeks earlier, they'd been in first place. Then in February, All-Star defenseman Brad Park collapsed to the ice with a broken ankle, and the Rangers collapsed with him. Park returned to the lineup after a month's absence and helped the Rangers to a pair of wins, but after a demoralizing 6–2 loss at Detroit on April 4, their playoff hopes grew dim.

The only thing keeping the Rangers alive was the fact that the two-time defending champion Montreal Canadiens were also struggling. Like the Rangers, they were looking to clinch the fourth and final playoff berth in the Eastern Conference.

The Blueshirts took the ice on that Easter Sunday afternoon knowing they had to score at least five goals in order to have any chance of making the playoffs. Anything less would have automatically eliminated them since the Canadiens had a five-goal edge in goals scored. That would be the first tie-breaker if the Rangers finished with the same number of wins and points as Montreal.

"We knew what we had to do," Jean Ratelle said later.

And they got right to work, firing a club-record 65 shots at Red Wings goalie Roger Crozier. Rod Gilbert scored the first of his two goals 36 seconds into the game, Ron Stewart and rookie

Jack Egers each had a pair, Dave Balon had a hat trick, and defenseman Arnie Brown—typically not a big point producer—picked up four assists. Coach Emile Francis kept the shifts short and rolled all four lines to keep the Rangers on the attack for the full 60 minutes.

The Rangers were so desperate to run up the score that Francis pulled goalie Ed Giacomin to get an extra attacker on the ice in the final minute when the Rangers had a 9–3 lead. The strategy didn't work, and the Red Wings scored twice as Giacomin watched from the bench.

Later that evening, Rangers players turned on their radios to hear Chicago blow out the Canadiens 10–2. Montreal and New York finished the regular season tied with 38 wins and 92 points, but the Rangers had a two-goal edge in goals scored: 246 to the Canadiens' 244.

The playoff race was decided. The Habs were out, and the Rangers were in.

What If?

We're suckers for "what if" scenarios involving the Rangers—blockbusters that would have dramatically altered the course of the team's history but, for one reason or another, fell apart at the last minute. The aborted 1992 trade with Quebec for Eric Lindros was certainly the biggest. Here are some other doozies:

Rangers Trade Earl Ingarfield to Bruins for John Bucyk
Rangers coach and general manager Emile "The Cat" Francis came within a whisker of landing star left-winger John Bucyk from the

Bruins. You remember Bucyk—he was the guy carrying the Stanley Cup off Madison Square Garden ice and into the visitors' locker room after Boston defeated the Rangers in Game 6 of the 1972 finals.

"In 1965," Francis recalled, "the Bruins brought in a guy named Hap Emms to be their new general manager. On their first trip into New York that season, I called Emms and said I wanted him to drop by my office so we could go out to lunch. I took him to a hotel that was four or five blocks from the Garden, and we sat there for about three hours. By the time we left, we had made a deal—I was going to trade Earl Ingarfield to the Bruins for Johnny Bucyk."

A center who'd worked his way up to the top line between Andy Bathgate and Dean Prentice, Ingarfield was a nice player but the gap in talent to be exchanged was significant. The Cat was about to pull a fast one on Boston's rookie GM, and he knew it. He was already salivating as he imagined possible line combinations.

"What I was going to do with Bucyk," Francis said, "was put him on a line with Rod Gilbert and Jean Ratelle. That would have been a big deal. A *hell* of a deal."

There was just one catch—Emms wouldn't finalize the transaction without the approval of Bruins owner Weston Adams. Naturally, when Adams heard who the Bruins were giving up to get Ingarfield, he swiftly vetoed the trade.

Bucyk would play another 13 seasons for the Bruins, retiring as the highest-scoring left wing ever (a record since surpassed by Luc Robitaille) before easily being voted into the Hockey Hall of Fame.

Who knows? Had Bucyk ended up a Ranger, maybe he would have carried the Stanley Cup into the other team's locker room.

Rangers trade Niklas Sundstrom and Todd Harvey to Islanders for Zigmund Palffy and Rich Pilon

You could count on one hand the number of trades consummated between these bitter division rivals. This deal, negotiated in June 1999 by Rangers GM Neil Smith and his counterpart in Uniondale, Mike Milbury, would certainly have been the biggest of them all. In exchange for Palffy, a natural goal scorer, and Pilon, a rugged defenseman, the Rangers were prepared to give up a pair of two-way forwards in Sundstrom and Harvey plus a first-round draft pick, a minor league player, and $2.5 million in cash.

What would possess the woeful Islanders to trade their best player, a three-time 40-goal scorer, to their arch enemies across the river? Money. Palffy was entering the second year of a five-year, $26 million contract, and ownership wanted to slash payroll. Every other team in the league knew it, but only a handful could afford him. The only offers Milbury received were from the Rangers and Los Angeles Kings. Milbury liked the Rangers' offer better.

"They were really close," recalled Chris Botta, the Islanders' former PR chief, "but it never got to a point where I wrote a press release. I remember writing it in my head. I knew the particulars. But I remember thinking to myself, *How am I going to write this? How am I going to sell it? Especially to this team?* It finally broke down at the ownership level because our owners had some unique ideas of how to drain Jim Dolan of a whole bunch of other things in the deal."

When the league refused to allow any cash to change hands, Milbury went back to the Rangers and asked them to sweeten the package with additional players, prospects, or picks. Smith balked, forcing Milbury to accept the Kings' offer.

"I think trading Ziggy to the Rangers almost shamed our owners and exposed them," Botta said. "That's how bad we were from an ownership and a management perspective. It was indefensible. You don't trade your best player to your biggest rival. Our only defense was there was no other choice."

Rangers Sign Restricted Free Agent Joe Sakic

Joe Sakic, the Hall of Fame center who played in 12 All-Star Games and racked up more than 1,600 points in his 20-season career, almost became a Ranger.

Early in August 1997, a year after leading his team to its first Stanley Cup, the 28-year-old Avalanche captain was a restricted free agent. Mark Messier had just signed a free-agent contract with the Vancouver Canucks, leaving the Rangers with a gaping hole in their lineup. Neil Smith had money to spend and took the gutsy step of signing Sakic to an offer sheet worth $21 million over three seasons, more than doubling his salary.

Smith figured there was no way Colorado would match the offer. The Avs were in financial trouble and had just signed Peter Forsberg to a two-year deal worth $9 million, a lot of money at the time. Plus the Rangers' offer was heavily front-loaded with a "poison pill"—a $15 million signing bonus on top of Sakic's $2 million salary.

Sakic was blown away by the Rangers' offer. He told the *Denver Post* he was looking forward to playing with Wayne Gretzky, who had joined the Rangers the previous season. Still, Joe knew there was the chance, however slim, that the Avs would match. "I know I'll be playing here in a place I love, or I'll be going to the great city of New York," he said.

The Avs' owners, Ascent Entertainment, scrambled to come up with the money to keep Sakic, negotiating a lucrative new deal with their broadcast partner by convincing them that keeping a star of Joe's stature in Denver would be good for ratings.

After the Avalanche matched the Rangers' offer sheet, Ascent chairman Charlie Lyons sent MSG president Dave Checketts a framed copy of the famous picture of Nelson Rockefeller giving a crowd of hecklers the middle finger. The message was clear.

The Sakic contract set a new bar for salaries among top-end NHL players. Payrolls around the league ballooned, and the gap between the wealthy teams and the poor teams widened.

Colorado GM Pierre Lacroix told the *New York Times* that he expected the Rangers to continue their free-spending ways.

"The way they are going and the way they are acting," he said, "I'm sure they are going to be the first team to sign an alien and to have an alien play for their team. I just hope the planet of the alien will have a chance to match."

Rangers Trade for Steven Stamkos

When Tampa Bay's Steven Stamkos didn't immediately blossom into a megastar mere months after being chosen first overall at the 2008 draft, team co-owner Len Barrie concluded the kid must not be ready to play in the NHL. Rangers GM Glen Sather, correctly sensing that Barrie was a weak-minded fool vulnerable to Jedi mind tricks, suggested they work out a trade.

As reported by the *New York Post*, Barrie asked the Rangers for a package of two or three roster players from a wish list featuring Michael Del Zotto, Evgeny Grachev, Ryan Callahan, Brandon Dubinsky, and Dan Girardi (it's unknown which players out of that group would have gone to Tampa).

According to Sather, he and Barrie shook hands on the deal but when Barrie went back to share the good news with his partner, Oren Koules, and Lightning GM Brian Lawton, they were not happy. The trade quickly unraveled and the Rangers missed out on getting a player who, the very next season, would lead the league with 51 goals.

82 Burying the Hatchet

In time, the ecstasy of 1994 dwindled and it was back to business for the Rangers. The core of Mark Messier, Adam Graves, Brian Leetch, and Mike Richter were still productive, so management decided to postpone (indefinitely) any rebuild to make another run at the Cup. Reuniting Messier with former Edmonton Oilers teammate Wayne Gretzky was part of that plan.

But the reunion was short-lived.

Messier was set to become an unrestricted free agent after the 1996–97 season. He was 36 now, and certainly not the player he used to be. When he said publicly that he wasn't looking to break the bank on a new long-term contract, Garden ownership and Rangers management took him at his word.

Believing Messier's value would continue to diminish in the years ahead, and seeing no logic in continuing to pay for 1994, the team took a calculated risk by offering Messier a one-year deal worth $4 million—the same salary as Gretzky but $2 million less than he'd made in his previous contract. Messier and his hard-bargaining agent/dad, Doug, were insulted.

The team eventually came up a smidge on the dollars but wouldn't budge on the term. Then the Vancouver Canucks blew all other suitors out of the water by offering Messier a mammoth three-year deal worth $6 million per year. It was, as Garden president Dave Checketts termed it, "crazy money." And impossible to turn down.

And just like that, Messier and the Rangers were done. There were hurt feelings on both sides—Mark and his camp complaining about a lack of loyalty and respect, the Rangers doing the same. Everyone was shocked at how the relationship unraveled, none

Applaud the Captain...But Applaud Gently

"I broke my hand in January 2006, just four days before the Rangers were going to retire Messier's number at the Garden. I didn't tell work because if I'd called out sick, I wouldn't have been able to attend the game. At the time, I was a cop in the NYPD and when you call out sick, you're only allowed to be out of your house for four hours a day and no later than 8:00 PM. After 8:00, they check up on you and if you're not home, you get suspended. So I worked for four days with a broken hand. The day after the ceremony, I called out sick and missed the next five weeks."

Rob Coppola, Phoenix, Arizona
Rangers fan since 1976

more than Gretzky. "If I had known he would leave," Wayne said, "I never would have signed here."

Three years later, Glen Sather replaced Neil Smith as Rangers general manager. As soon as Mark's contract with the Canucks expired in July 2000, talks began on bringing him back to New York.

Messier celebrated his return to the Rangers at a press conference during which he and Checketts symbolically buried a hatchet in a glass box—a fish tank, really—full of topsoil. Brian Leetch was there, too, delighted to give the captaincy back to his old friend.

Then it was time for the man of the hour to take the podium. Shedding tears that have since become as much a trademark as the iconic No. 11 on his jersey, an emotional Messier promised to restore pride in a team that had fallen on hard times in his absence. He vowed the Rangers would return to the playoffs, and he spent the next four years trying in vain to keep that oath.

Mess was the league's oldest player at 44 years, two months when he took his last shift on Garden ice in 2004, and he officially retired a year later as the second-leading scorer in NHL history with 1,887 points (691 as a Ranger, fifth on the club's all-time list).

Messier's time in New York was undeniably a godsend, the transformative effect he had on the organization unprecedented. But was it all champagne and parades? No. The team made the playoffs only five of the ten years he spent on Broadway. There was the messy, not-so-private clash with Coach Roger Neilson in the early 1990s that led to Neilson getting fired. Although his willingness to play through injuries was commendable, his tendency to hide said injuries from the coaching staff sometimes did more harm than good. Mark's gung-ho style wore thin in the locker room with some of the players tuning him out, particularly in the later years. His desire to be consulted on personnel decisions was a source of tension. Even his decision to quit the Rangers front office in 2013, right after losing out on the head coaching job to Alain Vigneault, smacked of sour grapes.

But here's the bottom line: Mark Messier delivered the Stanley Cup to New York City, the hockey equivalent of successfully climbing Mount Everest in flip-flops. And that's as good a way to silence the critics as any.

83 King Kwong

Willie O'Ree became the first black player in NHL history when he suited up for the Boston Bruins in 1958. But the league's color barrier was actually broken 10 years earlier when Larry "King" Kwong, a Canadian of Chinese descent, played his first and only NHL game for the Rangers.

Born in British Columbia to Chinese immigrants, Larry and his 14 siblings faced all manner of discrimination. At the time, Chinese-Canadians weren't even allowed to vote, and it was hard

Herb Carnegie

In 1948, the same year Larry Kwong made his NHL debut, the Rangers took an interest in Herb Carnegie, a young black player tearing up the Quebec Provincial League. They offered Carnegie a tryout and minor league contract, but because the money was less than what he made in Quebec, he turned them down.

for them to find work. A local barber once refused to cut Kwong's hair just because he was Chinese.

Sports provided Kwong with an outlet for his frustrations—and an equal playing field. A great all-around athlete, he was an amateur tennis champ and an accomplished sprinter. He also played lacrosse, softball, and soccer.

At 16, he added hockey to his list of athletic pursuits and excelled at the game. Two years later, he was skating for the Trail Smoke Eaters, one of the top senior league teams in Canada.

During World War II, Kwong entered the Canadian military and played hockey as entertainment for the troops. Someone from the Rangers saw him play and was impressed enough with his skating, puck handling, and passing skills to offer Kwong a pro tryout in 1946. He didn't make the Rangers but was assigned to their top farm team, the New York Rovers of the Eastern League, who played their home games at Madison Square Garden.

The 5'6", 150-lb. winger scored a goal in his debut for the Rovers against the Boston Olympics in Boston on October 27, 1946. Word of Kwong's exploits quickly spread through New York's Chinese-American community. Before one Rovers game, a local restaurateur named Shavey Lee, the unofficial "Mayor of Chinatown," and two showgirls from the China Doll nightclub honored Kwong at center ice.

Kwong, who'd since picked up the nicknames "King Kwong" and "The China Clipper," was leading the Rovers in scoring late in the 1947–48 season when he and teammate Ronnie Rowe were summoned by Rangers coach Frank Boucher. Three of Boucher's regulars—Neil Colville, Phil Watson, and Ed Slowinski—were sidelined with injuries, so Kwong and Rowe took a train to Montreal where the Rangers were getting ready to play the Canadiens. The date was March 13, 1948.

Wearing uniform No. 11, Kwong was used sparingly that night—reportedly just a single shift late in the game—and beyond a cursory mention in the newspapers the following day, the occasion didn't receive much fanfare. A few days later, he was sent back to the Rovers.

Those who saw him play insist Kwong had what it took to be an NHLer. But in a six-team league, the competition for every roster spot was just too fierce.

As much as Kwong enjoyed his time in New York, he sensed there was no long-term future for him with the Rangers. So after the season, he quit the Rovers and went back to Canada to play for a team he knew wanted him: the Valleyfield Braves of the Quebec senior league. There he'd get to play against future NHL stars like Jean Beliveau and Jacques Plante, and in 1951, he led the Braves to a league title.

Kwong made a living playing the game he loved—a victory unto itself—but he spent the rest of his life wondering why he didn't get another opportunity to showcase his talents in the NHL.

In 2013, shortly after celebrating his 90th birthday, Kwong was finally recognized for breaking hockey's color barrier when he became the first Chinese-Canadian athlete to be inducted into the British Columbia Sports Hall of Fame.

84 Visit the Farm

Rangers fans are lucky. When they want to see their team's top prospects in action, all they have to do is take a two-hour drive up I–84 to see the American Hockey League's Hartford WolfPack.

You'll find all the charms and trappings of minor league hockey here: cheaper tickets ($12-$45 range), kitschy promotions, event staff throwing balled-up T-shirts into the crowd, fans howling like wolves, and a friendly lupine mascot named Sonar. It's good family fun.

The team formerly known as the Binghamton Rangers moved into the Hartford Civic Center in 1997 after the Hartford Whalers relocated to North Carolina to become the Hurricanes. Playmaker Derek Armstrong, sniper Brad "Shooter" Smyth, team captain Ken Gernander, and brawler P.J. Stock were early fan favorites.

In 1999–2000, a mostly veteran squad coached by John Paddock won 49 games before eliminating local rivals Springfield, Worcester, and Providence en route to defeating Rochester in the Calder Cup Finals.

Since then, many Rangers have gotten their start off-Broadway in the building once known as "The Mall" but rebranded in 2007 as XL Center, including Marc Savard, Dan Cloutier, Dominic Moore, Artem Anisimov, Ryan Callahan, Brandon Dubinsky, Dan Girardi, and Cam Talbot.

Believing he could boost revenues and reinvigorate sagging ticket sales, former Whalers owner Howard Baldwin came back to town in 2010 and negotiated with the Rangers to take over the WolfPack's business operations. Playing to the locals' sad devotion to the long-departed NHL team, he renamed the WolfPack the Connecticut Whalers midway through the 2010–11 season and brought back the Whalers' famous theme song, "Brass Bonanza." The gimmick resulted in a temporary spike in attendance.

By 2013, Baldwin was gone and the team returned to its original name, uniform, and colors. The Pack was back.

Here's an abbreviated history of the Rangers' farm system:

Springfield Indians (1926–33, 1959–62)

A founding member of the Canadian American Hockey League. Andy Aitkenhead, Ott Heller, Cecil Dillon, and Charlie Rayner all saw action for the Indians, who played their games at the Eastern States Coliseum (aka, the Big E Coliseum), a 5,900-seat arena in West Springfield, Massachusetts.

Philadelphia Ramblers (1935–41)

The Ramblers were often terrible and occasionally dominant but rarely mediocre. The club won the 1936 Can-Am League title. Bryan Hextall, Kilby MacDonald, Neil Colville, Butch Keeling, and Phil Watson all played for the Ramblers before graduating to the Rangers, with whom they won a Stanley Cup in 1940.

New York Rovers (1943–51)

The New York Rovers shared Madison Square Garden with the Rangers, typically playing on Sunday afternoons. They were nicknamed "the Redshirts" because—you guessed it—they wore red jerseys. The Rovers' Atomic Line of Cal Gardner, Rene Trudell, and Church Russell took the Eastern League by storm. They were so good that in 1945–46 the entire line was promoted to the Rangers.

Providence Reds (1955–58, 1971–76)

Led by future Rangers star Camille Henry, the Reds stormed into the 1956 Calder Cup Finals where they swept the Cleveland Barons. Ron Greschner and Rick Middleton starred for the Reds in the 1970s. The team played at the Rhode Island Auditorium on Main Street before moving to the Providence Civic Center (now the Dunkin' Donuts Center).

St. Paul/Minnesota Rangers (1963–66)

The St. Paul Rangers were a founding member of the Central Hockey League and winners of the 1965 Adams Cup. In 1966, the team relocated to Omaha, Nebraska, in anticipation of the start of the NHL's Minnesota North Stars in 1967.

Omaha Knights (1966–72)

The club was named for the Knights of Ak-Sar-Ben, a local philanthropic organization. Notable alumni include Syl Apps, Andre "Moose" Dupont, Billy Fairbairn, and Steve Vickers. The Knights won two league titles during their time as a Rangers affiliate in 1970 and 1971.

Buffalo Bisons (1967–70)

The AHL's Bisons played at Memorial Auditorium (aka "The Aud") and were owned by brothers Ruby, Al, and Sam Pastor, who also owned the Pepsi bottling plant in town. This explains why the Bisons' logo featured a red, white, and blue soda bottle cap. With future Rangers star Gilles Villemure in goal, the Bisons won the 1970 Calder Cup. The club ceased operations after that season to make way for an incoming NHL expansion team, the Buffalo Sabres.

New Haven Nighthawks (1976–81, 1984–87)

New Haven has a long and storied history of supporting minor league hockey, dating back to the 1920s. The Nighthawks played at New Haven Coliseum, an eyesore of a structure that had a parking garage built directly above it. Quite a few Rangers got their start as pros in New Haven, among them Dave Gagner, Ed Johnstone, and Doug Soetaert. Veterans like Mike Rogers and Nick Fotiu also played there later in their careers. John Tortorella was an assistant coach with the team, but not while it was a Rangers affiliate.

Denver/Colorado Rangers (1987–89)

Notable alumni included Tony Granato, Peter Laviolette, Mike Richter, Brad Stepan (Derek Stepan's dad), Mark Tinordi, and Darren Turcotte. One of the scariest injuries a hockey player has ever suffered occurred to Denver's Mark Janssens. In 1989, Janssens was involved in a fight with Martin Simard of the Salt Lake Golden Eagles when he lost his balance and fell. His bare head bounced off the ice and he went into convulsions. Unconscious and writhing uncontrollably, Janssens swallowed his tongue but trainers were able to dislodge it, likely saving his life. He woke up in a hospital with a badly bruised brain and a fractured skull. Miraculously, Janssens made a full recovery and played a complete 80-game schedule for the New York Rangers the following season.

Binghamton Rangers (1990–97)

In the 1990s, if a young player didn't perform up to expectations with the parent club, he was likely to be threatened with banishment to Binghamton, hockey's version of Siberia. The Baby Rangers played at Broome County Veterans Memorial Arena, a 4,700-seat barn where locals watched Tie Domi, Alexei Kovalev, and Sergei Zubov before they became NHL regulars. In 1992–93, Binghamton dominated the AHL regular season by winning 57 games but lost in the second round of the playoffs. In 1997, the New York Rangers purchased the club and relocated it to Hartford, Connecticut, to become the Hartford WolfPack.

85 The Stadium Series

Following the disgraceful, inexcusable, and utterly unnecessary owner-imposed lockout that wiped out half of the 2012–13 season and resulted in the cancelation of the 2013 Winter Classic, the NHL promised to do something big to win back disgruntled fans.

Free merchandise? Lower ticket prices? A new commissioner? Of course not. Instead, they rolled out the Stadium Series—four outdoor regular season games separate and distinct from the Winter Classic and Canadian-based Heritage Classic outdoor games. Two of the four events were slated for Yankee Stadium, and both would feature the Rangers taking on a local rival.

Preparations began two weeks before the first game with the construction of a rink in the middle of the field, stretching horizontally from foul line to foul line, as well as an auxiliary rink near home plate and three stages in the outfield.

Oddly, although the games were to be played in the Bronx against teams from outside New York City—the Islanders and Devils—the Rangers were designated as the road team for both contests. The *New York Times* reported that this was due to the special exemption that has freed Madison Square Garden from paying property taxes since 1982. A provision of the agreement states that if the Rangers (or their cohabitants, the Knicks) play a home game outside the Garden, the exemption is forfeited. There was no way CEO Jim Dolan was going to let that happen.

January 26, 2014: Rangers 7, Devils 3

Allowing six goals on 21 shots and getting replaced by Corey Schneider was not the showing Martin Brodeur wanted to have against Henrik Lundqvist and the Rangers, especially in a nationally televised game and in front of 50,000 fans.

The game-time temperature was 24 degrees, and snow began to fall steadily during the second period when the Rangers scored four unanswered goals, including two from left winger Mats Zuccarello.

Derek Stepan scored on a penalty shot to cap off New York's scoring in the third period.

Lundqvist, whose goalie mask had Yankee pinstripes down the front and images of Babe Ruth, Joe DiMaggio, and Lou Gehrig on the right side, made 19 saves in the win.

Rangers, Kings Beat the Odds in Vegas Exhibition

On September 27, 1991, the Los Angeles Kings played the Rangers in the parking lot of Caesar's Palace in Las Vegas. The preseason matchup, which the Kings won 5-2, was the first outdoor game in NHL history.

In 80-degree heat, 13,000 fans packed in the stands wearing shorts and T-shirts to watch this truly bizarre event, which began with the ice being badly damaged by a protective tarp that had been draped over it.

"It was one of our first exhibition games of the year," John Vanbiesbrouck recalled, "and when you have Luc Robitaille and Wayne Gretzky and other great players out there facing you, of course you don't want to be embarrassed. But we dressed a solid lineup and were a very good hockey club that year. We were going to contend for the Presidents' Trophy, so we were no slouch."

Of all the challenges league officials expected to encounter in staging an outdoor hockey game in the desert, there was one they could not have anticipated: bugs. A lot of them.

"These bugs were called grasshoppers," Vanbiesbrouck said, "and they came in like locusts, like a plague. They hit the ice, and a lot of them stuck to the ice. The big joke from that game was when Tie Domi had a breakaway on Kelly Hrudey, he lost control of the puck and actually slipped and fell. He said to us later that he couldn't get a shot off because he slipped on a grasshopper."

January 29, 2014: Rangers 2, Islanders 1

With the Northeast in the grips of a deep freeze, the first puck wasn't dropped until 7:45 PM when the temperature was 22 degrees (and falling) with a single-digit wind-chill factor. Spectators bundled up like Eskimos witnessed a much tighter contest than the one preceding it.

Both teams struggled to control the puck on the choppy outdoor ice, and it took nearly 39 minutes for a scoreless deadlock to be broken when Brock Nelson put one past Lundqvist to give the Islanders a brief 1–0 lead. The Rangers' Benoit Pouliot tied the game just 40 seconds later. Dan Carcillo's goal four minutes into the third period would prove to be the game-winner, and the Rangers improved to 3–0 in outdoor games.

Rangers fans and Islanders fans don't see eye to eye about much, but they were overwhelmingly united in their displeasure with the evening's entertainment—R&B artist CeeLo Green, who came out during the first intermission in a full-length fur coat to perform a few of his hits. It was the wrong audience and the wrong venue for Green, who was booed relentlessly throughout his set. (Imagine James Taylor performing at an NBA All-Star Game. It was that bad.) CeeLo claimed to have enjoyed the experience, but the double-bird he flipped the crowd before leaving the stage suggested otherwise.

86 Lights, Camera, Action

From starring roles to blink-and-you'll-miss-them cameos, here's a partial list of appearances by the Rangers on the silver screen and the small screen:

Movies:

13 Going On 30 (2004): In this romantic comedy/fantasy, Jennifer Garner plays the adult version of a 13-year-old girl who is mysteriously transformed into a 30-year-old woman. As an adult, she discovers that she is dating a fictional New York Ranger named Alex Carlson (Samuel Ball).

At First Sight (1999): After having his vision restored through an operation, a formerly blind man (Val Kilmer) takes in a game between the Rangers and Sharks at Madison Square Garden.

Big Daddy (1999): Adam Sandler's character, Sonny Koufax, is seen wearing an Adam Graves Rangers jersey, but the "G" and "S" were digitally removed for contractual reasons because the producers of the film wanted to avoid paying licensing rights for the use of the jersey.

Broadway Brawler: Bruce Willis was set to star in this romantic comedy about a washed-up hockey player who becomes involved in the lives of a single mother and her two children. Game footage was shot at Madison Square Garden during the 1996 preseason, with Bruce Driver temporarily wearing a Rangers jersey with the name of Willis' character, Eddy Kapinsky (the Pinnacle card company even produced a limited number of Eddy Kapinsky hockey cards, which are quite valuable among collectors). But *Broadway Brawler* was never completed. Unhappy with director Lee Grant, Willis exercised his right as co-producer and fired the entire crew, ending production only three weeks into filming.

Face-Off (1971): Art Hindle plays a star for the Toronto Maple Leafs who falls in love with a pop singer (Trudy Young). The film includes game action between the Leafs and Rangers. Former Ranger Derek Sanderson, then a member of the Boston Bruins, appears as himself.

Manhattan Melodrama (1934): This Clark Gable film includes a scene in which Gable's character, Blackie, murders Assistant District Attorney Richard Snow (Thomas Jackson) in a Madison Square Garden bathroom during a game between the Rangers and Montreal Canadiens.

Manhattan Murder Mystery (1993): Woody Allen and Diane Keaton star in this comedy about a couple who suspect that their next-door neighbor has murdered his wife. The film opens with a scene at Madison Square Garden during a Rangers-Capitals game.

Mystery, Alaska (1999): An all-star cast including Russell Crowe and Burt Reynolds headline this underdog tale about an amateur hockey team that accepts a challenge to play an exhibition game against the Rangers. Although former Rangers player, coach, and GM Phil Esposito appears in the film as himself, the filmmakers were not able to recruit any active Rangers to appear in the film. As a result, the Rangers' roster in the movie is entirely fictional.

The Forgotten (2004): Julianne Moore plays a woman struggling to cope with the loss of her young son in this sci-fi/thriller. Her character befriends a retired Ranger named Ash Correll, played by Dominic West. Correll's apartment is filled with mementos from his playing career, including a framed Rangers jersey.

The Great Canadian: In 1939, Metro-Goldwyn-Mayer arranged with Rangers coach and manager Lester Patrick to film some location shots for a Clark Gable hockey flick at Madison Square Garden. Phil Watson and Babe Pratt were going to appear as doubles in the hockey scenes, with Watson set to double for Gable. In *The Patricks: Hockey's Royal Family*, author Eric Whithead recalls that Pratt complained to Lester about the casting, saying that Watson was "too ugly" to stand in for Gable. *The Great Canadian* was eventually canceled and it is not believed that any filming ever took place at the Garden.

The Rocket: The Legend of Rocket Richard (2005): Originally released in Canada as *Maurice Richard*, this French-language biopic follows the rise of the Montreal Canadiens legend. Sean Avery has a small role in the film as hard-nosed Rangers defenseman Bob "Killer" Dill, whose battles with Richard are well chronicled. The film re-creates with reasonable accuracy the December 17, 1944, game between the Canadiens and Rangers in which Dill goaded Richard into a fight. Richard won the bout decisively and then beat Dill again in the penalty box after the two exchanged words. Interesting fact: *The Rocket* was shot two years before Avery actually joined the Rangers.

Safe Men (1998): A comedy about two hopeless lounge singers who are mistaken for ace safecrackers by a local mob boss. Brian Mullen appears as himself in the film, signing autographs at a gaudy Bar Mitzvah. In the same scene, Jewish gangster "Big Fat" Bernie Gayle (Michael Lerner) and his son, Bernie Jr. (Michael Schmidt), are wearing Rangers jerseys. Bernie Jr. also sports a Rangers yarmulke.

Television:

Beverly Hills 90210: In the season-seven episode "Face-Off" (1997), Brandon (Jason Priestley) plays in a charity hockey game with retired pros Ron Duguay and former Bruin Cam Neely, both appearing as themselves.

Friends: In the first-season episode "The One with George Stephanopoulos" (1994), Joey and Chandler take Ross to a Rangers game to take his mind off of the anniversary of his first time having sex with his ex-wife Carol. The evening takes an unfortunate turn when Ross suffers a broken nose after getting hit in the face with a puck.

How I Met Your Mother: In the fifth-season episode "Definitions" (2009), Robin (Vancouver native and real-life Canucks fan Cobie Smulders) takes a date to a Rangers-Canucks game.

How I Met Your Mother: In the sixth-season episode "Glitter" (2010), Marshall (Jason Segel) takes Lily (Alyson Hannigan) to Madison Square Garden to meet the Rangers' organist. Their visit coincides with a Rangers-Flyers game.

The Late Show with David Letterman: Rangers players have frequently appeared on David Letterman's NBC and CBS late-night programs, including a June 15, 1994, appearance by Mark Messier, Brian Leetch, and Mike Richter, who brought the Stanley Cup with them, and a 2009 appearance in which Chris Drury, Henrik Lundqvist, Sean Avery, and others read the Top 10 List, "Things Never Before Spoken by a Hockey Player."

The Martha Stewart Show: In a November 2010 episode of the cooking, entertaining, and homemaking program, Henrik Lundqvist stops by to help Martha bake an apple crostata (an open-faced pie).

The Nanny: In the third-season episode "The Hockey Show" (1996), Fran (Fran Drescher) dates fictional Ranger Michael LaVoe (Anthony Addabbo). Mike is highly superstitious and blames Fran for losing the game when she wears red shoes to the arena. Ron Greschner and John Davidson appear as themselves.

Rules of Engagement: In the fourth-season episode "The Score" (2010), Russell (David Spade) and Timmy (Adhir Kalyan) attend a Rangers-Bruins playoff game at Madison Square Garden. Russell gets angry at Timmy for rooting against the Rangers.

Ryan's Hope: Ron Greschner makes a cameo appearance in a July 1980 episode of the long-running ABC soap opera, which was set and produced in New York City.

Seinfeld: In the sixth-season episode "The Face Painter" (1995), Devils fan David Puddy (Patrick Warburton) paints his face before attending a playoff game at Madison Square Garden between the Devils and Rangers. After Elaine (Julia Louis-Dreyfus) threatens to break up with him if he paints his face again, Puddy and other characters go to the next game with their chests painted instead.

Spin City: In the second-season episode "Deaf Man Walking" (1998), Deputy Mayor Mike Flaherty (Michael J. Fox) attends a photo shoot at a city rink with Adam Graves, Pat LaFontaine, and Dan Cloutier, all appearing as themselves. In the scene, Mike fires a slap shot at Cloutier, who easily catches the puck with his bare hand, then accidentally crashes into Graves and LaFontaine, injuring both.

Spin City: In the fifth-season episode "Hey Judith" (2001), Carter (Michael Boatman) and Stuart (Alan Ruck) are at a Rangers game when Stuart wins a chance to compete in a shot from center ice contest. Amidst a sea of Rangers fans, he is the only person wearing a Detroit Red Wings jersey, a reference to Ruck's role in the film *Ferris Bueller's Day Off*.

Up All Night: In the first-season episode "Week Off" (2011), stay-at-home dad Chris (Will Arnett) pulls up to his driveway and sees his life-size, cardboard cutout of Brendan Shanahan in the garbage. "Why is Brendan Shanahan in the garbage?" Chris asks wife Reagan (Christina Applegate). "Because Brendan Shanahan was blocking an air conditioning vent," she replies. Cardboard Shanny returns a week later in the episode "First Christmas" when Chris decides to sell all his hockey memorabilia so he can have enough money to buy Reagan a very special Christmas present.

87 Marek Malik's Miraculous Shootout Goal

The use of the shootout to decide regular season games tied at the end of overtime was adopted by the NHL in 2005. It was probably the most dramatic and controversial rules change since the league implemented four-on-four overtime seven years earlier.

Traditionalists dismissed the shootout as a gimmick. What's so bad about a tie, they reasoned. Why should a hard-fought contest be resolved by a skills competition?

Others defended the tiebreaker for breathing new excitement into the game, as evidenced by how it seemed to bring fans out of their seats. That was certainly the case on November 26, 2005, when the Rangers hosted the Washington Capitals.

Henrik Lundqvist and Olaf Kolzig were strong in their respective nets during regulation and nearly impenetrable through overtime and the first 14 rounds of the shootout.

By then, the teams had selected so many players to shoot that they were being forced to send out their weaker defensemen. Bryan Muir of the Caps scored in round 14, and Jason Strudwick answered for the Rangers to tie the score again. The next Caps shooter was stopped, which set the stage for Marek Malik.

Skating in on Kolzig, Malik deked to the goalie's glove side, pulled the puck back, put his stick through his legs, and flipped the disc in over Kolzig's blocker to score and win the game. After the shot, he raised his arm and shrugged as if to say, "Was there ever any doubt?" before being mobbed by his teammates.

Malik's sleight of hand was the sort of jaw-dropping wizardry that fans would've expected from, well, virtually anyone other than Malik, (6'6", 238 lbs.) who would spend much of his three seasons in New York being criticized for his lack of physical play and tendency to turn the puck over in his own zone.

But on this special night, Malik was still a Ranger newbie, and as far as the Garden faithful were concerned, his slate was still clean.

At 15 rounds, the Rangers-Capitals shootout is still the longest one ever. The goal that ended it was ranked as the play of the year by TSN's *SportsCentre*, and it was certainly the play of Malik's career.

Marek Malik (right) slips the puck past Washington Capitals goaltender Olie Kolzig in a shootout to win the game on Saturday, November 26, 2005, at Madison Square Garden in New York. (AP Photo/Julie Jacobson)

88 Worst. Loss. Ever.

When the Rangers lost 14 of their first 15 games to open the 1943–44 season, the only way players and fans could cope was to tell themselves that things couldn't get much worse.

And then, on January 23, 1944, they got worse.

It was a Sunday night at the old Olympia in Detroit and the Rangers, still reeling from the loss of so many key players to the war effort, delivered a performance so putrid that the stench of it still hovers over Lake St. Clair.

The contest opened on an encouraging note for the New Yorkers, with Bryan Hextall nearly scoring on a breakaway. His shot seemed to enter the net, but the scoring light didn't go on. The Rangers argued, but referee Norm Lamport supported the ruling of no goal and the game continued.

Then the Red Wings scored twice, taking a 2–0 lead into the first intermission—not an insurmountable deficit for the Rangers. But during the next 40 minutes, the Detroit skaters launched an all-out assault on New York's 23-year-old rookie goalie, Ken McAuley, scoring five times in the second period and eight times in the third. Syd Howe (no relation to Gordie) capped off the slaughter with a third period hat trick.

Final score: Red Wings 15, Rangers 0. It remains the most lopsided game in the history of the NHL.

When he returned to the visitors' dressing room after the game, McAuley—who'd made 43 saves despite allowing all 15 Detroit goals—was in no mood to talk. And really, what was there to say? That he was humiliated? That it had been the worst experience of his hockey playing career? That his teammates had abandoned him?

Remembering Dudley "Red" Garrett

Yes, the war years were tough on NHL teams, but "tough" is a relative term when you stop to consider the roughly 100 players who left the league to serve in the military. Some even saw action. A few never returned.

One of them was Dudley "Red" Garrett, a hard-nosed defenseman from Toronto who broke into the NHL with the Rangers in 1942–43. During the season, Red was called to serve in the Canadian Navy. The Rangers and their fans were disappointed to lose the promising rookie but also hopeful that once the war was over, he would return and continue his development into a full-time NHL defenseman.

But Dudley never saw New York again. He was stationed up in Atlantic Canada where the Canadian Navy often provided armed escort ships for vessels carrying supplies to Allied troops overseas. It was dangerous work since these supply boats were targets of German submarines.

On November 25, 1944, Dudley was serving on the HMCS *Shawinigan* when it was torpedoed by a German submarine off the coast of Newfoundland. The *Shawinigan* sank with the loss of all hands on board. Dudley was 20.

In 1947, the American Hockey League established the Dudley "Red" Garrett Memorial Award to honor the top AHL rookie as voted by the media and players.

Veteran defenseman Wilfred "Bucko" McDonald tried to ease the tension by assuring the kid that of all the goalies who had ever played in the NHL, none of them ever set a record like that.

McAuley was finally able to laugh about the episode in a 1972 interview with *Sports Illustrated*. He said, "I ask people when they remind me of that night, 'Where would the Detroit Red Wings have been without me?' I gave them the confidence to become big stars."

McAuley lasted only one more season in the NHL before returning to his native Edmonton to play senior hockey. Ironically, he later went to work for the Red Wings as a coach in their farm system.

89 Support the Garden of Dreams

There are many worthwhile charities in the world doing good work for those less fortunate. One of those is the Garden of Dreams Foundation, a non-profit organization that works closely with the Rangers and the rest of Madison Square Garden Company to bring a little magic into the lives of kids facing some of the biggest hurdles imaginable.

Thanks in large measure to the generous support of individuals in the community, Garden of Dreams has made a difference in the lives of thousands of children in crisis throughout the tri-state area—kids suffering from devastating illness, homelessness, abuse, hunger, extreme poverty, or tragedy. Working with local children's hospitals, community-based organizations, and other charities in the area, Garden of Dreams creates once-in-a-lifetime experiences for kids and their families through exclusive access to MSG celebrities and venues. Rangers players have been heavily involved with the Foundation since it was started in 2006.

Henrik Lundqvist was named the Foundation's official spokesperson. In 2012, he commissioned an extra mask for the Winter Classic, which raised $35,000 for the charity. Then he launched his own signature line of sports apparel called "The Crown Collection," with proceeds from sales benefiting the Foundation. He also hosted a private benefit concert with tennis legend (and wannabe rocker) John McEnroe joining him on stage, an event that raised another $48,000.

The Foundation's premier fundraising event is Casino Night, a black-tie affair where fans get to play casino games alongside Rangers players, coaches, and alumni and bid on unique auction items. In 2014, the event helped raise almost $300,000 for the charity.

"It's fun to dress up and go to a classy event," Rangers fan Randi Gruber said. "Even though the players are technically working, they seem to be more laid back than they might be at a typical fan meet-and-greet. It was fun to talk to them and mingle. They all seemed pretty gracious. I went with three other people, but we had a friend who couldn't go because she was very pregnant at the time. We were Facetiming with her when Benoit Pouliot reached over, took the phone, and started talking to her. That was awesome. Then Derek Stepan showed us a picture of the dog he brought back from Sochi. It really was a great night."

Tickets for Casino Night aren't cheap—you can't get in the door for less than $500—but if philanthropy is really your goal, the Foundation will accept gifts of any size.

To make a gift to the Garden of Dreams, or to learn how to become a volunteer, visit donate.gardenofdreamsfoundation.org or give the Foundation a call at (212) 465-4170.

90 Gratoony the Loony

The Rangers have had plenty of colorful characters over the years but none quite as colorful as goaltender Gilles Gratton, whose many idiosyncrasies earned him the nickname "Gratoony the Loony."

But was Gratton really loony or just misunderstood?

The signing of Gratton as a free agent in the spring of 1976 was part of an ongoing rebuilding process overseen by coach and GM John Ferguson. Fergy had heard some of the strange stories circulating about Gratton—like that he'd once asked out of a start because the moon was in the wrong part of the sky—but didn't seem to care.

That summer, when Ferguson and other Garden executives were recruited to telephone prospective season ticket holders to help boost sales, a fan said to Ferguson, "I understand you signed a flake in Gilles Gratton."

"I don't believe he's a flake," Fergy replied. "Sure, he does his own thing, but I'm only interested in knowing if he can stop the puck."

Judged on those grounds alone, Gratton's brief Ranger career would have been forgotten long ago. With a bloated 4.22 goals against average, he won only 11 times in 41 appearances, all during the 1976–77 season.

We're still talking about Gratton all these years later because he's a legend among aficionados of goalie mask art—more on that later—and because he possessed some eccentricities that seem bizarre when viewed within the context of his job as a hockey player but wouldn't illicit more than a shoulder shrug if he'd been a Starbucks barista or the manager of a New Age bookshop.

Gratton was said to have believed in reincarnation. He told people that in a past life he was a soldier during the Spanish Inquisition who was killed when he was run through by a lance. He also dabbled in meditation, as former teammate Nick Fotiu can attest.

"I roomed with Gratton on Long Island during training camp," Fotiu recalled. "I remember taking a shower, and when I got out of the bathroom, I nearly jumped in the air because I saw this guy in the corner of the room. He had the bed sheet wrapped over his head with his eyes closed. I yelled at him, 'What the f--- are you doing?' He said, 'I'm meditating.' I said, 'F---ing meditating? I'm going to kill you. You scared the s--- out of me!'"

Gratton was also one of those free spirits who found clothing to be burdensome. The late John Halligan, the Rangers' intrepid publicity man, recounted an evening at the old New Haven Coliseum

Painted Faces

Ever since Boston's Gerry Cheevers drew stitches on his mask to mark each spot where a puck had hit him, goalies have been expressing themselves by personalizing their masks.

John Davidson commissioned a "Lone Ranger" motif for his mask. Artist Greg Harrison painted a blue mask over the eyes, a cowboy hat and Ranger shield on each side, a brown and grey rifle bullet on the forehead, and a red sheriff's star over the nose and mouth.

New York has long been known as the Big Apple, so Wayne Thomas had one painted on the front of his mask.

On display at the Hockey Hall of Fame, Steve Baker's mask was one of the earliest to feature a specific geographic location—in this case, the Empire State Building.

John Vanbiesbrouck expanded on that theme by getting the entire Manhattan skyline painted on his mask, with a twist: a swarm of bees (for "Beezer") flying overhead. He only got to wear it for one season, 1992–93, which was also his last with the team.

Steve Valiquette's Spider-Man mask paid homage to one of Marvel's most popular New York–based heroes.

Henrik Lundqvist changes his mask design about as often as he changes his socks. At various times his mask has featured a mosaic of Rangers logos, his No. 30 crown insignia, lightning bolts and other 3D effects, and even Swedish icons Greta Garbo and Ingrid Bergman.

Cam Talbot's *Ghostbusters* mask earned him the nickname "The Goalbuster."

But the most famous Rangers goalie mask of them all, the Lady Liberty mask, belonged to Mike Richter. Its designer, Ed Cubberly, also created the Hannibal Lecter mask worn by Anthony Hopkins in *The Silence of the Lambs*. Cubberly delivered the mask to Richter during a practice, and initially the goalie was reluctant to wear it because it was a different style than he was used to. When practice was over, Richter asked teammate Bernie Nicholls to fire some pucks directly at his head to see if the new mask could do the job. It did, and the rest is history.

when an almost naked Gratton found a piano in an area off-limits to the public and regaled bystanders with a tune.

"One time," Fotiu remembered, "before a game in Philadelphia, Gratton said to me, 'I'm going in net and I'm going to take all my clothes off. I'm going to strip in the Spectrum.' He told me he was going to do it. I said, 'You're not going to do it. I'll come off the bench and tackle you. You're not going to do it.' He never did it."

Even if you believe only a fraction of the crazy tales that have circulated about Gratton, some of which have surely been exaggerated for effect, there seems to be near-unanimous sentiment that Gratton's mask was the coolest ever worn by an NHL goalie. The bold and imaginative design has been the source of some debate.

Gratton has insisted that the ferocious feline face painted on the front is that of a tiger, while hockey lore has long held that it's actually a lion. The artist who painted the mask, Greg Harrison, claimed the idea for the design came from Gratton's Zodiac sign, Leo. Believe who you will.

In honor of the 2012 Winter Classic, Martin Biron commissioned a special mask as a tribute to the one made famous by Gratton, a fellow Quebec native.

91 Stepan Up

There's more to the measure of a player's toughness than his penalty-minute totals. Take Derek Stepan. Back in the lineup four days after surgery to repair a broken jaw, and sporting a protective facial shield that made him look like a Rock 'Em Sock 'Em Robot, Stepan scored twice in a 7–4 loss to the Montreal Canadiens in Game 5 of the 2014 Eastern Conference Finals.

Even in defeat, that performance spoke volumes about Stepan's character. And character is a big reason why, at the 2008 NHL Entry Draft, the Rangers had the Shattuck St. Mary's High School star ranked higher than Central Scouting did. They chose him in the second round, 51st overall—so much earlier than he expected to go that he was actually at home watching on TV when his name was called—then saw him off to the University of Wisconsin to continue his development.

Two years later, on October 9, 2010, a Saturday night in Buffalo, Derek became the first Ranger to record a hat trick in his NHL debut, beating Ryan Miller three times in a 6–3 win over the Sabres. Stepan scored his first goal midway through the first period,

Derek Stepan (21) wears a protective shield around his jaw prior to Game 6 of the Eastern Conference Finals between the New York Rangers and the Montreal Canadiens at Madison Square Garden in Manhattan, New York on May 29, 2014. The Rangers won 1–0 to advance to the Stanley Cup Final.
(Kostas Lymperopoulos/Cal Sport Media via AP Images)

Who Was Lars-Erik Sjöberg?

A legend in his native Sweden where he played defense for various club teams and was a mainstay on the Swedish National Team for a decade, Lars-Erik Sjöberg also won three championships with the WHA's Winnipeg Jets.

Sjöberg was working as a scout for the Rangers when he died of cancer in 1987. To honor him, the Rangers created the Lars-Erik Sjöberg Award, which is presented annually to the best rookie in training camp. Past winners of the award include Derek Stepan, Marc Staal, Niklas Sundstrom, and Mike Richter.

redirecting a point shot by Dan Girardi, and then he added two more in the second.

What was it about the 6', 196-lb. center from Hastings, Minnesota, that first caught the Rangers' attention? Well, as a kid, his physical attributes were merely average. Maybe even a little below average. He was never the best player on his team at any level because of his smallish build and mediocre skating ability.

Derek hung around the game because he had "hockey sense" nurtured by an influential coach who happened to live under the same roof. Derek's father, Brad Stepan, was a left winger and junior hockey teammate of future Rangers legend Adam Graves. New York's fifth-round draft pick (91st overall) in 1985, Brad attended several Rangers training camps and spent the 1988–89 season with the team's IHL affiliate in Denver but never made it up to the NHL. He instilled in his son the importance of being an unselfish player, going so far as to forbid Derek from scoring after he had scored a few goals so that he would focus on setting up his teammates.

"He's like a Mark Messier, guys who aren't the most skillful but are the most important cogs for good teams, who play entire shifts goal line to goal line and block shots, win draws, and are incredibly reliable," Derek's high school coach, Tom Ward, told the *New*

Did You Know?

Derek Stepan was just the fourth player in NHL history to score a hat trick in his first big league game. The others were Alex Smart of the Montreal Canadiens (January 14, 1943), Réal Cloutier of the Quebec Nordiques (October 10, 1979), and Fabian Brunnström of the Dallas Stars (October 15, 2008).

York Times. "A complete player who might be a leading scorer, but he's more interested in winning. We call it 'hockey sense,' and he's blessed with it."

92 Tim Horton

It was late in the 1969–70 season when the Rangers suffered a wave of injuries to their defense corps. Fearing his undermanned club might drop out of the playoff race, Emile Francis telephoned his counterpart in Toronto, Punch Imlach, to inquire about the availability of the legendary Tim Horton (yes, the same Tim Horton whose name adorns a coffee and sandwich shop at the Madison Square Garden taxi ramp).

Horton, a staple on the Maple Leafs blueline for 20 seasons, was a shade under 6' tall and weighed less than 200 lbs.—merely average by today's standards. He was, however, considered to be the strongest player in the game. In one oft-told tale, Horton got into a scrap with Derek Sanderson and broke two of the Boston winger's ribs simply by enveloping him in a crushing bear hug.

"I knew Toronto wanted to get rid of Horton because he had gone to arbitration and was awarded a $70,000 contract," Francis recalled. "Well, we had nobody making that kind of money in

New York, but I knew that our season hinged on the fact that if we didn't get a defenseman or two, we were going to be in trouble."

On March 3, 1970, the Rangers acquired Horton from the Maple Leafs for future considerations (left wing Denis Dupere).

"Salary," Francis said. "That's the only reason we were able to get Tim Horton. Oh shit, he was a great defenseman. One of the best defensemen that ever played for me. He was a right-handed

Veteran NHL player Tim Horton was a star with the Toronto Maple Leafs before coming to the Rangers. (AP Photo/Lederhandler)

Jeff Beukeboom

Any conversation about the hardest-hitting Rangers defensemen has to include Jeff Beukeboom. That wonderfully descriptive name—Beukeboom—so accurately described the rugged style of this blueline behemoth who used every ounce of his 230-lb. frame to the maximum. His bone-jarring hits became a staple at Madison Square Garden, and fans loved it.

"It wasn't a blueprint to go after Edmonton players," Neil Smith said in 1991 of acquiring yet another ex-Oiler. "But on a battlefront, the best soldiers are the ones who've been in battle before. Winners usually repeat."

And so it was that Beukeboom, reunited with Oilers alumni Mark Messier, Glenn Anderson, Craig MacTavish, Kevin Lowe, Adam Graves, and Esa Tikkanen, won his fourth Stanley Cup in 1994.

An intimidating presence on Broadway for eight seasons, Beuk was the perfect complement to the more offensive-minded Brian Leetch, with whom he was partnered for much of the decade. His steady, stay-at-home style allowed Leetch to join the rush and kept opposing players out of Mike Richter's goal crease.

Lingering effects of post-concussion syndrome forced Beukeboom to call it quits in July 1999.

shot on defense, which we didn't have, and there were only about six in the league. And he was the strongest defenseman that I had ever seen. I once saw Bobby Hull go flying down on the left wing. Horton put out his right arm and stopped Hull right in his tracks."

While Francis was scrambling to address the Rangers' immediate needs on defense, he was also trying to overhaul the culture of an organization that hadn't won a playoff round since 1950. That sometimes meant doing away with past practices and experimenting with new ones, like putting the team up in a hotel right across the street from Madison Square Garden the night before a home game if they had played the previous night on the road.

"It was one of those nights that Horton left his hotel room to go get a Coke from the soda machine," Francis said. "He put in a dollar and nothing came out. And he put in another dollar and nothing came out. So he goes back to the room and calls the guy at the front desk and says, 'I just put two dollars into the machine to get a soda and nothing came out.' The guy at the desk said he was too busy to do anything about it. You know what Horton did? He went down the hall, picked up the machine, brought it over to the elevator, and sent it down to the first floor. Now he calls the guy at the front desk and says, 'You were too busy to come up here, so I sent the machine down to you. Either give me my Coke or give me my money back.' That's how strong he was."

Horton was claimed from the Rangers by Pittsburgh in the 1971 intra-league draft. From there it was on to the Buffalo Sabres.

At 44 and playing in his 24th NHL season, he was already the second-oldest player in the league behind Minnesota's Gump Worsley. With the growing success of the restaurant chain he'd started a decade earlier, Tim was ready to get out of the game and focus more on business.

But he never got the chance. On February 21, 1974, he died from injuries suffered in a car accident in St. Catharines, Ontario.

Three years later, Horton was inducted posthumously into the Hockey Hall of Fame.

93 Hockey's True Iron Man

You may know that Doug Jarvis, who played for the Montreal Canadiens and Hartford Whalers, holds the record for most consecutive NHL games played. But did you know that pro hockey's true Iron Man is actually Andy Hebenton, a plugging right wing who played more than 1,000 professional games without a single miss? That remarkable stretch included 560 games with the Rangers.

Andy was a hard-nosed player who began his career as property of the Canadiens. The high-flying Habs of the 1950s considered him too slow, so he languished in the minors. But Muzz Patrick, newly anointed as general manager of the Rangers for the 1955–56 season, had scouted Hebenton in the Western Hockey League and knew what he could do. Muzz made Hebenton his very first acquisition, paying $10,000 to Montreal for his services. It was money well spent.

Hebenton quickly developed into one of the NHL's best back checkers and penalty killers. He also had a knack for scoring, netting 20 or more goals in five of his eight seasons on Broadway. In 1956–57, he won the Lady Byng Trophy for clean, effective play. He also won the Rangers' Players' Player Award three straight seasons from 1959 to 1961.

But it was Hebenton's durability that most impressed teammates. The man simply refused to take a night off. Once, during a Saturday game against Montreal, he took a stick in the mouth that knocked four of his teeth halfway down his throat. It was a nasty injury, but he finished the game, played again the next night, and finally saw a dentist on Monday.

The Rangers lost Hebenton's services in June 1963 when the Boston Bruins grabbed him in what was then called the Intra-League Draft. He played one season for the Bruins—all 70 games, of course—before returning to the Western League to continue a career that would extend past his 45th birthday.

All told, Hebenton played 1,062 games as a pro without a miss, a number that will probably never be matched. It was only the death of his father that finally snapped the streak on October 18, 1967.

94 Remember the Boogeyman

When it comes to the subject of fighting in hockey, the authors of this book are guilty of a certain hypocrisy—celebrating the epic bouts of players like Tie Domi and Lou Fontinato on one page and on another, mourning the death of a young man who might still be on this earth if not for his job as the NHL's most feared fighter.

Derek Boogaard was a 6'7" 260-lb. behemoth who couldn't score goals, couldn't take faceoffs, and couldn't kill penalties. But what he could do was beat up other enforcers. At that, he might've been the best in the business. Often, though, he didn't have to fight. His mere presence in the lineup was like a nuclear missile sitting in its silo, a deterrent against any would-be aggressor. Even as one-dimensional players like "The Boogeyman" were becoming obsolete in the salary cap age, Derek clung to his role because he knew it was the only reason he'd made it to the NHL.

"I wouldn't trade it for the world," he said shortly after signing a four-year, $6.5 million contract with the Rangers in July 2010—a lot of years and a lot of dollars for a player who hadn't scored a goal in five seasons. But Glen Sather felt the team needed a heavyweight after Jody Shelley departed as a free agent to sign with the rival Flyers.

Derek was used sparingly under Coach John Tortorella— mostly fourth-line minutes when he wasn't a healthy scratch—but was well-liked by teammates because he was an upbeat, fun-loving guy. Many of those who played with him on the Rangers and his previous team, the Minnesota Wild, described him as a "gentle giant." In New York, he created "Boogaard's Booguardians," hosting military members and their families at Madison Square

Garden for all Rangers home games. He also worked with the Garden of Dreams Foundation.

Derek suffered an unknown number of concussions playing hockey, but the one he got during a fight with Ottawa's Matt Carkner in December 2010 put him out of commission for the rest of the season.

On May 13, 2011, Boogaard's brothers found him dead in his Minneapolis apartment. His death was later ruled an accidental overdose of pain medication and alcohol. Derek, 28, had a history of abusing prescription painkillers and spent time in the league's substance abuse program.

After Boogaard's death, his family agreed to donate his brain to Boston University where researchers would study it for signs of chronic traumatic encephalopathy, also known as CTE, a progressive degenerative disease similar to Alzheimer's. CTE is believed to be caused by repeated blows to the head. It can only be diagnosed posthumously, but scientists say CTE manifests itself in symptoms like memory loss, depression, and even addiction.

The Boogaards waited months for the results. And while they waited, two more NHL enforcers died—reportedly suicides—stirring up a debate about the toll that fighting takes on hockey players.

Eventually, scientists concluded that Derek's brain was ravaged by CTE. Had he survived, he might've ended up like Reggie Fleming, a Rangers enforcer in the 1960s who died in 2009 after three decades of dealing with behavioral and cognitive impairments. He had CTE, as did former Red Wings brawler Bob Probert, who died of heart failure a few months after Boogaard.

NHL players and executives are still overwhelmingly opposed to a ban on fighting. But if the time comes when fans start tuning out because of the violence, and corporate partners move their sponsorship dollars elsewhere, then the league and its players' union will have some very difficult decisions to make. Until then, hypocrisy reigns.

95 One Roof, Two Rivals

The Rangers have had many rivals but only one, the New York Americans, failed so miserably in their efforts to outskate, outscore, and outdraw the Blueshirts that they were driven out of existence.

In 1925, the NHL announced the sale of the defunct Hamilton Tigers to Prohibition bootlegger "Big Bill" Dwyer, who moved the team to New York and renamed it the Americans.

Dwyer was a shady character known around town as the "King of the Bootleggers," a distinction that frequently landed him in trouble with the law. In fact, when the Americans made their New York City debut at Madison Square Garden on December 15, 1925, versus the Canadiens, Dwyer missed the game because he was either still in the slammer or had just been released.

"Yonkers" Billy Burch, one of the few U.S.-born players in the league at the time, was an early star for the Amerks, as the newspapers called them. They wore red, white, and blue stars and stripes uniforms and were an instant hit among the high society types who frequented the Garden. But the Amerks' reign as New York's latest, greatest attraction was short-lived.

In 1926, Madison Square Garden ownership decided to bring in an expansion team of its own to share quarters (rent-free) with the Amerks, despite the fact that Dwyer had previously received assurances that his team would have exclusive rights to the New York area. The new team, later dubbed the Rangers, stole the Amerks' patriotic color scheme and, eventually, much of their fanbase.

How's that for starting a rivalry?

In their first season as cohabitants of the Garden, the Amerks finished eight games under .500, while the high-priced Rangers won their division. The Americans' struggles continued the following year as they finished in last place, while the Rangers, in just their second season, won the Stanley Cup. The Blueshirts were suddenly the toast of the town, relegating the Amerks to also-rans forever.

Strengthened by the acquisition of goalie Roy "Shrimp" Worters, the Americans bounced back in 1928–29 and qualified for the playoffs for the first time. The diminutive Worters, listed at just 5'3", went on to become the first goalie to win the Hart Trophy as league MVP. That spring, the Americans and Rangers faced each other in the playoffs. If ever there was an opportunity for Dwyer's "Star Spangled Skaters" to win back the hearts of New York's hockey fans, this was it. But after the teams battled to a scoreless tie in the first game of a two-game, total-goals series, the Rangers scored the only goal in the second match, in overtime.

As the 1920s gave way to the '30s, the Americans slid deeper into irrelevance while the Rangers continued to thrive.

Meanwhile, Dwyer was losing a fortune as the end of Prohibition crippled his illegal hooch business. In 1936–37, having been unable to find a sucker to take the team off his hands, Dwyer simply abandoned the Americans, though conflicting reports from the day suggest he may have been forced out by the league. Mervyn "Red" Dutton, a former Amerks player who'd since become coach, took over management of the team.

Dutton tried to change the Amerks' fortunes by signing veterans Hap Day and former Rangers defensive stalwart Ching Johnson, and it paid off. In 1938, the club finished in second place, setting the stage for another postseason meeting with the Rangers.

The Americans won the first game 2–1 on Johnny Sorrell's overtime goal. Then the Rangers tied the series, forcing a decisive third game. In that match, the Rangers jumped out to a 2–0 lead. But the Amerks stormed back in the third period, tying the game on goals by Lorne Carr and Nels Stewart. Then early in the fourth overtime, Carr scored again to give the Americans the upset victory.

Did You Know?

To add a little spice to the Rangers-Americans rivalry, the MacBeth Trophy was awarded annually to the club with the best record in head-to-head competition. Presented by the New York Hockey Writers' Association, the trophy was named for William J. "Bunk" MacBeth, a sportswriter credited for convincing Bill Dwyer to bring pro hockey to New York City.

After the Amerks folded in 1942, the hockey writers continued to award the trophy to the Rangers' Most Valuable Player in the playoffs.

Finally beating the mighty Rangers—in the playoffs!—was the last great moment for a franchise that had enjoyed precious few.

In 1940, Dutton and his boys could only watch with envy as the Rangers celebrated their third Stanley Cup.

By then, Dutton was so desperate to drum up interest in his failing hockey club that he renamed it the Brooklyn Americans, believing that he could grow a new fanbase in the outer borough. But that stunt didn't fool anyone. The Amerks were still playing their home games at Madison Square Garden, even though they practiced out in Brooklyn and wore new sweaters with "Brooklyn" spelled out across the chest. The few fans the Amerks had left in Manhattan were turned off by the rebranding, and there was little incentive for a hockey fan living in Brooklyn to schlep into the city to watch a last-place team.

In 1942, the Americans ceased operations due to a wartime player shortage and because the team was still carrying debts owed by Dwyer. Dutton tried to revive the franchise after the war, but the league wouldn't let him. Although he couldn't prove it, Dutton believed that Garden ownership had pressured the NHL into not reinstating the Amerks.

The legend—and it's never been verified as a direct quote—is that an embittered Dutton swore the Rangers would never win another Stanley Cup in his lifetime.

And they didn't.

Dutton, who died in 1987 at age 88, spent the rest of his life answering questions about his so-called curse. His name was forever linked to Rangers failure, and that tickled him immensely.

96 The Five-Timers Club

It's a super-exclusive fraternity that hasn't admitted any new members in more than 30 years. You can't buy, lie, bully, or sweet talk your way in. Fact is, until another Ranger scores at least five goals in a single game, Don Murdoch and Mark Pavelich will have the Five-Timers Club all to themselves.

If there are common traits to be found among those who've scored a hat-trick-plus-two in the National Hockey League, it's that they tend to have what the kids call "mad skills" and the good sense to acknowledge that the feat requires an epic stroke of luck. Murdoch and Pavelich had that in common, and little else. The former was a free-spirited, club-hopping kid from Cranbrook, British Columbia, who gleefully and unapologetically embraced New York's myriad pleasures to excess. The latter, quiet and shy out of uniform, preferred the solitude and tranquility of ice fishing back in his native Minnesota.

Replacing veteran Bill Fairbairn in the lineup in 1976–77, Murdoch was put on a line with Walt Tkaczuk and Greg Polis and scored twice in his first pro game. Even as a rookie, he had a way of making it look easy.

"Donnie," observed former roommate Dave Maloney, "was one of the top three natural goal scorers I ever played with."

One of Murdoch's greatest assets was his deceptive stride. Appearing heavier than his 180 lbs., he didn't look especially quick

Ranger Killers

The Blueshirts have been on the receiving end of some bravura goal-scoring performances:

Player	Team	Goals	Date
Syd Howe	Red Wings	6	February 3, 1944
Bernie Geoffrion	Canadiens	5	February 19, 1955
Bryan Trottier	Islanders	5	December 23, 1978
Tim Young	North Stars	5	January 15, 1979
Mario Lemieux	Penguins	5	April 9, 1993
Marian Gaborik	Wild	5	December 20, 2007

or agile, but he knew how to fake an opposing player into over-committing himself. Gaining speed, he'd glide around flat-footed veterans who, out of sheer frustration, might reach out and grab him or dive into his skates—anything to prevent him from getting off a shot.

On October 12, 1976, Murdoch's five goals led the Rangers to a 10–4 drubbing of the Minnesota North Stars. It was the most ever scored by a Ranger in a single game, and it tied an NHL record for most goals in a game by a first-year player.

"I've never had as many goals in one game, in juniors or anywhere," a giddy Murdoch said afterward, politely declining to mention that he and his mates had been aided by an absolutely brutal Minnesota defense that allowed 49 shots.

Just more than six years later, on February 23, 1983, Pavelich would match Murdoch's feat in an 11–3 rout of the Hartford Whalers.

Of all the "Miracle on Ice" men who jumped to the NHL, Pav was among the most successful because he adapted easily to the pro game. It helped that the Rangers, with whom he signed as a free agent in 1981, played a wide-open style and were run by a pair of familiar faces: Herb Brooks, coach of the 1980 Olympic team, and Herbie's former assistant, Craig Patrick, who had just been hired as the youngest general manager in Rangers history. They knew better than anyone what the 5'8" center could do, and in New York he finally put to rest any concerns that he might be too small to handle the NHL grind.

"I didn't try for the NHL originally because I didn't think I'd get a fair shot," Pavelich said. "Even the teams that wanted me to come to their training camps warned me that my size would be against me."

But by using his quickness and anticipation to beat bigger players, Pavelich could dodge hits in open ice by ducking or darting around opponents. And when he ran out of room, he was tough enough to absorb a stiff check in order to make a play. The rough stuff didn't faze Pav. In fact, he seemed to enjoy it.

His first three Ranger seasons were offensively prolific. Often playing alongside Ron Duguay, Dave Silk, or former Olympian Rob McClanahan, Pavelich scored at close to a point-per-game clip during the regular season and playoffs.

His five goals against the Whalers, allowed courtesy of goalie Greg Millen, were scored from five different angles. Later, photographers prodded Pavelich into holding up five pucks—a somewhat clichéd ritual, but the introverted star obliged.

"Holding five," Pav said as camera shutters clicked, "is tougher than scoring five."

97 Sing the Rangers' Victory Song

When the Rangers win on home ice, it is customary for the arena music director to play the Rangers' Victory Song, a festive, bouncy little number written specifically for the Rangers by musician and hockey fan J. Fred Coots.

The Rangers' Victory Song

Listen to the cheering of the people in the stands
Twenty thousand hockey bugs and each a Ranger fan!
It's plain as day to see
They want a victory!
All together now strike up the band!
Just keep your stick on that puck
And don't lay down on your luck;
That's the Rangers' Victory Song!
Get through the enemy's goal
With all your heart and your soul;
That's the Rangers' Victory Song!
You've got to fight, Rangers fight
With a grin on your chin!
Tonight is the night
So get in there and win!
This game is worth any price;
Go out and put it on ice
That's the Rangers' Victory Song!

Born in Brooklyn in 1897, John Frederick Coots learned to play the piano from his mother. His first job in music was as a pianist and stock boy in a music shop, and by the age of 20 he had his first song published. He then went into vaudeville—early variety shows produced for the stage—playing the piano and writing songs for other performers.

Coots' star continued to rise as he wrote music for numerous Broadway shows and films. He penned more than 700 songs throughout his career, but his biggest hit by far was the classic Christmas carol, "Santa Claus Is Coming to Town," a collaboration with lyricist Haven Gillespie written in 1934.

Six years later, Coots penned the Rangers' Victory Song as a tribute to the team that finished the 1939–40 season as Stanley Cup champions. He officially dedicated the song to Lester Patrick and his players.

For nearly a quarter century, the Victory Song was played live on the Madison Square Garden organ by the legendary Gladys Goodding and by a string of successors. A recorded version—sans vocals—has been in use since the 1980s.

A member of the Songwriters Hall of Fame, Coots died in 1985 at the age of 87, but his love for the Rangers lives on in a way that would've been most meaningful to him: through his music.

98 "Broadway" Bobby Hull

It was 1981 and Bobby Hull, the legendary left wing who'd victimized goaltenders across the NHL for 16 seasons (plus seven more in the WHA) was wrestling over whether to stay retired or try to squeeze one more year of hockey out of his 42-year-old body.

When an interviewer asked Hull which team he'd like to play for if he came out of retirement, Hull said there was only one—the Rangers, for only the Rangers could give him the chance to reunite with Anders Hedberg and Ulf Nilsson, the Swedish stars who had been his linemates for four high-flying seasons on the Winnipeg Jets.

When Coach Herb Brooks learned of Hull's comments, he invited Hull to try out for a spot on the Rangers when the team opened training camp that September.

Following this development with heightened interest was Garden president David "Sonny" Werblin, who generally loved anything that would keep the Rangers in the news. "Broadway" Bobby Hull was an angle no beat writer would be able to resist.

Of course, the question on everyone's minds was whether Hull, whose 100-mph slap shot and furious dashes up the ice used to

Barnstormin' Bobby Breaks Out With Blueshirts

Bobby Hull's 1981 comeback bid wasn't the first time his name appeared on a Rangers roster. In 1959, a Swiss winemaker sponsored a European barnstorming tour featuring the Rangers and Boston Bruins. The Rangers' leading scorer, Andy Bathgate, couldn't make the trip, so Hull went in his place. Another Chicago player, center Ed Litzenberger, accompanied Hull on the trip, and they played on a line with Eddie Shack. On the larger ice surface, the 20-year-old Hull was able to showcase the speed and booming shot that would make him a superstar. A year later, he won his first Art Ross Trophy as the NHL's scoring champ.

make opponents back off and fans roar, could still play. He had been out of the game for more than a year, quitting the Hartford Whalers in the spring of 1980 to deal with a glut of personal issues including a costly divorce suit brought against him by his former wife and then having to care for a partner who had been hurt in an automobile accident.

But on the practice ice at Rye Playland, Hull didn't look like a has-been going through the motions to cash in on one more contract. He scrimmaged with all the enthusiasm and intensity of a rookie half his age.

The Blueshirts were gearing up to play an exhibition schedule in Finland and Sweden, and Brooks was looking forward to seeing if Hull still had the magic with Hedberg and Nilsson. The reunion plans were at least partially spoiled when Nilsson, the Rangers' oft-injured center, underwent surgery to fix a dislocated knee, an injury that would ultimately end his career.

Even without Nilsson as his center, Hull made the most of his comeback opportunity, skating well in five preseason games but certainly not with the blazing speed that had decades earlier earned him the nickname "The Golden Jet." His timing was a bit off, too, though his wrist shot still looked accurate. His lone goal of the preseason was scored on Mike Palmateer in a 4–1 win over the Capitals in Sweden.

The Rangers were impressed by Hull's character but not overly so by his diminished hockey skills. They encouraged him to stay in Westchester and keep training, leaving the door open for him to try to earn a spot on the team later.

But Broadway Bobby knew his playing days were done.

"Time was too valuable to hang around," Hull told a reporter as he prepared to head back to his home in Ontario. "I've got a lot of things to do. I haven't dug up my potatoes or turnips or picked my Brussels sprouts yet."

99 The Great Farewell

Professional sports is littered with burned-out stars who play a season or two longer than necessary just to pad their stats or fatten their bank accounts.

But Wayne Gretzky, the league's all-time leading scorer, was too proud and too competitive to go out that way. He would not have signed with the Rangers in 1996 if he didn't sincerely believe he could help bring another Stanley Cup to New York.

He also came at the urging of good buddy and fellow Edmonton Oiler alum Mark Messier, who sold The Great One on the joys of playing in New York City and spoke from firsthand experience about how winning a championship there would be unlike anything Gretzky had ever experienced. Messier's presence also ensured that Gretzky would not be the focal point of the team, something the nine-time MVP found appealing.

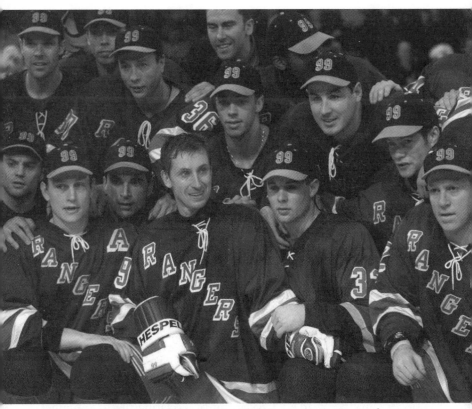

Wayne Gretzky is surrounded by his New York Rangers teammates as they pose for a group photo following his last game in the NHL on Sunday, April 18, 1999, in New York. (AP Photo/Paul Chiasson)

When he was introduced for the first time as a Ranger on October 6, 1996, Gretzky received an earsplitting "better late than never" reception from the Madison Square Garden crowd.

Pacing the club with 25 goals and 97 points in his first Ranger campaign, the biggest drawing card in the history of hockey proved he was worth the wait. He continued to shine in the 1997 playoffs, rifling three slap shots past Florida's John Vanbiesbrouck in Game 4 of the quarterfinals, a series the Rangers won in five games.

After a five-game dismantling of the Devils in the division semis, the Rangers advanced to face Philadelphia in the Conference Finals. Playing on the wing alongside Messier, Gretzky registered his second hat trick of the postseason in Game 2 to tie the series. When someone suggested that Wayne was lucky to be performing so well out of position, Messier shot back, "His luck's been good for 20 years."

But mounting injuries took their toll on the Rangers, who lost the next three games and the chance to play for the Stanley Cup.

Gretzky, not at all happy about having to shoulder more of the scoring load after Messier's free-agent defection to Vancouver, played two more seasons in New York, winning his fifth Lady Byng Trophy along the way. But he and the team were never again able to reach the heights achieved during that 1997 playoff run.

As the 1998–99 campaign drew to a close, the weight of 21 seasons and more than 1,400 NHL games—not to mention the certainty of another year out of the playoffs—prompted Gretzky to announce that he would retire at season's end.

Prior to Gretzky's final game on April 18, 1999, NHL commissioner Gary Bettman set a precedent by declaring that the number

Extra Garlic

"I was eating at Il Vagabondo, this little Italian place on the East Side when, all of a sudden, Gretzky walks in to pick up some takeout. He had an apartment somewhere in the neighborhood. He didn't see me. I asked Charlie, the manager, what Wayne had ordered and he told me chicken and broccoli with extra garlic. That night, during the game, Gretzky came out on the ice and was talking to me about something. I said, 'The chicken and broccoli is okay but you should back off the extra garlic a little bit. Move about 12' back will ya?' He looked at me with this confused expression. 'How did you know I had chicken and broccoli?'"

Paul Stewart
Former NHL referee

> **One More for the Books**
> In his final game, a 2–1 overtime loss to the Pittsburgh Penguins, Wayne Gretzky collected an assist on Brian Leetch's power play goal. It was the 1,963rd assist and 2,857th point of Gretzky's NHL career.

99 would be retired throughout the league. The announcement, which was met by a deafening Garden ovation, only confirmed what everyone already knew in their hearts: there would never be another Gretzky.

100 Pass It On

You've read all there is to read about the Rangers. You've memorized all the stats, built a proper fan cave in your basement, screamed "Potvin sucks!" until your vocal chords were raw, made "Slapshot" (aka The Goal Song) the ringtone on your phone, and froze your tuchas off at the Stadium Series.

Now, there's just one thing left to do: pass it on. Teach what you have learned. Share the joy—and painful burden—of being a Rangers fan. In many families, love of Rangers hockey is a tradition carried down from generation to generation.

Marcie Braverman remembers watching her older brother, David, play street hockey with his friends on the cul-de-sac where they grew up in Edison, New Jersey.

"They were all wearing Ranger jerseys," she said. "I remember thinking, 'Oh, this is the game I watch on TV.' And then it would start to get dark around 6:30 or 7:00, and the street lights would

A Special Gift

"I was the youngest in a family that wasn't crazy about hockey, so I really didn't know how to share my love for the game and the Rangers. From the second my nephew was born in 2000—the first boy of a new generation in the family—I envisioned watching, playing, and going to games with him...even during those tough years under John Muckler. Once he was old enough, I took him to a game at the Garden every year for Christmas. In 2008, for a school project, he wrote and illustrated a story about going to the games with me, and it's one of the most amazing things I've ever been given. I had it laminated, and now it's displayed proudly with the rest of my Rangers memorabilia."

Adam King, Coram, New York
Rangers fan since 1988

come on. All the kids would go home and we'd go inside and watch the games together as a family."

Marcie's grandfather, Irving Graf, was a Rangers fan "by default" who had faithfully followed the old New York Americans until that team went under in 1942. He adopted the Rangers because he still loved hockey and needed a team to root for. Once his daughter, Nancy, was old enough, Irving took her to hockey games at the old Garden between 49th and 50th Streets. She became a rabid Rangers fan.

Years later, on one of their earliest dates, Nancy took Sandy Braverman to his first Rangers game. He was hooked...on Nancy. And Rangers hockey, of course. Three kids and one Stanley Cup later, the Braverman clan still bleeds Ranger blue.

"Family dinners can get a little crazy with all the hockey talk," Marcie said, "especially around the Jewish holidays. Rosh Hashanah and Yom Kippur aren't impacted by the Rangers that much because they usually fall in September. But Passover always falls around the same time as the playoffs. Whether the Seder was at our house or my aunt's house, at some point during the dinner, my immediate family would have to get up from the table to watch the game. With our cousins who are more religious and don't allow televisions to be on during the Seder, it became a problem. Now, thanks to modern technology, we all get updates on our phones so we don't have to leave the table quite as often. My brother would still sneak off to the bathroom and stream the game live on his phone. From the dining room table we'd hear him yell, 'Score!' and sort of give each other that knowing look. We knew what he was doing."

Now a new generation of Bravermans is being indoctrinated— or, if you prefer, welcomed—into the fold. David's son, Jackson, is not yet three but has already been to his first game. His little sister, Liv, can't be far behind.

"As pissed as I get at the Garden sometimes for the high ticket prices and the way they blast Rihanna so loud between stoppages you can't even talk to the person sitting next to you," Marcie said, "Rangers hockey is a part of me and always will be. When I think about how it brought us together as a family, I get goose bumps. I get choked up. It's ingrained in all of us."

All except Marcie's twin sister, Jessica.

"She had to watch the games with the rest of us because she had no choice," Marcie said. "She was outnumbered."

Acknowledgments

Russ and I would like to thank all those who helped make this book possible, beginning with our new friends at Triumph Books: Tom Bast, for finally saying "yes," Adam Motin for his efforts to keep us on schedule, and Karen O'Brien for throwing that schedule out the window.

Thanks, also, to our literary agent, Laurie Hawkins, for sticking by us through the good times, the bad times, and all the times in between.

We are eternally grateful to all who shared their insights and anecdotes in interviews, especially the great Emile Francis, whose graciousness and candor in recalling what might be termed the "middle era" of Rangers history brought to life events that we had previously only read about or were too young to remember.

Thanks also to Mario Morgado and his able-bodied assistant, Leo, for that fun hike through Chelsea, and to Angelo Cataldi and the Morning Team at WIP, Bruce "Scoop" Cooper, Shane Malloy, and Mark Rosenman, for their editorial support and cooperation.

Our most heartfelt thanks are reserved for our friends and families for their steadfast support, patience, and encouragement…and the Silver Fox Club, for keeping us humble.

—A.R.

Sources

Boucher, Frank with Trent Frayne. *When the Rangers Were Young*. Dodd, Mead & Company, 1973.

Carpiniello, Rick. *Messier: Hockey's Dragon Slayer*. McGregor Publishing, 1999.

Eskenazi, Gerald. *A Thinking Man's Guide to Pro Hockey*. E.P. Dutton & Co., 1972.

Esposito, Phil and Peter Golenbock. *Thunder and Lightning*. Triumph Books, 2003.

Gilbert, John. *Herb Brooks: The Inside Story of a Hockey Mastermind*. MVP Books, 2008.

Halligan, John and John Kreiser. *Game of My Life: New York Rangers*. Sports Publishing, 2006.

Howe, Gordie and Colleen Howe with Tom Delisle. *And … Howe! An Authorized Autobiography*. Power Play Publications, 1995.

Hunter, Douglas. *A Breed Apart*. Penguin Books, 1998.

Hynes, Jim and Gary Smith. *Saving Face: The Art and History of the Goalie Mask*. John Wiley & Sons Canada, 2008.

Joyce, Gare. *The Devil and Bobby Hull*. Wiley, 2011.

Park, Brad and Thom Sears. *Straight Shooter: The Brad Park Story*. Wiley, 2012.

Sloman, Larry. *Thin Ice: A Season in Hell with the New York Rangers*. William Morrow and Company, 1982.

Villemure, Gilles and Mike Shalin. *Gilles Villemure's Tales from the Ranger Locker Room*. Sports Publishing, 2002.

Whitehead, Eric. *The Patricks: Hockey's Royal Family*. Doubleday, 1980.

Newspapers and Magazines
The Hockey News
New York Daily News
New York Post
New York Times
The Sporting News
Sports Illustrated
The Wall Street Journal

Websites
HockeyDraftCentral.com
Hockey-Reference.com
IIHF.com
NewYorkRangers.com
NHL.com